Normality

Normality

Theoretical and Clinical Concepts of Mental Health

Revised Edition

Daniel Offer and Melvin Sabshin

WITH THE ASSISTANCE OF JUDITH OFFER

WITH A FOREWORD BY

Roy R. Grinker, Sr.

BASIC BOOKS, INC., PUBLISHERS

NEW YORK

Library of Congress Cataloging in Publication Data

Offer, Daniel.
Normality.

Bibliography: p.
1. Mental hygiene. I. Sabshin, Melvin, joint author. II. Title.
RA790.035 1974 155 74-79288
ISBN 0-465-05147-2

Printed in the United States of America
74 75 76 77 78 10 9 8 7 6 5 4 3 2 1

Contents

Foreword

An aroused interest in definitions of mental health and dimensions of psychological normality indicates a decided shift away from the traditional psychiatric focus on mental illness. Although we can trace the transitional events that led professional disciplines to modify their concepts and operations, the wide and rapid public acceptance of health, rather than illness, as a crucial issue raises questions regarding the social dynamics involved.

A previous era of public acceptance of "mental hygiene" in the 1920's had disastrous results when the promises of the mental-hygiene movement could not be kept. Today we are in a more precarious situation because we have gradually extended the dimensions of mental illness to the point where the attainment of utopian mental health, although impossible, would require the exclusion of much of human behavior.

Society, especially the middle and upper classes, has been extensively indoctrinated through mass communications with information about psychiatric therapy, psychoanalysis, and psychotherapy, much of which is available to only a fraction who need and ask for such services. Training programs for professionals can never supply enough therapists to meet the demands, much less the needs, as we judge them to exist. An informed public therefore turns its attention to the next generation and wants to be directed in the child-rearing practices that will ensure that the developing children will be healthy or normal. So, when we talk about mental health or normality, primary prevention, or early case-finding, the public is receptive and willing to respond with tax money, private donations, and a listening, cooperative attitude.

Profound changes have taken place in psychiatry in the past two decades. The original struggle for adequate state-hospital facilities fought by Dorothea Dix, Clifford Beers, and Adolph Meyer was successful; but, unfortunately, the result was custodial care for thousands, rather than rehabilitation. World War II indicated that many more humans not in hospitals failed at adaptation to conditions of stress, and medical practice continually demonstrates that in some manner emotional disturbances play a role in the onset, course, and outcome of many diseases of the body.

Lethargy and inaction among psychiatrists abruptly ended through the efforts of psychiatrists in the military services during World War II who sparked the establishment of the Group for the Advancement of Psychiatry (GAP). In 1955, a Joint Action Committee was established that made concrete recommendations in an extensive report in 1961 with interspersed monographs on special subjects. The American Medical Association established a Council on Mental Health, which published reports and held yearly meetings attended by physicians from the grass roots.

The term "mental health," which has a sweet sound and a hopeful connotation, rapidly replaced the feared words "mental illness." Clinics were no longer called "psychiatric," but "mental-health centers." Even anachronistic "detention hospitals" are becoming "mental-health clinics" though their stench remains. Governmental funds were allocated for planning for mental health with the promise of liberal support later for mental-health community centers devoted to prevention.

Social psychiatry, utilizing both social science and psychological-psychiatric concepts, began as a "*new*" discipline to study the social matrix of mental illness. Finally, community psychiatry sprang full-blown as an operational specialty. The world of mental illness is expected by many to dissolve before the juggernaut-like bandwagon of community psychiatry onto which social scientists, psychologists, psychiatrists, ministers, and a variety of people with good intentions are clambering.

The known problems are difficult enough, although easily stated; but usually they do not include the core questions: What is mental health? What is mental illness? General definitions are difficult enough; but, to add to the confusion at the extremes of life, when transitions of growth and decline are necessary (in childhood, in adolescence, and in the aged), health is not unalloyed, but seems to be associated with evidences of turmoil in behavior, in feeling, and in psychological tests. Among adults in the wide span of middle age, psychiatrists and psychologists have treated patients suffering from mental or emotional disturbances with unclear ideas of how their goals of better health or of normality can be defined, and each theoretical school seems to have its own implied concepts of health and illness.

It seems clear, then, that, for a conceptual framework and for an operational system concerned with primary prevention, early treatment, and rehabilitation, the time is appropriate for a consideration of what we really mean by normality. Does it exist? Is it the polar opposite to illness? Are there one or several types of mental health? Is mental health a transaction among genetic, personality, and environmental processes? Is mental health a capacity for adaptation to multiple environments in an era when the average expectable environment is the unexpected?

The authors of this book have laboriously collated the definitions of normality from many frames of reference and from the literature of several disciplines that use the concept of normality. They have organized their material into four perspectives of normality through which its dimensions may be profitably viewed. The results are definitive statements solidly based on current knowledge that can be profitably utilized by theoreticians and investigators, as well as by activists who are trying to make the world "mentally healthy."

ADDENDUM TO FOREWORD

Since the above was written in 1966 as a foreword to the first edition, many investigators have been inspired to study normality and healthy coping strategies. Offer himself has completed a lengthy longitudinal study of the modal adolescent from first year high school through college and even beyond. My own sample of homoclites have been followed up by questionnaires fourteen years later and found to be even healthier than during the first study. They constitute a precious group of 134 normal male controls available for investigators to use for their own controls.

This revised edition, I am pleased to state, indicates the authors' progress in thinking in that they designate normality as a transactional system under the umbrella of General Systems Theory instead of normality as "process." Only longitudinal studies of humans who progress through the continuity of life cycles will furnish data with predictive powers. Thus this second edition constitutes a decided advance over the first.

Roy R. Grinker, Sr., M.D.
Director, Institute for Psychosomatic and Psychiatric Research and Training,
Michael Reese Hospital and Medical Center, Chicago
Professor of Psychiatry,
Pritzker School of Medicine,
University of Chicago
December 1973

Preface

> You seem very sure of yourself. Who can say where the normal stops and the abnormal begins? Can you personally define these conceptions of normality and abnormality? Nobody has solved this problem yet, either medically or philosophically. You ought to know that. —E. IONESCO (1960)

Twenty years ago, it would have been decidedly abnormal for psychiatrists to write a book on the dimensions of normal behavior. Indeed, as recently as ten years ago, there were relatively few psychiatrists actively engaged in studies of normal behavior. One measure of changing times is that, in the mid-1960's, it seems much less strange or deviant for the authors to attempt such a book. In recent years, there has been a sharp increase in studies of so-called normal populations by psychoanalysts and psychiatrists, but the investigations have often faltered because of conceptual or methodological ambiguity.

Although psychologists and social scientists had been studying nonpatient populations for years, they had, in general, little interest in or knowledge of psychopathology and psychiatric illness. This contributed to the relative lack of appropriate interdisciplinary communication between psychiatrists and psychoanalysts on the one hand and psychologists and social scientists on the other. The lack of adequate communication not only hampered the development of new methods of study, but also reinforced the tendency to view health and normal behavior from multiple vantage points. Indeed, even casual inspection of the literature reveals an enormous diversity of concepts and approaches to these issues. This book is written with the intention of specifying the dimensions of these multiple perspectives and, also, with the hope of clarifying the dimensions and of achieving a more integrated and empirical understanding.

Our own involvement in the problem of normality and health has grown from our clinical experience and research. It was in the course of studying adolescents hospitalized in the psychiatric section of a general hospital [1] that we became increasingly interested in the distinction between healthy and maladaptive responses in this age group. Like Strauss, Schatzman, Bucher, Ehrlich, and Sabshin (1964), we felt that:

> . . . psychiatrists are singularly ill equipped to deal with the nonpathological characteristics of adolescence, that is, those associated with adolescents as age-graded Americans in an age-graded culture. It seems safe to add that teen-agers inside a hospital are even more difficult to manage—as teen-agers—than teen-agers outside. For the staff, a perplexing ambiguity attends adolescents' hospitalization. They are sick, but they are also youngsters. How is one to distinguish pathological behavior from normal mischief? And if the two are mixed, to what degree and in what ways?

In order to differentiate more clearly between normal and abnormal behavior in adolescence from an empirical standpoint, we began a study on "The Modal Adolescents." [2] In this project, we have studied a group of one hundred typical or normal adolescents who had been carefully selected in two suburban high schools. One of the major dilemmas that con-

[1] Offer & Barglow (1960); Falstein, Feinstein, Offer, & Fine (1963); Fine & Offer (1965); Marcus, Offer, Blatt, & Gratch (1965).

[2] See Offer & Sabshin (1963) and Offer, Sabshin, & Marcus (1965) for details.

fronted us in choosing such a population was to define clearly what we meant by a normal teen-ager. As we searched for a satisfactory answer in the available literature, we felt an increasing need for new concepts, methods, and data in arriving at a meaningful definition of normality or health. We became aware that the literature on adolescent behavior utilized distinctly different approaches to normality. The choice of the approach was frequently related to particular scientific disciplines, theoretical systems, and methodological procedures. Yet, at times, individuals of diverse backgrounds and disciplines surprisingly shared a similar approach. In order to clarify the methodology for our research, it became worthwhile to review the various perspectives, to classify them, and to show differences and similarities between them. The book was thus originally related to questions emerging from our own research.

We believe that this volume has transcended our study of adolescent behavior in that the perspectives described are central to much of current psychiatric research. It cannot be overemphasized, however, that, as psychiatrists and individuals, we have our own biases, thought patterns, and techniques of conducting research. We have not written from an Olympian position, surveying all that we see around us in a completely objective manner; rather, our conclusions are based on our own personal and professional experiences. However, taking these experiences into consideration, the reader will be able to note how the variations in our perspective play a role in the questions asked. As psychiatrists and as investigators interested in research models, we believe that this book is a contribution to psychiatric research.

The book is divided into two parts. In Part One, we survey selective approaches to normality in the following disciplines: medicine as a whole, psychiatry, psychology, psychoanalysis, anthropology, sociology, and biology. In Part Two, we focus on the issues that transcend the individual approaches and help us view the problem of normality and health as a whole. Though we have not achieved a full synthesis, we do point toward the emerging trends.

Throughout, we tend to use the terms "normality" and "health" interchangeably. We have found that investigators, on the whole, do not consistently differentiate between these two terms. This does not mean that the terms have identical meaning throughout the literature or that they generally represent identical concepts. In our opinion, however, at the present stage of knowledge, the distinctions between normal and healthy behavior are based on hypotheses, rather than on empirical evidence.

In the Appendix, the interested reader will find detailed definitions and the opinions of a select group of investigators to whom we refer. These quotations serve as a supplement to the concepts of normal behavior presented in the text.

Re-reading our manuscript seven years later, in 1973, it seemed to us that many of our original observations are still relevant today. There has been a steady increase in empirical studies of mentally healthy populations which have added considerably to our understanding of the vicissitudes of normality and mental health. What is lacking is a deeper theoretical understanding of normal personality development and the psychodynamic understanding of the coping process. It is our prediction that the next decade will see more theory building based on the empiricism of the late sixties and early seventies.

For the revised, second edition, we rewrote the "Normality as Transactional Systems" perspective in Chapter 6. We completely rewrote Chapters 8 and 9 and brought them up to date. We are grateful to Dr. Roy R. Grinker, Sr., who has rewritten the Foreword.

Acknowledgments

This book was written while one of us (Dr. Offer) served as a Mental Health Career Investigator for the U.S. Public Health Service's National Institute of Mental Health at the Institute for Psychosomatic and Psychiatric Research and Training, Michael Reese Hospital and Medical Center, Chicago. The authors are grateful for the support given by the N.I.M.H., U.S.P.H.S. Grants Nos. 4870 and 08714.

We have learned a great deal from our discussions with our colleagues at the institute at Michael Reese Hospital, and at the University of Illinois, throughout the years. We would like to thank specifically those who have made valuable criticisms and suggestions at various stages of the book: Drs. J. Bowman, R. Bucher, A. Burstein, R. Cartwright, D. Ehrlich, E. Haggard, H. Heath, F. L. K. Hsu, C. Kligerman, A. Kling, S. Kobrin, R. LeVine, J. F. Masterson, Jr., D. Oken, D. M. Schneider, A. Strauss, G. Vogel, and M. Zald.

We are especially grateful to Messrs. S. J. Baskin and G. E. Miller and Drs. S. L. Baskin, W. Hirsch, R. P. Wolff, and R. R. Grinker, Sr., who read the entire manuscript and made many valuable suggestions and recommendations. In addition, Dr. Grinker, the director of the Institute for Psychosomatic and Psychiatric Research and Training of Michael Reese Hospital has helped us in broadening our own perspective of modern psychiatry.

The revision of the book was done while one of us (Daniel Offer) was a Fellow at the Center for Advanced Study in the Behavioral Sciences in Stanford, California. We are grateful for the support received and the ambience of quiet scholarship that the Center offered.

Parts of Chapter 8 have been published in our article, "Normality," in the second edition of *The Comprehensive Textbook of Psychiatry* edited by A. M. Freedman, H. I. Kaplan, and B. J. Sadock and published by the Williams & Wilkins Company (Baltimore, 1974). We are grateful to the editors for permission to reprint these sections. Finally, we would like to thank our secretary, Ms. Jean Antonini, who helped us in the process of revising the book.

DANIEL OFFER
MELVIN SABSHIN

Stanford
December 1973

PART ONE

The Disciplines

1

Medical-Psychiatric Thinking and Gross Normality

> To work good, to feel good, to expect good—these might be called the primary dimensions of health (When I say good, I mean well).
> —J. C. WHITEHORN (1959)

The subtleties, complexities, and degrees of normality have only recently emerged as a central question in medical thinking. Physicians have, of course, been interested in studying the normal, or healthy, state of tissues for many centuries. In these studies, however, the overwhelming tendency has been to assume that the state of health can be conceptualized in gross terms as the absence of clearly defined pathology. When a medical student dissected a cadaver or examined normal mucosa under the microscope, he was doing this almost exclusively as a prelude to the study of demonstrable deviations. Although variations in anatomic structure and in physiologic function are extremely common, the student was rarely stimulated to focus his attention on a structural or functional classification of the so-called state of health. Rather, he was taught to view health and normal functioning as essentially gross or homogeneous for almost all practical purposes.

It should be understood, however, that there was good historical reason to view pathology as sharply distinct from the normal condition. In most cases, sickness was thought to be manifested in stark, dramatic form so that even the layman could note its presence. Plague and pestilence were and still are so striking that, during episodic scourges, it is quite pragmatic to view normality as essentially equivalent to the absence of the dreaded disease. There was little reason to measure degrees of being without the plague, and this pragmatic model dominated medical thinking until the latter part of the nineteenth century. It was natural for such an approach to affect the development of all medical specialties, including psychiatry. Although psychiatry is as old as medicine itself, its evolution as a medical specialty had become almost a revolution by the latter part of the nineteenth century. Thus, modern psychiatry was spawned in an era that still conceived of illness and health as sharply disparate. This tradition, born of medicine, continues to have a pervasive influence on much of mid-twentieth-century psychiatry, despite the turbulent psychiatric and medical revolutions of the past hundred years.

In this chapter, we shall outline the ebb and flow of these developments in medicine as a whole, as well as the evolution of modern psychiatry insofar as these developments affected perspectives on normal behavior. Although we shall illustrate how the concept of gross normality has been debated and ultimately altered in psychiatry and in its parent medical profession, we shall also emphasize how much of the earlier tradition has remained as a vital force. Indeed, the current debates about the extension of psychiatry into its new directions and new roles cannot be understood without such historical emphasis.

Traditional Medical Concepts of Gross Pathology and Gross Normality

The physician is trained to eliminate or attenuate illness and to help the sick person return to a "healthy" state. It is wholly understandable that the individual doctor's concern has always been primarily with pathology and abnormality. Pathology has been the basic science most nearly approaching clinical practice. The individual physician could not spend his limited time working with adequately functioning people who neither manifested disturbing symptoms nor experienced pain. Quite practically, those people who had no manifest need of medical care could be considered healthy or normal. Thus, the state of health has been and in many ways still is defined roughly as freedom from gross pathology, defects, ailments, or suffering. Man was conceived of as functioning in a healthy manner, and this health was generally possessed by the majority of the population. Illness, on the other hand, involved the exceptional or unnatural state. Over the centuries, the concepts of normality and health became synonymous. This concept satisfied the overwhelming needs of physicians and patients through the past century. It continues to have operational value in the twentieth century, so that it is important to note both the traditional and the new approaches to the problems of health and illness in modern medicine.

The latter part of the nineteenth century saw the emergence of a debate between investigators who maintained the distinction between gross normality and gross pathology and those who developed ideas that blurred the boundaries between states of illness and health. The medical discoveries of Robert Koch and Louis Pasteur, for example, were used to substantiate the existing concepts of qualitatively differing states of normality and abnormality. Paradoxically, the brilliant discoveries of these great pioneers of medicine served as a resistance against further change. Both Koch's and Pasteur's discoveries led to the view that individuals either harbored bacteria that gave rise to illness or were free of such bacteria.[1] Generations of medical students have been raised with Koch's postulates and, thus, have maintained the boundary between disease and health. No more perfect example of this distinction can be made than is afforded by these postulates. Medical investigators, following the tradition induced by the postulates, searched vigorously for the virulent organism that had invaded the host and caused illness.[2] For such investigators, normality was the antonym of virulent infection. In proving a case of illness, little attention was paid to the intervening variables that are now regarded as equally important events leading to a clinical-pathological syndrome. The impetus of Koch's discoveries had a pervasive effect on medicine, and the infectious-disease model was generalized far beyond itself. Even today, the search for the specific organisms necessary for the production of pathology goes on, for example, in major areas of cancer research.

[1] Koch's postulates are: (1) The bacterium must be observed in every case of the disease. (2) The bacterium must be isolated and grown in pure culture. (3) The bacterium in pure culture, when inoculated into a susceptible animal, must give rise to the disease. (4) The bacterium must be observed in and recovered from the experimentally diseased animal (Burrows, 1954).

[2] This is, of course, an oversimplification, as was demonstrated by Koch's contemporary, Pathology Professor Pettenkofer, who, in order to disprove Koch's claim of the totally virulent nature of the cholera bacillus, breakfasted on a sandwich spread containing a pure culture of the bacilli (supplied by Koch). Since he suffered no ill effects, it became obvious that the bacillus alone was not sufficient cause for the illness. Other factors, such as constitution, state of health, and the emotional state, could not be disregarded.

Evolution of New Trends in Medicine Leading to Present Preventive Medicine

Although anatomists, biologists, physiologists, and physicians were not altogether satisfied with the gross concepts of normality and pathology, it was not until the latter part of the nineteenth century that clear alternative models developed in a usable fashion. Claude Bernard (1865) stands out as a symbol of a newer theory of illness and health. His formulations of the internal milieu and his studies of the dynamic equilibrium of living organisms helped to develop new trends. Cannon's (1929) concepts of homeostasis also directed attention to the complex interactions of the various bodily systems (for example, the central nervous system and the endocrinological systems). Not only the presence of invading organisms but also the disruption of systems previously in balance could bring about malfunctioning. This new way of visualizing malfunction added considerable depth to the medical-physiological perspective. Although it is true that Bernard and, later, Cannon developed new models of disease, it should also be understood that other factors contributed to the recession of the older models' predominance in medical thinking. In actuality, the discoveries of Koch, Pasteur, and many others led to techniques that could control infectious illness.

The very success of the application of principles derived from the earlier conceptual models played a key role in the fading of the dichotomy between health and illness. By the time Cannon enunciated his concepts of homeostasis, the soil in which such an approach could be nourished had been developed. This is not to say, however, that all traces of the health–illness dichotomy have been lost. In practice, it is exceedingly difficult to utilize the new models consistently. Even the current generations of physicians prefer to deal with what they consider real, or demonstrable, pathology. Much of the gratification in the practice of medicine comes from providing meaningful aid to a person who is disorganized by disease. Furthermore, it is apparent that there is a differential rate of the development of medicine throughout the world. In many countries, epidemics continue to plague mankind, and physicians in these countries must retain more than just a trace of the older approach. In the presence of endemic malaria, it is difficult to think of the more subtle and chronic illnesses. Even in the developing countries, however, many physicians have been affected by the newer approaches of preventive medicine and public health. Indeed, there is reason to believe that such approaches may facilitate the impact of modern medicine on a world-wide basis.

Thus, the current picture is complex. Medicine has moved toward an extension of the concept of illness that includes subclinical syndromes. It has also moved toward a greater interest in the antecedents of demonstrable diseases. The concern with prediction of chronic illnesses, for example, in the pathogenesis of essential hypertension, has had a great impact in the middle of the twentieth century. Physicians are interested in studying laboratory and clinical findings that may predict the development of disease. These findings have become the basis for a number of therapeutic interventions, such as the treatment of early signs of coronary disease and hypertension. There is also an increasing concern with aiding individuals who are symptom-free to function on an optimal level. Thus, the goals of medicine are not limited to the restoration of the patient's previous equilibrium. Although it seems likely that residuals of the older dichotomy will continue, it also seems predictable that preventive approaches will become increasingly strong throughout all of medicine. This, in turn, is leading to much greater emphasis on the nuances of health and normality.

Illustrative of the current trends is the suggestion that a new branch of medical science be established and be called "propetology" ("leaning toward"). Propetology aims to discover the proneness to disease of various types of individuals. The leaders in this new preventive medicine (Williams & Siegel, 1961) suggest the necessity of collecting a vast amount of data on the distinguishing characteristics of individuals. Propetology analyzes measurement trends, observes intra-individual variations, and analyzes data utilizing complex measurement patterns. Isolations of single significant items and correlations of multiple variables will be undertaken. The hope is that such analysis and accumulation of data will lead to techniques that permit earlier intervention. The development of propetology does not signify a lessening concern with pathology. As a matter of fact, it is possible that the major impetus of this approach will be the redefinition of the borders of pathology to include a much wider range of phenomena heretofore omitted. It is also possible, of course, that out of such developments as propetology new ideas going beyond the broadened definition of pathology will develop. Whatever the new direction, it is clear that much more attention will be paid to the normal part of the spectrum than has been in the past.

Within the past twenty years, the move toward the preventive approach and the other changes described in the foregoing has led to newer models of adaptation and disease. The work of Cassel, Patrick, and Jenkins (1960) is related to the homeostatic models of Cannon and yet shows some significant differences in its emphasis on open systems. In developing a model, these authors have pointed out how freedom from illness cannot be placed in complete contrast to manifestations of illness. They describe the recent shift in medical thinking which no longer stresses the single cause–effect relationship, but rather attributes each biological event to a network of causative factors. They also point out how the biological approach itself is insufficient without understanding the role of social and psychological factors in the evolution of illness. With increasing information about the complex systems of the organism, it becomes more difficult to speak of one standard of health or of one type of health. There is a growing recognition that specific patterns of maladaption and subclinical syndromes can be present in an individual who seems "normal" to others. The impact of modern physics and of relativity theory has had its effect in medicine in that man can only be viewed as relatively free from illness. Although this model, which is indeed prototypic of much advanced medical thinking, differs strikingly from that of Koch as described before, it represents a transition from the older approach to even more radical departures.

Ryle (1947) has been in the vanguard of those who have attempted to delve deeply into the meaning of normality in medicine. He has emphasized that variation is so constantly at work in man and animals that no rigid pattern of normality is conceivable. In developing the central roles of variability and environment in determining our concept of normality, Ryle utilizes a cogent example. He points out how a bank clerk and a miner function in radically different environments, each using special skills and equipment. The bank clerk may be free from symptoms of disease while working in his urban office. If, however, he moves to a radically different environment, be it that of a polar explorer or a soldier in combat, he may "break" physically and/or emotionally despite his apparently normal previous adaptation. The miner, who may have suffered from the combined effects of poor heredity, malnutrition, and occupational stress in adolescence, may nevertheless be better able to function as a miner than a robust individual who is brought into the mine without preparation.

Thus, the crucial question emerges, "fitness or adaptability for what"? Ryle summarizes his position when he states:

> The study of human variability within the normal range is important: 1. as a fundamental biological study; 2. as supplying necessary standards in medicine for the recognition of health and illness in borderline states; and 3. because the extremes within the normal range of variability in respect to certain functions may help to explain certain innate resistances and predispositions to disease and thereby place the study of diathesis on a firmer footing. . . . Variability, both in time and in species, is one of the most distinctive and necessary attributes of life, which thus admits no constant and no norm (pp. 4–5).

The major impact of this approach is: (1) to point out the limitations of a simple statistical definition of normality for medicine—the variability must be included; (2) to emphasize the relativity of the concept of normality from cultural and epidemiological points of view; and (3) to suggest the limitations of a simple dichotomy of health and illness. What characterizes Ryle in contradistinction to many of his contemporaries is the deep concern with the context in which adaptation is required. This leads to a much wider interest and a host of processes previously excluded from medical studies. This approach also agrees well with major developments in the behavioral sciences—developments that will be discussed in this chapter and other sections of the volume.

Psychiatric Concepts of Gross Pathology and Gross Normality

The scientific foundations of modern psychiatry were given major support by developments in the latter part of the nineteenth century. During this period, a series of remarkable empirical investigations were undertaken. As a result, psychiatry began to understand dementia praecox, the manic-depressive psychoses, and other syndromes as broad but consistent clinical entities. An empirical framework for psychiatric classification became feasible, and this framework stimulated a renewed search for causative factors in mental illness. Among the other syndromes elucidated near the end of the century was the so-called dementia paralytica. When it became clear that this syndrome constituted a manifestation of central-nervous-system syphilis (paresis) caused by the Treponema pallidum, the entire medical world was infused with new hope. Perhaps the cause of each psychiatric illness could ultimately be understood in a manner analogous to the pathogenesis of paresis. The search for a single, pre-emptive, causative agent, whether external to the organism (for example, bacteria, viruses) or internal (for example, metabolic defects, constitutional aberrations), began in earnest. Since these developments followed shortly after the discoveries of Koch and Pasteur, psychiatry was in the mainstream of changes taking place in all of medicine. The major task involved the isolation of specific etiological agents so that effective therapeutic endeavors could be discovered. In the thinking of the great pioneers of this exciting period there was little concern with the definition of normality or health. One either had clear-cut symptoms that fitted the newer classificational system or one did not have symptoms and hence could be considered healthy for all practical purposes. The syndromes under investigation were gross and objective, and little attention was paid to the subtler varieties and manifestations. It was wholly natural that the search for pre-emptive causal agents was tied to gross psychopathology. Also relevant to the areas of concentration was the fact that psychiatric practice of the latter part of the nineteenth century was hospital-based. Very few psychiatrists spent the bulk of their time in out-patient practice. Their work was done in the hospitals and involved primarily the care of people manifesting clearly demonstrable psychopathology. Absence of the cardinal symptoms of dementia praecox, affective and organic disorders, and related gross illnesses was sufficient grounds to permit an individual to be classified as psychologically healthy.

Many psychiatrists of the mid-twentieth century continue to make as sharp a distinction between health and psychopathology as did their predecessors fifty years previously. Often this perspective is still accompanied by the hope and expectation that most of the psychiatric syndromes will be explained ultimately by a major single cause. Energetic search for the etiology of schizophrenia continues, despite an ever-increasing repository of discarded hypotheses and disproven propositions. Notwithstanding a few exceptions, the search for "another" Treponema pallidum has failed to yield an explanation of a major psychiatric syndrome such as dementia paralytica.[3] Consequently, a large number of psychiatrists have become discouraged with the single-cause model and have found alternative concepts more attractive. Where medicine in general has achieved spectacular success in unraveling etiology through an infectious-disease model, the psychiatric specialty as a whole has not been so successful. Thus, a combination of factors has weakened the popularity of the traditional approach to

[3] For example, the discovery of phenylpyruvic oligophrenia (Jervis, 1953), in which a particular mental aberration was specifically linked to a metabolic defect, is a case in point.

psychiatric illness and has concomitantly weakened the older tendency to recognize a sharp dichotomy between illness and health. Psychiatry has also been deeply influenced by the work of Cannon and Bernard, so that a more complex multi-causal approach dominates the thinking of a majority of American psychiatrists.

On the European continent, however, a gross model still holds sway. Even the newer interests in existentialism and phenomenology in psychiatry have not radically altered this approach. For the existentialist, normality stands out, not as the opposite of abnormality nor as the absence of all abnormalities, but rather as a complex entity qualitatively different from those entities composing abnormalities. Indeed, for the existentialist, the qualitative transition from normality to disease means a total change in one's world. It is the world itself that is made alien, but nevertheless it is a qualitatively different world. Though the world of the mental patient can be understood, we cannot participate in it, and it differs intrinsically from the world of the "normal" person because the communality of the "living world" (*Lebenswelt*) is lost in mental illness. A mental patient, therefore, has given up his former world, which he no longer knows as a human experience—hence the qualitative difference between the "normal" person and the mental patient. (See Straus, 1963, Straus, 1966, and Nathanson, 1963, for details.)

Another sign of the retention of the older approach to normality in psychiatry is the fact that psychiatric textbooks in general do not attempt to define normality or health. Few textbooks even attempt a clinical, albeit phenomenological, description of normal behavior. Textbooks rarely mention "normality" in their indexes.[4] It is impressive that even the excellent and comprehensive *American Handbook of Psy-*

[4] For examples, see the following textbooks: Henderson & Gillespie (1950);

chiatry (Arieti, 1959) does not provide a definition or description of normal behavior. There are a few exceptions, however; for example, Laughlin (1956) does state that "emotional health is truly a relative matter." He describes an emotionally healthy person as one who has "effected a *reasonably* [authors' italics] satisfactory integration of his unconscious instinctual drives." Laughlin goes on to state that such a person has worked out harmonious solutions that are acceptable to himself and to his social milieu. This definition is, in effect, a statement about functional adequacy. The person who is healthy has reasonably well-balanced psychological systems and hence masters his own internal and external environment to a point of adjustment. This approach is a typical one for psychiatrists who have attempted a definition of normality or health.[5]

Although psychiatry has changed a great deal in recent decades, the gross concept of normality clearly still has strong adherence, just as this traditional concept is strong in medicine as a whole. A number of papers perpetuate this point of view, and we would like to cite two statements reflecting it. L. L. Havens, as quoted by Barton (1959, p. 11), emphasizes the value of statistical norms and also goes on to question some of the definitions of health as equivalent to ideal functioning. He states:

Noyes & Kolb (1958); Dunbar (1959); Meyer-Gross, Slater & Roth (1960); and Gregory (1961).

[5] For similar approaches, see Kolle (1961); Frank (1961); and Lewis (1958), who unambivalently states: "A rather silly but often repeated truism says that the aim of psychiatric treatment is to promote mental health. It is hard to tell what the latter phrase means. Mental health is an invincibly obscure concept. Those who have attempted to define it in positive terms have twisted ropes of sand. This clutter of words is groping towards an ideal, a sociobiological ideal: but much of it can have no operational referents and it abounds in terms which are undefined and at present undefinable" (p. 170).

> Usually in medicine we say an organ is healthy if it does its job within the normal range and over the usual time. We do not expect too much, although the usual range is not the range of the average man, but of the average healthy man. Statistical norms are useful in this context and should not be dismissed despite the difficulties of agreeing on a normal population in the mental health area. Without such a point of reference, one cannot tell what is a toxic experience and what is normal tolerance. Without norms there is also the danger of unreal goals of treatment. This may be a significant health hazard. Ideal or even potential health criteria are too easily spun out of theories or brief glimpses of people at their momentary best.

In Havens' opinion, it is quite easy to expect "too much" of the living organism and living behavior. A need for a reasonable basis for judging adequate performance is thus renewed in his definition. Barton (1959) raises issues about the same point when he states:[6]

> It is difficult for me as a clinician to separate the presence of health from those preventive measures that reduce the likelihood of the development of disease and illness. I believe most patients would settle for the absence of illness. If they are not sick, they are well.

Like Havens, Barton has been concerned about the utilization of absolute, positive criteria for normality. In a sense, Barton advocates the utilization of a structual- or functional-adequacy concept. Freedom from disabling symptoms is, in his view, a reasonable definition of health or normality. Barton makes a pragmatic plea that we consider people mentally normal if they manifest no evidence of gross psychic inconsistency or disorders of thinking or communication. As the reader will see in subsequent chapters, this point of view is

[6] See Appendix under W. E. Barton.

debated rather sharply, and we will cite contrasting opinions. It should be noted here, however, that the advocates of the traditional approach do not often state this position in print. Although we have cited two quotations advocating the position, explicit statements about it are rare. Nevertheless these attitudes are, in our opinion, still representative of a large sample of American psychiatrists and psychiatrists all over the world.

Newer Perspectives in Psychiatry

In recent decades, the psychiatric approach to normality has been influenced not only by the radical changes in medicine as a whole, but also by developments in psychoanalysis, dynamic psychiatry, psychosomatic medicine, and the social sciences. The changes also have broad implications for the various perspectives on normality. In illustrating these implications, we have selected prototypic examples from each of the four areas.

The advent of psychoanalysis in the earlier part of the twentieth century had a profound impact on approaches to psychopathology, and the reverberations have continued up to the present. The psychoanalyst is interested in specific kinds of psychopathology amenable to his treatment approach. From a broader perspective, the kind of patient best treated by a psychoanalyst is one whose disorder does not necessarily affect his capacity to adjust to society. In this sense, it is a subtle illness or an early form of illness. Thus, psychoanalysts by and large do not work with those who have extreme psychopathology; they are more involved in the treatment of "the psychopathology of everyday life." Many patients treated by psychoanalysts endure a good deal of difficulty and suffering, but a significant number of them would not be viewed as sick by the majority of Americans. Indeed, many of the more tradition-minded psychiatrists would argue that most patients being psychoanalyzed are "well." [7] It follows from the above that psychiatrists do not altogether agree on the nature of health and illness and that there are considerable differences of opinion among psychiatrists as to what exactly constitutes normality or abnormality.

In Chapter 2, we discuss the specific psychoanalytic interpretations of normality. It is important to note, however, that concepts derived from psychoanalysis have been widely accepted by American psychiatrists who practice "dynamic psychiatry." The concepts evolved in such practice are closely related to definitions of health and normality and have been enunciated in numerous publications. Analysts involved in psychiatric training at graduate and undergraduate levels have contributed much to these definitions. Levine (1942), who has been a leading psychiatric educator for many years, writes in his book, *Psychotherapy in Medical Practice*, as a psychoanalytically trained psychiatrist. He begins his discussion of psychiatric normality with a definition of physical normality. In Levine's view, it must include the concept of the absence of specific disease, must consider the concept of a statistical average, and must include the concepts of health and maturity. Having accepted both the traditional and the newer medical methods of determining normality, he states that the diagnosis of psychological normality involves the same problems encountered in the diagnosis of physical normality but that the former is more complex and comprises a "higher level of integration" (p. 286). Levine then presents his own characterization of normality, which we present in its entirety because it is prototypic

[7] This position has been espoused by other behavioral scientists, for example, Dunham (1965).

of definitions by psychoanalytically oriented or dynamic psychiatrists. Normality is:

1. Non-existent in a complete form, but existing as relative and quantitative approximation.
2. In agreement with statistical averages of specific groups, if that is not contrary to standards of individual health and maturity.
3. Physical normality; absence of physical disease; presence of good structure and function and maturity.
4. Intellectual normality.
5. Absence of neurotic and psychotic symptoms. [Levine elaborates later that the normal individual is only relatively free of neurotic and psychotic symptoms.]
6. Emotional maturity (especially in contrast with neurotic character formation).
   (a) Ability to be guided by reality rather than by fears.
   (b) Use of long-term values.
   (c) Grown-up conscience.
   (d) Independence.
   (e) Capacity to "love" someone else but with an enlightened self-interest.
   (f) A reasonable dependence.
   (g) A reasonable aggressiveness.
   (h) Healthy defense mechanisms.
   (i) Good sexual adjustment with acceptance of own gender.
   (j) Good work adjustment.

Interestingly, Levine's first requirement rules out the possibility of ever achieving mental normality. But at the end of this discussion he is careful to show that the above criteria, especially the components of emotional maturity, are relative and quantitative. Levine defines normality in terms of absence of abnormalities (criteria 2, 3, 4, 5) and of the successful adjustment of a person to himself and his environment. The problem of who shall judge degrees of adjustment or what is meant by "reasonable" has not been satisfactorily resolved. Who shall be the judge to decide finally whether a behavior seen universally in a particular culture is indeed "contrary to standards of individual health and maturity"? Perhaps, in accordance with psychoanalytic traditions, Levine's clinical impression of the normal man is a reflection of his own clinical experiences in the sense that his six criteria of normality are culturally derived and not quantitative in nature but rather are qualitative and necessarily value-laden. We do believe that Levine's discussion of normality and health is a good statement of the position to which a large number of contemporary American psychiatrists would subscribe.

Another newer trend in psychiatry since World War II involves the rapidly increasing interest in psychosomatic medicine. Individuals working in this area have attempted to isolate psychological variables that interact or transact with somatic systems in precipitating or causing the clinical manifestations of illness. Psychosomaticists come from multiple traditions in psychiatry, but they all are attempting to bridge somatic medicine and psychological factors. Engel (1953, 1960, 1962) is typical of those who attempt to integrate psychoanalytic and psychiatric concepts in an approach to psychosomatic medicine.

From the standpoint of our interest in normality, it is impressive to note that Engel's book (1962), summarizing many of his current concepts, is entitled *Psychological Development in Health and Disease*. In this work he attempts to come to grips with definitions of health and illness by linking the biological and the psychological fields. Discussing health and disease as successful and unsuccessful adaptations respectively of an organism to its environment, he examines the roles of physical and mental conditions in determining the degree of success of this adaptation. Citing tuberculosis as an example, he questions the completeness and utility of a given theory that focuses exclusively on the tubercle bacillus as the cause of the syndrome known as tuberculosis.[8] Here he closely follows recent changes in medicine, emphasizing the need to accept the presence of the tubercle bacillus as only one of the conditions necessary for the development of tuberculosis. After elucidating the principle of multiple causation of pathogenesis, Engel (1962) analyzes *seven* different psychological and organic vectors that are necessary for the pathogenesis of tuberculosis.

The sharp boundary line between health and illness is also questioned by Engel (1961). He examines grief as an excellent example of the conceptual problem in such a boundary line. From the perspective of the total health of a person, grief cannot be considered as a normal reaction. From Engel's standpoint, we would benefit from viewing grief as an illness and studying the healthy, reparative, and adaptive responses of an organism as compared to the type of stress that commonly produces a grief reaction. In regard to stress, Engel (1962) writes that psychological stress refers to all processes, whether originating in the external environment or within the person, that impose a demand or requirement upon the organism, the resolution or handling of which necessitates work or activity of the mental apparatus before any other system is involved or activated. Engel is thus prototypic of the modern psychosomaticist who wishes to extend the definition of illness from gross malfunctions to more subtle and complex behavioral forms under stress.

The past decade has witnessed the development of what has come to be called social and community psychiatry (Sabshin, 1965). To a significant extent, this change within psychiatry has been the product of a pragmatic movement intended to

[8] We refer the reader to our discussion of Koch's postulates in the first section of this chapter.

provide better mental-health care for disadvantaged segments of the U.S. population. During the 1950's, the need to improve the internal and external social relationships of large state mental institutions gave major impetus to the advances. Thus, in the 1960's, we have seen the rapidly increasing permeability between the inside of the hospital and the outside world, as is reflected in the day and night hospitals, half-way houses, and community centers where psychiatrists are functioning in a plethora of new roles. In these roles, psychiatrists, in growing numbers, have come into contact with elements of the population not previously seen in their offices or in their hospitals. In the process of being involved in these new activities, the social psychiatrist is often called upon to make decisions that relate to a definition of health or illness. What should be done in an industry to promote "good mental health"? What should teachers do in keeping the mental-health interests of their students in clearer perspective? Who should be selected to carry on an unusual mission, such as that of an astronaut? (See, for example, Ruff & Levy, 1959, and Ruff & Korchin, 1962.) What kind of health is necessary for any of these roles? In providing answers to such questions, community psychiatry has begun to develop a number of research programs. Psychiatric research carried on in the new settings has already catalyzed the interest in definitions of health and normality. The authors of this book became involved in these definitions in the course of their own work on so-called typical or modal adolescents (see Chapter 8). It is wholly predictable and natural that a new generation of behavioral scientists interested in social and community psychiatry will become centrally concerned with such definitions.

The interest in social psychiatry and concern with definitions of health and normality are typified by the work of Redlich (1957).[9] He points out that psychiatrists are far from agree-

[9] See Appendix under Fredrick C. Redlich.

ment on the meaning of the term "health." This inconsistency exists because there is no "completely satisfactory and universally accepted theory of behavior. The predominant psychiatric approach is clinical, that is, health is the absence of disease." Thus does Redlich express dissatisfaction with the negative, clinical definition of normality that we have identified as a traditional one for psychiatry. Redlich is also critical of an equation of the statistical and the clinical norm. He questions, for example, the interpretation of Alfred C. Kinsey's finding that 40 per cent of middle-aged married men masturbate as proving that masturbation is a normal occurrence in these men. He follows up Ryle's (1947) question "normal for what?" with the question "normal for whom?" This question cannot be adequately answered without integrating the statistical and the clinical norms.[10] The plea for investigations by psychiatrists on non-patient populations is prototypic of the approach by social psychiatrists interested in a more empirical definition of normality. Such empirical investigations are, according to Redlich, the only way to develop the groundwork for a more operational definition of normality and health.

As the social psychiatrists have moved in new directions, they have helped to raise many questions about the conceptual and practical models within their own field. There is concern both within and outside psychiatry about the overextension of the concept of illness. This situation may pose ethical as well as conceptual problems. Szasz (1956, 1960, 1961a, 1961b, and 1963) has been a chief critic of these new, as well as some of the older, directions in psychiatry.[11] He is concerned most specifically with a broadened base of a definition of illness. According to Szasz, all mental illness is fundamentally a problem of communication. More than any other psychiatrist of his generation, Szasz advocates the abandonment of the concept of

[10] See Chapter 8, where this problem is discussed in detail.
[11] See Appendix under Thomas S. Szasz.

mental illness. He says (1961b): "It is customary to define psychiatry as a medical specialty concerned with the study, diagnosis, and treatment of mental illness. This is a worthless and misleading definition. Mental illness is a myth." Szasz is concerned about the confusion among medical values and the values of social, ethical, and legal concepts.[12] In discussing this problem, he states (1960, p. 113):

> Finally, the widespread psychiatric opinion that only a mentally ill person would commit suicide illustrates the use of the legal concept as a norm of mental health. The norm from which deviation is measured, whenever one speaks of a mental illness, is a *psycho-social* and *ethical* one. Yet the remedy is sought in terms of *medical* measures which—it is hoped and assumed—are free from wide differences of ethical value. The definition of the disorder and the terms in which its remedy is sought are therefore at serious odds with one another. The practical significance of the covert conflict between the alleged nature of the defect and remedy can hardly be exaggerated.

It is important to note that Szasz is not simply critical of new developments in social psychiatry; he is also critical of many of the traditional approaches. Thus, he has criticized the current basis for commitment and for hospitalization as being indicative of a confusion of legal and medical values. He is also critical of some of the psychoanalytic definitions when they are equated with "illness." In 1960, he stated, for example, that:

> Notions such as excessive repression or acting out an unconscious impulse illustrate the use of psychological concepts for judging (so-called) mental health and illness. The idea that chronic hostility, vengefulness or divorce are indicative of mental illness would be illustrations of the use of ethical norms. . . .

Szasz believes that psychiatry has already inadvertently ingested and unwittingly combined the social sciences with ethi-

[12] See Chapter 7 for a fuller discussion of the ethical issues.

cal and legal maxims. It seems to us, though, that Szasz has taken a very strong position on a movement that is far more complex than he seems willing to concede. Psychiatry is indeed struggling to redefine its position in the behavioral-science field, and its attempts to analyze and define normality and health should be seen as part of this movement. Undoubtedly, these new directions occasionally will blur useful distinctions between health and illness. Szasz helps us focus on this problem in his writings. In the opinion of the authors, the gains inherent in social and community psychiatry far outweigh the problems consequent to their development. One of the major advances involves new conceptualizations of health as well as of illness. Ultimately, the issue should be clarified rather than blurred. This book has been dedicated to such a clarification, and the authors are optimistic about psychiatry playing a major role in it.

We have pointed out that the concepts of gross normality and gross pathology have been traditional in medicine as a whole and in its specialty of psychiatry. In our presentation, we emphasized the positive value of the traditional approaches, as well as the development of criticism about these positions. We also emphasized that the traditional approaches have considerable influence even in the 1960's and perhaps remain the dominant, pragmatic models. We have shown, however, that the solution of certain major problems has helped move medicine as a whole from a traditional concept of gross normality to modern propetology, which studies propensity for illness rather than illness itself.

Thus, there is a slow but definite trend in medicine to study and treat illnesses at an earlier stage in order to forestall more serious pathology. This trend implies a broadened definition of illness to include more subtle manifestations of dysfunction, but it also implies the necessity for new concepts and methods to study normal behavior. Psychiatry has participated in the old and new approaches to mental health and illness. A current cross-sectional overview of modern psychiatry reveals a complex combination of the traditional and the newer approaches. Thus, many psychiatrists retain the older perspectives of gross psychopathology and believe that their primary role is to deal with the seriously disturbed. Others, such as the psychoanalysts, work with patients who have less obvious psychopathology. Therapeutic goals for such patients relate less to restoration of previous equilibrium than to helping the patient to achieve a superior intrapsychic balance for himself and thus to live a more productive and gratifying life.

In this chapter, we have begun to discuss the relation of such psychoanalytic goals to definitions of health and illness. In Chapter 2, these issues are discussed in even more detail. We have also emphasized that other trends developed since World War II have affected psychiatric definitions of normal and abnormal behavior. Dynamic psychiatry has had a profound effect on such concepts, as have psychosomatic medicine and the social sciences. More recent developments in social and community psychiatry appear to offer a number of opportunities for clarifying basic definitions of health. Critics of these approaches have stressed the dangers of extending medical interests in areas beyond our competence. Although the concerns have a basis in reality, we have attempted to point out some of the major advantages of the new developments. In increasing numbers, psychiatrists are working in locales other than hospitals or private offices. They are coming into much greater contact with segments of the population not previously seen by them. In our opinion, such a development bodes well for new ideas and for new approaches to mental health based on a sounder empirical analysis.

2

Epigenesis of Normal-Neurotic Behavior: Psychoanalysis

> Seeking for so-called "normality" is like looking for gold at the end of the rainbow.
> —L. W. DARRAH (1939)

Since its inception, psychoanalysis has been dedicated primarily to the study of man's internal psychic processes and their interrelationships. As psychoanalysis developed its theoretical structure, six major points of view emerged: the topographic, the dynamic, the economic, the genetic, the structural, and the adaptive. These metapsychological perspectives overlap and are complementary to each other but, taken as a whole, form the nuclear theory of psychoanalysis (Rapaport, 1960). Each of these propositions relates to psychopathology and to general psychology. However, despite the fact that the psychoanalytic investigations have resulted in extending the boundaries of general psychology, most psychoanalysts would agree with Jones (1961) that "psychopathology opened a route to psychology in general, perhaps the most practical route." This rootedness in pathology may be the reason why psychoanalysts often shy away from discussing mental health and why the psychoanalytic literature on normality is relatively small. When psychoanalysts discuss the issues of normality and health, the metapsychological propositions are rarely the basis for the theoretical conceptualizations.[1] The discussions often center around general psychological issues, philosophical vantage points, and value judgments.

In reviewing the psychoanalytic literature, we have found three major trends regarding normality and health. We have labeled the first trend *Normality as an Ideal Fiction*. This trend commenced with Sigmund Freud and is still the most popular position on normality among psychoanalysts. A second trend we have labeled *Normality as Optimal Integration*. It overlaps with the ideal-fiction model, but it is differentiated from it in assuming that optimum integration is possible and, indeed, occurs in a significant number of individuals. The third trend we have called *Normality as Adaptation within Context*. This perspective follows the adaptive metapsychological position and in so doing includes contextual factors in approaching a definition of normality. It denies that normality is a fiction or that a definition of it must imply optimal functioning. Rather, it focuses on a pattern of adaptation that is more common and that depends to a significant degree on the environmental interaction.

In discussing the issue of normality on the basis of the division outlined in the foregoing, we are not doing full justice, we realize, to psychoanalytic theory. Obviously, no short chapter could accomplish this task. Our purpose has been to organize psychoanalytic concepts around major axes in order to illustrate how psychoanalysts have approached this problem rather than to outline in detail all of the possible psychoanalytic approaches to normality. In our discussion of psychoanalysis, we will also consider those psychoanalysts who originally studied and worked with Freud but later developed their own independent systems or points of emphasis. We are referring

[1] Eissler (1960) is the only psychoanalyst who has explicitly discussed normality from all six metapsychological points of view.

specifically to Alfred Adler, Carl G. Jung, and Otto Rank. Despite their unique qualities and break with Freudian psychoanalysis, they share with their more classically oriented colleagues many basic notions concerning normality.

Normality as an Ideal Fiction

The acceptance of the universality of neurosis was one of the cornerstones of Freudian theory. In establishing the interpretability of dreams, Freud (1900) was able to demonstrate the universality of unconscious conflicts as reflected in the dreaming process, and he related this to the psychopathology of everyday life (Freud, 1901). The general applicability of the Oedipus complex, childhood repression, and amnesia likewise was postulated (Freud, 1905). All of this indicates that Freud was a theorist whose scope was not limited to those with severe mental disturbance. Rather, he postulated great ranges of functioning that depended on constitutional, as well as developmental, criteria and potentials. In a more subtle fashion, however, his concept of the universality of unconscious conflicts is derived from his viewing normality as an ideal, an absolute, the end of the range, and, hence, non-existent. To put it in other words, Freud's (1901) work sets the stage for his axiomatic assumption that all men are at least partly neurotic. When discussing normality, Freud (1937) stated: "A normal ego is like normality in general, an ideal fiction." In "Analysis Terminable and Interminable," Freud (1937, p. 337) further observes:

> Every normal person, in fact, is only normal on the average. His ego approximates to that of the psychotic in some part or other and to a greater or lesser extent; and the degree of its remoteness from one end of the series and of its proximity to the other will

furnish us with a provisional measure of what we have so indefinitely termed an "alteration of the ego."

Jones (1931), like Freud, believed that we can never fully answer the question "what constitutes a normal psychic apparatus?" He felt that a normal mind does not exist and wondered whether it can ever exist. But Jones attempted, nonetheless, to formulate a theoretical basis of the normal mind. He lists the following as necessary constituents of the normal mind. First, the normal mind must have a capacity for adaptation to reality. Second, relation with one's fellow men must include a sufficient quantity of affectionate and friendly feelings. Narcissism and ambivalence must be transcended in the development of the personality. The success of this transcendence may be estimated by evaluating the "internal freedom" that the individual possesses. Third, there should be mental efficiency wherein the more primitive drives are tamed and the resultant, available energy is effectively utilized. Thus, behavior of the more normal person would demonstrate this taming by evidence of more socially appropriate action (as in sublimation) rather than the overt or even subtle shifting of primitive drives from one object to another (as in displacement).[2] Fourth, happiness must be present, together with a capacity for enjoyment and self-contentment. The "capacity to endure" and to be free of anxiety (*Angstfrei*) must be part of the normal mind. Jones (1948) thus sees normality as a fiction composed

[2] The distinction between sublimation and displacement is a very complicated one. For the psychoanalyst, activities that superficially may be similar can reflect either sublimation or displacement. For example, the butcher in the slaughtering process may be displacing raw, murderous, and aggressive impulses. On the other hand, the same behavior may involve the taming of what was originally raw, aggressive energy into an occupational choice that is both socially acceptable and is somewhat autonomous from its original drive source, within the mental apparatus of the butcher.

of all the enumerated utopian capacities and states of mind, which are never encountered in any one individual. Although his necessary psychological prerequisites can never be fully attained, they may be employed as criteria for determining degrees of normality. Even though these four criteria are theoretically clear and concise, they are operationally difficult, if not impossible, to assess.

In a similar fashion, Eissler (1960), on the basis of his psychoanalytic study of the efficient soldier, concludes that the term "normality" cannot be defined from a psychoanalytic point of view.[3] He believes that Freud's views on normality are based on the following categorizations: 1. descriptive meaning (normality as a subjective feeling); 2. structural meaning (absolute psychic normality); 3. economic meaning (fictitious normality ego); 4. dynamic meaning (harmony of the ego); 5. functional meaning (degree of normality); and 6. social meaning (schematic normality). Eissler believes that theoretical frames of reference, such as Freud's, make the term "normality" impractical for clinical-psychoanalytic application. Eissler states:

> Health is a fictitious concept in the psychic stratum; perhaps it has a proper place in the biological. There are defenses which cause displeasure or pleasure and there are defenses which favor the survival of the individual or of the species or lead to the individual's destruction. We need the concept of health for practical purposes and the concept requires redefinition probably with each new developmental phase of the individual. I do not see how the concept can theoretically be defined in a meaningful way and still stay in accordance with the principles of scientific psychology. This, however, does not negate the need—nor, perhaps, the possibility of outlining the conditions under which man has the greatest chance to continue functioning even when

[3] See Appendix under K. R. Eissler.

> exposed to the weight of trying excessive stimulation coming from either external or internal sources. While the ability so to function may be made the cornerstone of the concept of health, I wished to demonstrate that such functioning can, and, as I surmise, even must, be bought at the price of unquestionably severe psychopathology. Thus this paper may be taken as an attempt at trying out the operational value of the concept of the psychopathology of normality.

In estimating the cost of normal functioning and health, apparently Eissler refers primarily to the person who is called normal by society, such as "The Efficient Soldier."

Despite his feeling that it is impractical to define normality, Eissler himself tries to discover a means of judging relative normality when he states that psychoanalytic therapy may be the best measure by which normality can be gauged. The healthier the person, the better candidate for psychoanalysis he is, and the healthiest person, with the strongest ego, is the best candidate of all. In Eissler's words (1953, p. 104):

> The description of the hypothetically normal ego (though never encountered in clinical reality) introduces a new concept into psychoanalysis. The whole troublesome question of normal behavior is thus taken out of the contexts in which it has been discussed up to now. It is no longer a question of whether or not a person has adjusted to reality, whether or not he has integrated current value systems or has achieved mastery over his biological needs. . . . Thus a normal ego is one which, notwithstanding its symptoms, reacts to rational therapy with a dissolution of its symptoms.
>
> It is necessary to follow up the implications of this concept. It implies that the normal ego also may suffer disease. . . . If we may assume that psychoanalytic treatment is the most comprehensive psychological therapy because its goal is to provide the ego with all the knowledge and all the support it needs to regain its full competency, then psychoanalysis becomes the only procedure by which "normality" can be gauged.

According to Eissler, the ability to free-associate without resistance and to benefit maximally from interpretation is paramount to a strong and normal ego. Even though absolute normality is unattainable, the degree of an individual's normality can be measured by the psychoanalytic method.[4]

Other psychoanalysts have criticized attempts at defining or describing normality. They confine themselves to regarding the feelings of being normal as a particular psychopathological defense. For example, the following two psychoanalysts describe, as did Eissler (1960) in "The Efficient Soldier," the psychopathological reactions of a "normal person" to his (the subject's) feelings of normalcy. Reider (1950) states that since "normal" is used interchangeably with "right" or "good," the reassuring feeling of being "normal" can serve as reaction formation or counterphobia in a defense against anxiety. Similarly, Gitelson (1954) describes how "normality" may be used as a narcissistic defense involving a rigid identification with the aggressor that the individual sees in society. By limiting the use of the term "normality" to a psychological defense mechanism, Reider and Gitelson are saying that people who see themselves as "normal" may be hiding behind a façade that, when analyzed, is found to contain pathological characteristics. Hence, a person who labels himself as "normal" and is also labeled "normal" by others is far from being free from psychopathology, and indeed may be quite neurotic. With Eissler (1960), we might categorize these views of the subjective feeling of normality as the "descriptive meaning" of normality. The question may arise as to whom these authors will define as "healthy" or "normal." Obviously, Reider and Gitelson's interpretation of normality is not the only possible one. We submit that they, too, have their clinical and theoretical yardsticks.

[4] This view is identical to Freud's (1937) statement that a fictitious normal ego "would guarantee unshakable loyalty to the work of analysis."

The clinical yardstick can be ascertained from the therapeutic goals that the psychoanalyst sets for patients undergoing treatment. It is the very spirit of psychoanalysis that demands functional as well as structural changes in the patient. Therefore, a "real cure" of a psychopathological patient is not confined to the disappearance of symptoms but includes the attainment of a permanent stabilization of the personality. But if an "ideal analytic case" is not seen in psychoanalytic practice and is only a theoretical construct, then it follows that normality cannot be defined practically. Hence, with Freud, normality is defined as an ideal fiction.

Normality as Optimal Integration

One of the most precise psychoanalytic descriptions of normality comes from the writing of Klein (1960). According to Klein, to be mentally healthy is to have a well-integrated personality. Of basic importance in attaining mental health, as she sees it, is the normal emotional development of the infant and the young child. She views the following five elements as the crucial components of an integrated personality:

1. Emotional maturity. This means that feelings of the loss (of childhood and youth) can be counteracted by a capacity to accept appropriate substitute gratification of infantile wishes. Furthermore, it entails the ability to enjoy pleasures with relative freedom.

2. Strength of character. For Klein, strength of adult character is primarily determined by very early infantile experiences with one's mother. If the loving and tender aspects of the mother's early care dominate the frustrating, hateful experiences, the infant internalizes (makes part of himself) these positive experiences and memories. As a consequence, his ego can develop its full potential of character strength.

3. Capacity to deal with conflicting emotions. Only "weak" people avoid inner or outer conflicts. Mental health "is based on an interplay between the fundamental sources of mental life—the impulses of love and hate—an interplay in which the capacity for love is predominant."

4. A balance between internal life and adaptation to reality. This balance

> depends upon some insight into the variety of our contradictory impulses and feelings and the capacity to come to terms with these inner conflicts. An aspect of balance is the adaptation to the external world—an adaptation which does not interfere with the freedom of our own emotions and thoughts. This implies an interaction: Inner life always influences the attitudes towards external reality and in turn is influenced by the adjustment to the world of reality.

5. A successful welding into a whole of the different parts of the personality. Here Klein primarily refers to the need for an integrated self concept. She postulates an inner drive stemming from unconscious sources for such integration. Because of hereditary givens and early experiences, all individuals have, to some degree, the unconscious feeling that parts of themselves are unknown. Klein believes that love is the stimulus and the binding force that provides the energy for integration of the unknown parts with the known parts.

In a summary statement, Klein says:

> Complete integration never exists, but the more it has succeeded, and the more the individual is able to have insight into his anxieties and impulses, the stronger will be his character, and the greater will be his mental balance (pp. 237 ff.).

Thus, at one end of Klein's implicit scale can be found individuals who have succeeded unusually well in completing the task of integration.

Erikson (1950; 1956), like Klein (1960), emphasizes the importance of successful mastery of the various stages in the normal development of the identity process and hence the character. In each stage, the ego faces numerous disruptions and potential crises. A mature and normal person is one who successfully overcomes the obstacles in each and every stage of his development. Saul (1960, p. 343), too, when describing "emotional maturity," emphasizes the importance of continual growth:

> Mental and emotional health is the adequate achievement of emotional maturity, which means the growth from helplessness and need for love to the capacity to love, to be a good, responsible spouse, parent, and citizen; and this depends upon good human relations in the earliest years, for the pattern of these feelings and relationships continue on through adult life.

The crucial factor in the emotional maturity of the individual is his "sound early experience." In this, Klein (1960), Erikson (1950; 1956), and Saul (1960) are all of the same opinion.

Kubie (1953, 1954, 1958) has also shown considerable interest in the problem of normality and its relation to neurosis and psychosis. He defines neurosis and psychosis in terms of the symbolic process and its differentiation. Every unit of symbolic thinking has "I" and "non-I" roots, corresponding to the universal adaptational tasks of distinguishing oneself from the outer world. When there is a disturbance at either of these roots, one is mentally ill. Disturbance in the "non-I" pole leads to impaired reality discrimination about the external world and hence to psychosis. Disturbance in the "I" pole has to do with the relation of the symbol to its substrate. It impairs reality discriminations about the body and its sensations and is the basis of neurosis. In introducing the subject of neurotic distortions, Kubie (1958, p. 20) defines health in the following way:

> The measure of health is flexibility, the freedom to learn through experience, the freedom to change with changing internal and external circumstances, to be influenced by reasonable argument, admonitions, exhortation and the appeal to emotions; the freedom to respond appropriately to the stimulus of reward and punishment, and especially the freedom to cease when satiated.

Hence, for Kubie, the essence of normality is flexibility in all the areas described above. Illness represents, then, the "freezing of behavior into unalterable and insatiable patterns." Each single behavioral event and reactions to it, rather than the total personality, are of importance. Kubie (1954, 1958) asks what are the forces behind a particular behavior or act. He says that, if an act is a result of unconscious forces, it has neurotic (or psychotic) overtones that force its repeated execution in a rigid compulsive manner. A normal repetition will be the result of conscious or pre-conscious forces, which are by definition free of conflict. Kubie (1954, 1958) is suggesting that it is more sensible to evaluate each behavioral act according to its origins (conscious or unconscious) rather than according to holistic terms, such as "total personality integration." The latter, according to Kubie (1954, 1958), makes scientific precision difficult. The dynamic interplay of the conscious and unconscious forces is of utmost importance, and it alone should serve us in our attempt to delineate the normal from the pathological.

Although Rank (1925) has a different definition of normality than those described in the preceding, the over-all conceptual model is very similar. He believes that all people fit into one of three categories.[5] The "normal," or adjusted, man is one who accepts the "popular will as his own." Such a posture does not necessarily reflect passive submission; it may be, and when healthy most certainly is, an active alignment with

[5] See Thompson (1957) for a detailed description of Rank's three categories.

the will of the group. The neurotic is the one with difficulties: he cannot positively identify himself with the group, nor can he stand alone, for standing alone produces feelings of inferiority and guilt. The third type, the creative artist, has succeeded in fully accepting and affirming himself. He is in harmony with his powers and ideals. According to Rank, it is the function of therapy to attempt to change the neurotic into the creative man rather than into the "normal and adjusted" man.

Rank (1932, p. 371) depicts human life as an endless chain of separations accompanied by traumas and a continuous necessity to struggle and to create:

> In the ceaseless struggle for liberation of self from the moral, social, aesthetic ideologies and the people who represent them, the individual goes through a disjunctive process of which I have regarded the process of birth as the prototype. But the process, though similar in principle to, is not a simple repetition of the trauma of birth; it is, broadly, the attempt of the individual to gain freedom from dependence of any sort upon a state from which it has grown. According to the stage of development, this separation will take the most varied forms and symbols, whereas the basic conflict is always the same: the overcoming of previous supporting egos and ideologies from which the individual has to free himself according to the measure and speed of his own growth, a separation which is so hard, not only because the victory is always at the bottom and in some form, won over a part of one's own ego.

Here Rank (1932) depicts the continuous struggle of the individual to free himself from the past that binds and limits him. Rank implies that only few and select individuals can separate themselves enough from their past to become fully creative, and these are the artists.

In Jungian psychology, the healthy person strives for perfection and tends toward completeness within the framework of his society. Thus, Fordham (1960, p. 237), a Jungian analyst, writes:

> Any concept of mental health must include the consideration of variables and emergent possibilities in a periodically unstable system. What is healthy, and what is not, depends upon the dynamic de-integration of the self into component structures of the ego and archtypes and the integration of them into the whole organism.

Jung (1971) differentiates between mental health for individuals and collective norms:[6]

> Individuation is always to some extent opposed to collective norms, since it means separation and differentiation from the general and a building up of the particular—not a particularity that is *sought out*, but one that is already ingrained in the psychic constitution. The opposition to the collective norm, however, is only apparent, since closer examination shows that the individual standpoint is not *antagonistic* to it, but only *differently oriented*. The individual way can never be directly opposed to the collective norm, because the opposite of the collective norm could only be another, but contrary, norm. But the individual way can, by definition, never be a norm. A norm is the product of the totality of individual ways, and its justification and beneficial effect are contingent upon the existence of individual ways that need from time to time to orient to a norm. A norm serves no purpose when it possesses absolute validity. A real conflict with the collective norm arises only when an individual way is raised to a norm, which is the actual aim of extreme individualism. Naturally this aim is pathological and inimical to life. It has, accordingly, nothing to do with individuation, which, though it may strike out on an individual bypath, precisely on that account needs the norm for its *orien-*

[6] See Appendix under Carl G. Jung.

> *tation* (q.v.) to society and for the vitally necessary relationship of the individual to society. Individuation, therefore, leads to a natural esteem for the collective norm, but if the orientation is exclusively collective the norm becomes increasingly superfluous and morality goes to pieces. The more a man's life is shaped by the collective norm, the greater is his individual immorality.
>
> Individuation is practically the same as the development of consciousness out of the original state of *identity* (q.v.). It is thus an extension of the sphere of consciousness, an enriching of conscious psychological life.

Jung (1971) believes in the existence of a collective norm that each person tries to approximate. He indicates that the person's own life and experience are always different from the collective norm. Since the collective norm, according to Jung, is an accumulation of all the individual ways, by definition, no single individual can approach the sum total. Thus, Jung calls this approximation of the norm the ideal toward which everyone strives but can never attain. Everyone develops his own psyche, which is related to the collective norm. The mature person has found a satisfactory relationship to this norm. Although this relationship is not by itself an assurance of mental health, without it one cannot attain a state of health. It appears that Jung's concept of individuation approximates his ideal for mental health.

Harms (1962) states that for Jung mental health is dependent on psychological awareness and is independent from collective subduing powers. The maturation and individuation procedures and rites are especially important, because mental health depends to a large degree on completing the development of one's personality.

The relativist position regarding definitions of normality is especially criticized by Money-Kyrle (1957).[7] He rejects outright a clinical concept of normality that will depend, even in

[7] See Appendix under R. E. Money-Kyrle.

part, on adaptation to society, for he believes that some people whom every clinician would classify as mentally ill would be regarded as normal in some societies.[8] The only criterion that Money-Kyrle feels is independent of cultural standards is insight. Hence, a normal, or healthy, mind is one that knows itself. Money-Kyrle thus states:

> Since in reality self-knowledge is always incomplete, it follows from our definition that there can be no completely normal person. But this conclusion, with which no analyst will quarrel, does not lessen the value of a term to denote a limit to which real people approximate in various degrees.

As we shall see in the next section, many psychoanalysts would quarrel with Money-Kyrle, and do not accept the premise that a definition of normality must contain a utopian element in it.

Normality as Adaptation within Context

One of the most significant contributors to the understanding of the psychoanalytic adaptive point of view is Hartmann (1960), who discusses the present contribution of psychoanalysis to the study of the essential elements of health.[9] He states that we could broaden our knowledge by studying normal behavior in both children and adults. Hartmann goes on to emphasize that ego psychology is important to our under-

[8] For a contrasting view, see the section on culture relativism in Chapter 4.

[9] In another publication, Hartmann (1939) deplores the use of value judgments implied in many mental health concepts. He objects to the indiscriminate use of terms like "good" or "bad" with "healthy" or "sick." In a similar fashion, Freida Fromm-Reichman (1946) criticizes society's failure to recognize that "mentally disturbed" and "mentally stable" are different in degree but not in kind. She feels that an understanding of this point would do much to correct the faulty association of mental illness and immorality. (See Chapter 7 for details.)

standing of mental health, because through ego psychology we are able to gain easier access to the relations between the biological and the socio-cultural aspects of human behavior. Hence, we can study the "interactions of adaptive and integrative tendencies." When these tendencies are interfered with, we should study the cases carefully, since the fuller understanding of the forces that upset the equilibrium will help us in the evaluation of mental health. Hartmann stresses, then, the contributions of new concepts of ego psychology to the understanding of mental health. There is a complex interaction among those factors having to do with basic biological mechanisms and the evolution of a mental apparatus geared to deal with socio-cultural realities. Hartmann's (1960) concept of ego autonomy emphasizes that each person starts life with certain capacities that are relatively free from conflict. Of course, they may be influenced by the ego's defensive functioning, which develops as a result of conflict. Throughout life, there is interaction between the relatively conflict-free and the relatively conflict-driven aspects of ego function. A person possesses various degrees of ego strength resulting from this interaction. Thus, ego strength determines the degree of the stability and the degree of environmental adaptation. Health emerges as synonymous with good adaptation of the person to his own mental and physical environment.

Glover (1956) differentiates between the "normal" person and the patient primarily on the basis of motivation, the former being inaccessible to therapy because he is not motivated or does not need therapy. By his tentative definition, the normal person is one "who is free from symptoms, unhampered by mental conflicts, who shows satisfactory working capacity, and who is able to love someone apart from himself." The "normal" man conforms to his environment and is adequately adapted to it. Glover is against idealization of normality, since such an idealized approach rewards conformity and seems to penalize diversity and heterogeneity. According to Glover, the normal man has successfully adjusted his personal psychic mechanism to the facts of objective reality, achieving a harmonious blending of the two.

Certain psychoanalysts who do attempt to define normality tend to emphasize the importance of cultural adaptation more than those psychoanalysts previously cited. One of the best known and most often quoted definitions of normality or mental health is Karl Menninger's (1945, p. 2):

> Let us define mental health as the adjustment of human beings to the world and to each other with a maximum of effectiveness and happiness. Not just efficiency, or just contentment—or the grace of obeying the rules of the game cheerfully. It is all of these together. It is the ability to maintain an even temper, an alert intelligence, socially considerate behavior, and a happy disposition.

As is apparent, this definition is an attempt to make normality feasible and within the grasp of man, and yet it has a familiar ring since it is laden with our Western social values.

Three basic patterns of defense that can be normal or pathological are stressed by Sapirstein (1948). They are flight, dependency, and self-sufficiency. These three basic patterns of defense enable us, according to Sapirstein, to "approximate normality in terms of adaptation rather than on the basis of *conflict* (internal or external) or the extent of *consciousness* of inner feelings." To be normal is to align our defenses in such a way that cultural adaptation is achieved.

In *Civilization and Its Discontents,* Freud (1930) discusses the collective neurosis of society. Since Freud does not define the environment as normal, adjustment to it cannot be utilized as a measure of mental health. In a similar fashion, Stärke (1921) speculates that if we consider civilization as operating as an obsessional neurosis, then the insane person might well reveal that which society finds intolerable, or, in other words, unmask the unconscious of society.

Fromm (1955) has attempted to argue by analogy and analyze society's ills in much the same way as a psychoanalyst handles a patient. In his comparison of a person's neurosis and "socially patterned defect," Fromm uses terms for the ills of society that are similar to those applied to a patient's psychopathology. Fromm's definition of mental health is:

> Mental health is characterized by the ability to love and to create, by the emergence from incestuous ties to clay and soil, by a sense of identity based on one's experience of self as the subject and agent of one's powers, by the grasp of reality inside and outside of ourselves; that is, by the development of objectivity and reason.

It is of interest to note that, although Fromm has shown great concern with the sanity of the social system, his description of the essentials of mental health are individually oriented and predominantly intrapsychic.

Alexander (1948) compares the intrapsychic systems to political systems.[10] He compares the neurotic personality to an autocratic government that suppresses all opinions that do not conform to its opinions. By analogy, the neurotic person spends much energy on suppressing desires and unacceptable impulses. Hence, the energy cannot be used for more constructive purposes. The healthy ego is compared to the democratic state, where individual needs are recognized and can be satisfied and conflicting interests are met by attempting to mediate and compromise. The democratic system by analogy

[10] See Appendix under Franz Alexander.

is a possible one for the psyche to follow, and with a strong and healthy ego it may often become a reality.

Together with the emphasis on social factors, the family, too, gains prominence in the writing of some contemporary psychoanalysts. Ackerman (1958) believes that not only internal freedom but also social relations are important to mental health. In his discussion of the goals of psychoanalytic therapy, Ackerman (1956, pp. 9–14) mentions three areas that are of concern to the psychoanalyst: "(1) What goes on emotionally within the individual. (2) What goes on between the individual and his significant small groups. (3) The social and value patterns of the individual's larger community." These are the areas, Ackerman (1956) feels, that must be considered when normal behavior of an individual is to be assessed accurately. In his discussion of "the future of mental health," Grotjahn (1960) equates normality with a "stable ego identity." This, according to Grotjahn, is influenced to a great extent by family relations. The family, having "free flowing communication which includes the conscious and unconscious of all family members," will produce the healthier individual.

Adler's individual psychology was, according to the Ansbachers (1956), a social psychology. It is not surprising, therefore, that Adler's criterion for normality is socially oriented. According to Adler (1939), the ideally normal individual is one who is of the greatest benefit to society. Adler says, in effect, that when one considers human normality, it is crucial to determine whether the individual is a burden or an asset to society at large and whether he is contributing to the progressive development of man.

The Ansbachers (1956, p. 102) further describe Adler's point of view:

> While the neurotic is more concerned with his self-esteem, and has a personal goal of superiority, the normal individual, due to his greater social interest, is more concerned with gaining satisfaction by overcoming difficulties which are appreciated as such by others as well. He has a goal of superiority which includes the welfare of others.

The normal person differs from the abnormal person in his motivation and interests. The neurotic man is self-centered and without a social conscience; the normal man has more common sense, is action oriented, and has the welfare of others at heart as well as his own. The normal man, then, can be different in kind from the abnormal person, but can be partially neurotic, suffer feelings of inferiority, and experience some of the same difficult situations encountered by the mentally ill patient.

We have presented conceptions of normality held by various psychoanalysts. In our opinion, the underlying and pervasive philosophical premise is that all men are at least part-neurotics. According to the dominant psychoanalytic motif, the normal man is the near-perfect man and perfection is an ideal that living man can never reach, albeit a few select individuals have, at times, come close to the ideal. It seems to us that those psychoanalysts who have evolved such a definition of normality attempt to convey, at least in part, a value-laden concept of man's most desirable characteristics. Although most psychoanalysts feel that normality is an ideal, they differ in their ideas of what comprises this highest good. Certain psychoanalysts think that mastery of the drives is the most crucial factor in attainment of normality. Others consider the necessary factors to be adaptation and the total integration of the personality; still others, stressing what may be called the operational approach, state that each single behavioral event has to be evaluated on its own merit. There are analysts who regard the successful mastery of the various developmental stages as crucial in becoming a mature person. Still others believe that a stable and satisfactory relationship of the individual to his family, his small groups, and society at large is the crucial factor in attaining normality.

We have discussed these differences, and yet we wish to emphasize the over-all agreement of most psychoanalysts. Thus, we conclude this chapter with the following comment by Michaels (1959), which best summarizes the psychoanalytic point of view:

> Medicine is gradually abandoning the myth of the normal person—although we still think of a person as being healthy—"normal"—if he is not sick. The statistical yardstick is still the measure of all things. From an analytic point of view, there is no such animal as the "normal" person except as an ideal—we are all relatively neurotic. The basic tenets of psychoanalysis affirm that conflict is the essence of life and that instinctual renunciation is the price of being a civilized human being. Paraphrasing Alexander Pope's phrase "To err is human," we would say "To be neurotic is human."

3

Normative and Ideal Concepts in Psychology

> One of the major methodological problems of clinical psychology concerns the relation between the "clinical" and "statistical" (or "actuarial") methods of prediction. . . . The problem is to predict how a person is going to behave. In what manner should we go about this prediction?
>
> —P. E. MEEHL (1954)

From the days of its emergence from philosophy, the field of psychology has been deeply and consistently concerned with the issue of norms and of normal behavior. Normative analysis of objectifiable and measurable behavioral units in animals and man has been a fundamental pillar underlying many significant developments in psychology. Although interest in psychopathology has heightened since World War II, it is largely viewed by psychologists as an outgrowth of, rather than as an antecedent of, theoretical constructs based on normative approaches. In contrast to psychiatry, whose medical roots placed pathology as *the* basic discipline, the profession of psychology has had a fundamentally different historical evolution. While differences between psychology and psychiatry have become somewhat obscured by the complex and heterogeneous developments in the 1950's and 1960's, the professions as a whole may still be distinguished by a number of major conceptual and practical dimensions, including their perspectives regarding health and normality. Segmentalization of psychology has proceeded at a rapid rate and the multiplicity of viewpoints and methods makes it difficult to characterize clear-cut over-all trends.[1] Nevertheless, it seems plausible to divide psychology's approach to normality into two major categories, one *statistical* and the other *clinical* in nature. We shall organize this chapter along this major axis and conclude by presenting the bridging formulations and criticisms.

Statistical and Normative Concepts

In this section, we will illustrate the relationship between the concept of the norm and some of the principles underlying measurements in psychology. It is here, in psychological tests and measures, that the concept of the average has had specific usefulness, though, as will be demonstrated, it has been interpreted differently by various psychologists. We shall begin

[1] According to the 1965 Directory of the American Psychological Association, there are presently twenty-two divisions of the A.P.A. They are: 1. Division of General Psychology; 2. Division on the Teaching of Psychology; 3. Division of Experimental Psychology; 5. Division of Evaluation and Measurement; 6. Division of Physiological and Comparative Psychology; 7. Division on Developmental Psychology; 8. Division of Personality and Social Psychology; 9. The Society for the Psychological Study of Social Issues—A Division of the A.P.A.; 10. Division on Esthetics; 12. Division of Clinical Psychology; 13. Division of Consulting Psychology; 14. Division of Industrial Psychology; 15. Division of Education Psychology; 16. Division of School Psychologists; 17. Division of Counseling Psychology; 18. Division of Psychologists in Public Service; 19. Division of Military Psychology; 20. Division on Maturity and Old Age; 21. The Society of Engineering Psychologists—A Division of the A.P.A.; 22. National Council on Psychological Aspects of Disability—A Division of the A.P.A.; 23. Division of Consumer Psychology; 24. Division of Philosophical Psychology.

by describing the utilization of the Bell-shaped curve for determining statistically normal distributions of behavior. By concentrating on the average, or norm, as applied in statistics, we do not mean to imply that there has not been, in recent decades, a considerable increase in methodological and analytical sophistication in psychology. Whereas the original use of norms pertained to relatively comprehensive measures, such as IQ, within the last few decades norms have been developed for more specific mental abilities and personality characteristics. One computational procedure that has contributed significantly in this area is the factor analysis, as pioneered by Thurstone (1947). This procedure enables experimenters to extract, from large batteries of tests, those factors that are groupings of tests or items that quasi-measure some basic function. Norms are now available for various types of factors, as, for example, is illustrated by the work of Cattel (1946) and Hathaway and Monachesi (1963).

In the field of psychophysiology, where variables are much less intangible than in psychology, the need for norms is less urgent, and relatively little concern has been expressed for their development. In fact, more interest has been evidenced in a need for norms for change scores than has been for levels. This has partially resulted from Wilder's (1958) emphasis on the Law of Initial Values, which points up the fact that a treatment cannot be expected to produce equal changes in individuals with different pre-treatment levels. Since these norms are lacking, various statistical manipulations have been devised to deal with change score data. One popular method for this is Lacey's (1956) Autonomic Lability Score, which uses the regression of post-treatment values on the pre-scores. A somewhat different treatment of change score data, suggested by Heath and Oken (1964), helps equate the variances of the responses in what they call "the quantification of 'response.'"

In the field of mental testing the concept of the "normal" is most often inexorably tied to statistical concepts of the average. The Belgian statistician Lambert Quételet (1796–1874) first applied Gauss's normal law of error, the Bell-shaped probability curve, to the distribution of biological and social human data. Quételet's theory was that Gauss's law could be applied to human variability, for he assumed that nature strives to duplicate a particular model in every man and misses by varying degrees. In discussing this theory, Boring (1950) states:

> We can understand Quételet's doctrine of "L'Homme Moyen," in which the average man appears as nature's ideal, and deviations toward the good, as well as toward the bad, appear as different degrees of nature's mistakes. The average is the most frequent value and nature's large errors are rare.

Quételet's doctrine assigns a purpose to nature's creativity and assumes that the average man is nature's biological ideal. On a somewhat more sophisticated level, the doctrine assumes that there is a great deal to be learned from studying what is normal or modal.

When Galton (1869) published *Hereditary Genius,* he accepted Quételet's use of "The Normal Law" as an explanation of the frequency of the occurrence of genius. As did Quételet, Galton based his theories on the supposition that the normal law is nature's law. Galton was the first to apply statistics to the measurement of mental ability. He investigated the statistically "normal" distribution of genius and postulated that the frequency of genius could be predicted. In 1905, Alfred Binet, together with Théodore Simon, developed the first standardized intelligence test for children that employed the concept of mental age. Binet's approach was operational. He developed his scales from observations of the actual behavior of a population of normal and subnormal children. The IQ scale is based on the assumption that the distribution of intelligence in the population, like many other human attributes, can be plotted on the Gaussian curve. Then, by definition, the median IQ will be 100, half the population falling below 100 and the other half above 100. An average IQ, again by definition, will be one between 85 and 115, which is one standard deviation from the mean. IQs between 70 and 130, a range including two standard deviations from the mean, encompass the overwhelming majority of the population. By and large, psychologists have found the IQ scale amenable to content standardization for different cultures and socio-economic groupings. Thus, the scale has been utilized extensively throughout the world (see Figure 3–1).

The application of normative models has become axiomatic in the constructions and validations of new psychological instruments. A good psychological test, for example, can be defined as one that separates the average from both extremes in a meaningful and consistent manner. Recently, however, we have witnessed an increased statistical sophistication in construction of psychological tests, so that the concept of the average, though still with us, has been replaced by more complex statistical analyses, such as factor analysis. As they were originally used by Thurstone (1947), these statistical devices have proven especially useful in situations where the investigator attempts to isolate specific variables that may apply to part of the personality but do not necessarily represent the whole personality structure (for example, anxiety as contrasted with anxiety neurosis). Each variable, or scale, is constructed on the principle of the Bell-shaped curve, so that the majority of the population will fall within a certain "normal" range and only the "disturbed" will fall in the extremes.

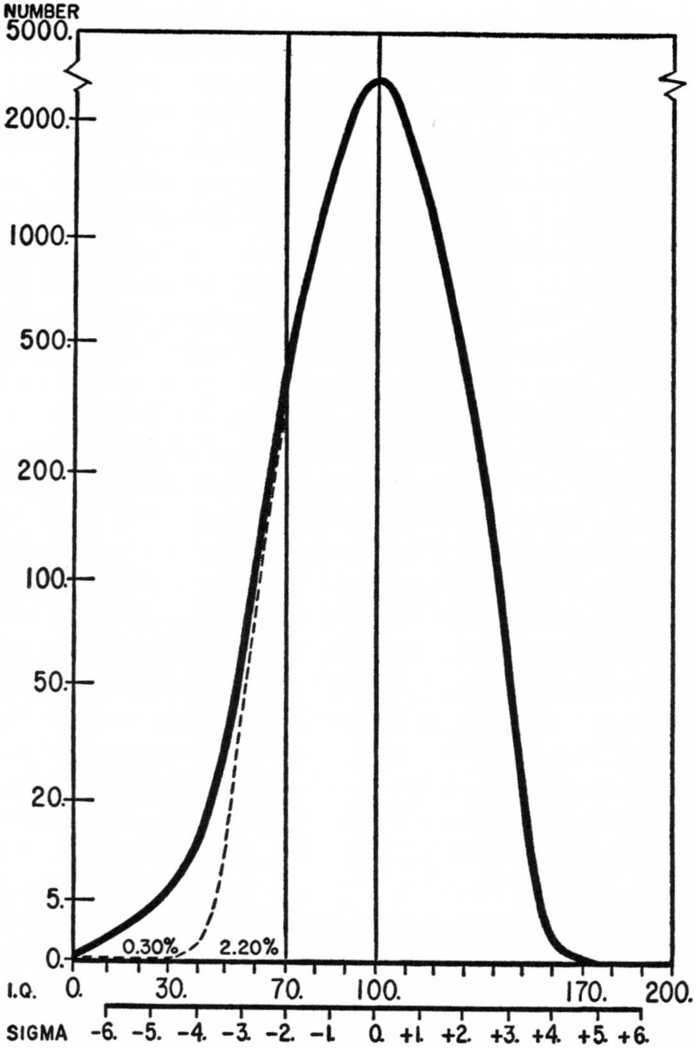

Figure 3–1. From *The Biology of Mental Defect* by L. S. Penrose (London: Sidgwick & Jackson Ltd., 1964), p. 29.

Basically, there are two different ways in which the norm, or average, is utilized in tests and measurements. The IQ, as described above, is prototypic of one type, in which the average, or norm, simply represents a statistical fact, namely that the majority of the population fall within one standard deviation of the mean. No more is claimed, though it is assumed that the higher a person's IQ, the greater his intelligence. There is a different principle in the second type of psychological tests; these are tests involving clinical evaluations, for example, Minnesota Multiphasic Personality Inventory (M.M.P.I.), Rorschach Test, and Thematic Apperception Test (T.A.T.). Here, too, the statistical principle of the Bell-shaped curve is utilized for defining averages and norms. Beck's (1944) utilization of norms in Rorschach testing corresponds to the model of the Bell-shaped curve. According to Beck, a subject is judged solely on the following basis: Do his associations fall within the norm or outside of the norm? The former are deemed to be normal or healthy, the latter disturbed.[2] As will be illustrated in this chapter, not all clinical psychologists interpret their results in this way. Our emphasis, though, is not on the mathematical rigidity of the scoring, but rather on the different interpretations of the values of varying clinical scores. It seems to us that in most clinical tests the average is defined as the clinically desirable, with *both* extremes connoting pathology. One either has too much anxiety or too little, with the desirable or even optimal quantity being somewhere in the middle. Another example is psychomotor activity; persons with too much psychomotor activity are defined as manics, those with too little are said to be depressed (or catatonic), and the optimal, average, or normal quantity is somewhere in between the two extremes. This principle, which we have

[2] It is important to note that by no means all types of associations fall within the Bell-shaped curve, although most do.

called "idealization of the norm," is incorporated into most clinical psychological tests.

This outline of the use of statistics and the concept of the norm in psychology is well known and exerts considerable influence, even beyond the area of tests and measurements. In Chapter 6, we indicate how it is being employed by other behavioral scientists, notably psychiatrists, who are deeply interested in collecting normative data on populations not individually treated or investigated by them. The major methodological premise behind the collection of normative data is the use of large numbers of individuals and even several populations. In the next section, we concentrate on an opposite methodological approach, namely the single case study.

Idiographic and Ideal Concepts

Many psychologists have come to believe that statistical and normative concepts are limited in generating hypotheses about human behavior. To paraphrase Sargent and Mayman (1959), we will present the thinking of those psychologists who believe that they "adequately" describe the individual. There is no question that the discipline of clinical psychology has been strongly influenced by psychoanalytic psychology. The influence has been so deep that purely psychoanalytical interpretations of normality are often incorporated within the psychological literature. Such psychological theories, which are not only influenced by but also are identical with psychoanalytic theories of normality, are not included in this chapter. We believe that they should be considered part of psychoanalysis proper. We have not included the thinking of those psychologists whose perspective is that of the psychoanalyst in this section.[3] Rather, we have chosen to discuss examples that have been influenced by psychoanalysis but differ from it in varying degrees.

Maslow and Mittelmann's (1951) text of abnormal psychology illustrates how psychological concepts have been influenced by the psychoanalytic point of view.[4] These authors state that there are three points that must be remembered in any study of the "normal." First, the dynamics of mentally sick and mentally healthy individuals differ only quantitatively. Second, the use of the term "normal" in statistics connotes the average. Third, normality has a direct relationship to cultural adaptation. Social status, age, and sex must also always be borne in mind. What may be normal for a boy of five or ten may be considered "immature" or even a sign of "mental illness" in an adult. Maslow and Mittelmann proceed to present a list of qualities that are, they feel, necessary to normal psychological health. They are:

1. adequate feeling of security;
2. adequate spontaneity and emotionality;
3. efficient contact with reality;
4. adequate bodily desires and ability to gratify them;
5. adequate self-knowledge;
6. integration and consistency of personality;
7. adequate life goals;
8. ability to learn from experience;
9. ability to satisfy requirements of the group;
10. adequate emancipation from group or culture.

Obviously, these criteria are difficult to assess. They seem to represent culturally bound and value-laden concepts since

[3] For example, such investigators as Erich Fromm, David Rapaport and Robert Waelder.

[4] See Appendix under Abraham H. Maslow & Bela Mittelmann.

they include terms such as "adequate," "efficient," and "ability." We have to ask: "Adequate for whom, according to whose judgment, and based on which criteria?" But more important, these criteria, like the psychoanalytic concepts, represent ideals not expected to be fulfilled in reality.

Maslow also represents the group of clinical psychologists who stress the importance of the creative aspects and the potentials of the individual. As Maslow (1954) states, he has been strongly influenced by Freudian and neo-Freudian psychology, as well as by Goldstein (1939, 1959), who in dynamic terms viewed the organism as endowed with built-in energy serving as a potential that could be actualized in time. Goldstein defines self-actualization as the over-all, all-encompassing goal of life. The healthy organism is one that upholds tension rather than one that strives to discharge it. But since the organism is not isolated from its environment, Goldstein (1959) states: "Man's self-realization is based on the condition of adequacy between the individual's behavior and the 'world's.' " Maslow (1954) claims that a study of people who have fulfilled their potentialities to the greatest degree will lead us to the formulation of a "positive psychology" and will rid us of negative approaches. The list of qualifications and attributes with which Maslow endows his self-actualizing people is indeed impressive. The spectrum is broad; it ranges from spontaneity, creativity, and a good sense of humor to identification with mankind, acceptance of self and others, and strong ethical principles. His examples of fulfilled personalities include such people as Abraham Lincoln, Ludwig van Beethoven and Albert Einstein, plus a few, select others.

Another approach, not dissimilar to the psychoanalytic one but stemming from a different clinical tradition, is that adopted by Rogers (1959).[5] Rogers developed his theoretical

[5] See Appendix under Carl R. Rogers.

framework in conjunction with his experience in "client-centered therapy." In his concept, the "fully functioning person" is strikingly similar to the person who, according to the psychoanalyst, functions "optimally." Rogers describes the "fully functioning person" as someone who is "continually in a process of further self-actualization." Although the major criteria that he uses are described in his own "Rogerian" terminology, they are not substantially different from either Maslow's or Levine's (see Chapter 1). The ten criteria are:

1. He will be open to his experience.
   a. The corollary statement is that he will exhibit no defensiveness.
2. Hence all experience will be available to awareness.
3. All symbolizations will be as accurate as the experiential data will permit.
4. His self-structure will be congruent with his experience.
5. His self-structure will be fluid Gestalt, changing flexibly in the process of assimilation of new experience.
6. He will experience himself as the locus of evaluation.
   a. The valuing process will be a continuing organismic one.
7. He will have no conditions of worth.
   a. The corollary statement is that he will experience unconditional self-regard.
8. He will meet each situation with behavior which is unique and creative adaptation to the newness of that moment.
9. He will find his organismic valuing a trustworthy guide to the most satisfying behaviors, because
   a. All available experiential data will be available to awareness and used.
   b. No datum of experience will be distorted in, or denied to, awareness.
   c. The outcomes of behavior in experience will be available to awareness.
   d. Hence any failure to achieve the maximum possible sat-

isfaction, because of lack of data, will be corrected by this effective reality testing.

10. He will live with others in the maximum harmony, because of the rewarding character of reciprocal regard.

Rogers equates his "fully functioning person" with the person at the end point of optimal psychotherapy. Rogers seems to expect those who have been adequately counselled to manifest optimal functioning in every area of life.

Buhler (1959), although critical of the psychoanalytical model, sums up her discussion of the healthy individual with a description of an "ideal" person. According to Buhler, there are "four basic biological tendencies of life." They are directed toward: 1. Need of satisfaction; 2. Upholding of the internal order; 3. Adaptation; and 4. Productivity. For an organism to achieve "healthy functioning," these four basic tendencies have to be balanced and integrated. According to her, the healthy individual can be described in the following way:

> Fulfillment to the healthy individual with a well-rounded personality is to have had "happiness." That is, the fulfillment of the most essential wishes; to have found sufficient self-realization in successful creative accomplishments; to have helped and not been detrimental to the welfare of others; and to have found "peace of mind" in the resultant internal order.

One can readily see the parallel between the "basic tendencies of life," from a biological frame of reference, and the psychological conceptualizations that they represent. Buhler believes that such an analogy is not only valid but also preferable, since only through correlation of biology and psychology will we achieve a fuller understanding of the constitution of health and normality.

Bridging Concepts and Criticisms

Many psychologists are dissatisfied with either an exclusively normative approach or an exclusively ideographic approach. In dealing with the question of normality, they have attempted to develop an operational system that transcends the straightforward clinical or statistical conceptualizations of normality. Experts in the use of projective testing have become increasingly dissatisfied with simple statistical analyses of their subjects' responses. Although many Rorschach specialists continue to interpret tests strictly along the dimensions of specific scores, other specialists make their diagnostic evaluations from a composite of the patient's behavior in the testing situation and the scores. The reverse tendency has also been manifested in increasing numbers. Thus, psychologists are now testing hypotheses based on single case studies on larger population samples.[6] This approach conveys dissatisfaction with concepts of health and illness based on ideographic approaches alone.

Many other psychologists, whose work has not specifically involved the definition of normal or healthy, have been profoundly interested in such definitions. In this section we shall discuss some of the concepts of these individuals, many of whom have emphasized the necessity for multiple perspectives in approaching the definition of normality. We have labeled all of the psychologists referred to in this section "bridgers" in order to highlight their attempt to integrate the two major approaches to normality underlying much of the current perspective in psychology. We shall also discuss viewpoints of psychologists who have been critical of various attempts by colleagues to define normality. These critics range from some

[6] For example, Symonds (1949); Ames et al. (1952); Koch (1956), and Murphy (1962).

who believe that attempts at such definitions are meaningless processes to those who have proposed new methods for achieving a more satisfactory definition.

The M.M.P.I., the Rorschach, and the T.A.T. can be evaluated solely on the basis of their exact numerical scores. When this is done, each test yields a mathematical measurement of the subject's deviations from a designated "average." As indicated earlier, the exact usefulness of this measurement is a central issue within clinical psychology (see, for example, Meehl, 1954). A significant group of psychologists utilize the psychological test only as a clinical instrument without giving it an absolute numerical value (see, for example, Schafer, 1954, and Engel, 1960). In the latter case, the complex transactions that take place between examiner and examinee are evaluated clinically as well as numerically. Engel (1960), for example, has formulated four parameters that are, she feels, crucial in the psychological evaluation of children. They encompass the issues of empathy, control, regression, and time and space. They were prompted "by a sense of incompleteness, arising not out of a disbelief in the significance of test scores (and norms) but out of a growing conviction that test results, considered apart from at least these few aspects of the child–examiner transaction, represent only a segment of the kaleidoscopic process that leads to diagnosis."

Shoben (1957) coins the term "integrative adjustment" and employs it as a working model for his definition of normality.[7] The model includes broad and general criteria of normality based on actual, observable behavior and intrapsychic harmony. Shoben points out that the normal person is not perfect. He may be, at times, self-defeating, shortsighted, and functioning below his capacity. He is not free from feelings of guilt, anxiety, or fear. The normal man may be able to enjoy a relatively high degree of self-respect and continue

[7] See Appendix under Edward Joseph Shoben, Jr.

in predominantly positive interpersonal relationships. He is able to learn from his mistakes, benefit from his experience, and so come closer to his own conception of the ideal. The advantages of his model are, according to Shoben, that it accounts for a wide variation in observed behavior engaged in by "normal" people. Although Shoben denies that his concept of "integrative adjustment" attempts to fit people into preconceived behavioral molds, he will find it difficult to evaluate degrees to which the person fulfills "the symbolic and social potentialities that are distinctively human." Shoben sees degrees of integrative adjustment as prototypic for normality. An individual may have a wide array of personal problems and conflicts, but it is his own style of functioning and coping that decides how well he is integrated. Thus, Shoben combines a model of his awareness of the limitations of man's actual behavior with depth psychology to include man's potential. The concept of "integrative adjustment," then, reflects all three areas of functioning.

The social psychologist Jahoda (1950, 1955, and 1959) has assessed the present status of concepts of mental health. In her book *Current concepts of Positive Mental Health* (1959), she reviews the psychological literature on mental health and then, in summary form, she presents six cardinal aspects of "positive mental health."[8] She believes these constituents to be operational in the sense that they can be proven empirically. Because Jahoda's work represents a digestion of much current psychological thinking in the field of mental health research, we present her criteria in their entirety. In the main Jahoda's criteria are:

1. Attitudes towards the self; they include the accessibility of the self to consciousness; the correctness of the self-concept; its

[8] See Appendix under Marie Jahoda.

relation to the sense of identity and the acceptance by the individual of his own self.

2. Growth, development and self-actualization; the extent the individual utilizes his abilities; his orientation toward the future and his investment in living.

3. Integration; the extent to which the psychic forces are balanced; a unifying outlook on life and a resistance to stress.

4. Autonomy; the aim here is to ascertain whether the self-reliant person will be able to decide with relative ease and speed what suits his own needs best.

5. Perception of reality; a relative freedom from need–distortion, and the existence of empathy.

6. Environmental mastery; under this heading is listed: ability to love; adequacy in love, work, and play; adequacy in interpersonal relationships; meeting situational requirements; adaptation and adjustment; and efficiency in problem solving.

In her book, Jahoda shows the various ways these factors are employed in the current mental-health literature. She also presents suggestions for future research that should help clarify the issues by bringing out further data. Eventually, the new data may broaden our understanding of the development of mental health and "how mental health in one stage leads to mental health in the next." In effect, Jahoda advocates a combination of an operational and a theoretical approach to the problem of mental health. She then bridges concepts derived mainly from case studies and from large-scale studies. This new synthesis could bring in additional data on new populations that have not been investigated in the past. Although Jahoda is aware of the cultural limitation of her six cardinal aspects "of positive mental health," she nonetheless does not clearly isolate the value-laden elements in her criteria.

M. B. Smith (1959) doubts whether the criteria for mental health of either Jahoda (1958) or Maslow (1954) have scientific merit. His criticism concerns especially the problem of values. He states:

> Neither the strategy of direct assault (for example, Maslow) nor that of multiple criteria (for example, Jahoda) turns out to give us much assistance on this problem, although the empirical relationships brought to light by research that follows either strategy may aid us in the volitional decision as to where to draw the boundaries. . . . So long as personality theory must be represented by *theories* of personalities (of Hall & Lindzey, 1957), we are in a poor position to set our boundaries according to guidelines suggested by any one of the several competitors. Here lies still another reason for the support of fundamental research in personality in the interests of mental health.

In another article, Smith (1961) strongly disapproves of simply erecting "competing lists" that categorize conceptions of positive mental health. By contrasting Jahoda's multiple criteria with those of Gordon W. Allport, he shows that they almost completely overlap. Smith (1961) recommends a "system theory as a frame of reference," which is to be utilized in the following way when seeking for dimensions of mental health:

1. They should be serious contenders in the arena of human values (though an impossible consensus is of course not required). The positive value should be explicit.
2. They should be capable of measurement or inference from identifiable aspects of behavior.
3. They should articulate with personality theory.
4. They should be relevant to the social context for which the chapter is being written.

Smith brings to light the obstacle that every worker in the field of normality or mental health has difficulty in overcoming, namely, the intermingling of one's own values and

Weltanschauung in the concepts one views as typical of the normal man. Therefore, he recommends that psychologists make explicit their own value orientation. He further states that the theories of normality should come from observable data, should not contradict present accepted theories of personality, and should be part of the larger social field from which they were drawn.

Amid the voluminous relevant literature on the concept of normality, we believe it worthwhile to cite the recent discussion between Friedes (1960), who advocates the elimination of the concepts of normality, and Korman (1961), who wants to retain it. Friedes believes that the multitude of different definitions of normality merely illustrates the uselessness of the concept. "Normality" is used sometimes as an absolute concept, sometimes as a cultural phenomenon, and only infrequently does it take into consideration the individuality of each person. Friedes feels that psychologists, rather than dichotomizing normality and pathology, should discard both terms and study the person, with his positive and negative psychological attributes, under different sets of experiences.

Korman (1961), in answer to Friedes, thinks that we should aim toward attaining a meaningful definition of normality. He advocates starting with an operational definition of normality, such as non-exposure to psychiatric diagnosis and treatment, then adding other indicators that will help "compose a matrix of significant relatedness. It is clear at this point that this approach, in contrast to the idealist or average views of normality, would lead us to an empirically based conceptualization of normality having the essential character of a theoretical construct." Although Korman asserts that this may not be a very reliable method, he feels it would provide for a good start that, "once this typological approach has begun to yield some fruits . . . , we will be able to shift to systematic studies of the processes which favor normal psychological growth."

In this chapter, some of the relevant psychological literature concerning normality has been reviewed. First, we have concentrated on statistical and normative concepts, in which the concept of the norm, or average, has specific usefulness, be it in IQ measurements or clinical psychological tests. Second, we have elaborated on ideographic and ideal concepts, where investigators stress the individuality of the person, his uniqueness, and the impossibility of using statistical criteria as sole judges of whether the individual is or is not normal. Rather, these psychologists see the normal individual as a non-existent theoretical ideal and thus compare each case to the idealized concept, with an attempt to judge how close (or distant) the person has come to attaining this ideal. Third, we have discussed the psychologists who can be best described as "bridgers" and critics. Probably the majority of psychologists fall in this group, in that there is, and has been, wide dissatisfaction with perspectives on normality. It should be noted, however, that despite these dissatisfactions and attempts to develop new guidelines, no systematic approach has as yet become widely accepted.

4

The Cross-Cultural and Cross-Societal Perspective

> The small proportion of the number of deviants in any culture is not a function of the same instinct with which that society has built itself upon the fundamental societies, but of the universal fact that, happily, the majority of mankind quite readily take any shape that is presented to them.
>
> —RUTH BENEDICT (1934a)

Most anthropologists and sociologists shy away when asked: "What is normal?" For many of these social scientists, the reluctance to attempt an answer reflects their wish to avoid taking part in such "moral" decisions. Yet, they have contributed and are continuing to contribute much to our understanding of the term "normality." In general use, however, the term "normality" has become so bound to culture that, unless otherwise defined, it is assumed that it is a relative term referring to a particular group value context. In contrast to those who tend to exclude the definitions of normality as part of their professional task, a number of anthropologists have demonstrated a deep interest in such definitions. This group consists mainly of those interested in the field of culture and personality but also includes other social scientists. We first analyze their comments and their own weighing of the importance of culture in determining normality. We then turn to those sociologists who, for the most part, let us glean their ideas on normality from their discussions on deviancy.

Anthropology

Cultural Relativism

In its purest form, a cultural-relativity position views all behavior as relative to its particular cultural context and states positively that no form of behavior is abnormal in all cultures. Although Ruth Benedict (1934 b) tended to subscribe to cultural relativity, she was not a purist and, according to Singer (1961), she believed that a universally valid criteria of normality might ultimately be found. Singer, in discussing Benedict's theory of personality and culture, makes the following points:

1. In every culture there is a wide range of individual temperament types (genetically and constitutionally determined) which recur universally.
2. Every culture, however, permits only a limited number of types to flourish, and they are those that fit its dominant configuration.
3. The vast majority of individuals in any society will conform to the dominant types of that society, since their temperaments will be sufficiently plastic to the molding force of the society. These will be the "normal" personality types.
4. A minority of individuals in every society will not "fit" the dominant types, either because their temperament types are too deviant from the ruling types or because they are "insufficiently endowed." There will be the "deviants" and "abnormals."
5. The classification and distribution of "normal" and "abnormal" personality types is relative to the configuration of particular cultures which define the criteria of "normality" and "abnormality" (p. 25).

Universally valid criteria for normality could possibly be found by further pursuing the wide range of temperament types postulated by Benedict as existing independent of cultural molding of this basic "raw material." The culturally influenced temperament is classified by each culture according to its needs.

In Linton (1956), too, can be found this double recognition of both relative normality and an absolute normality existing above and beyond cultural variances.[1] Linton, along with Kardiner (1939, 1945), has developed the concept of the basic personality structure that is not inconsistent with a cultural relativist bias.[2] They have stated that the personality of people within any particular society may be measured potentially by the degree of approximation to the basic personality type postulated for that society. Kardiner and Linton have described the culture's basic personality structure as the consequence of interaction between both "primary institutions" (the family, child-rearing techniques, and the like) and "secondary institutions," such as religion, art, and folklore. Kardiner has especially drawn attention to the fact that the ultimate character molding is based on unconscious perception of these institutions as well as on conscious processes. This basic personality structure seems to be not only influenced by the particular culture in which it develops, but also actually formed by cultural circumstances. Yet, according to Linton, physiological factors may account for the gross abnormalities of behavior seen in psychotic individuals, and these physiological processes are not culture-bound. While the symptoms of the psychotic may

[1] See Appendix under Ralph Linton.

[2] The concept of the "modal personality" for any particular culture (DuBois, 1944) is an elaboration of Kardiner's (1939, 1945) concept of the basic personality structure. Fundamentally a statistical concept, it describes the range of functioning in an average member of a culture.

vary from culture to culture, there would be an underlying core of similarity. Linton (p. 637) further states:

> Individuals having the institutional defects responsible for such abnormalities would be abnormal in any society. . . . The tests of absolute normalcy are the individual's ability to apprehend reality, as understood by his society, to act in terms of this reality and to be effectively shaped by his society during his developmental period.

The differences between the neurotic person and the so-called normal contrast with the differences between the normal and the psychotic person. In the latter case, absolute differences are postulated, whereas the differences between the neurotic and the normal are relative. In judging relative normality, it is necessary to assess the degree of the person's adjustment to his culture, together with the extent to which his personality approximates the basic personality structure of society. Furthermore, Linton interprets clinical studies to have revealed a high correlation between deviation from the basic personality structure and deviation from the usual childhood experiences in a particular culture. Put in another way, Linton's relative normalcy is "the extent to which the individual's experiences have given him a personality conforming to the basic personality of his society."

Universalistic Criteria

Could modal personalities or basic personality structures be compared cross-culturally and used for defining a utopian-type personality free from cultural and psychological maladjustment? In a symposium on "culture and personality," Herskovits (1954, p. 279) pointed out that, although not directly mentioned, such a definition of normality was being accepted by the discussants:

> In all our discussions of this question a hidden hedonistic premise invades much of our thought, almost a utopian premise that basically must be studied so that we can avoid maladjustment of any kind. That is, we hold the adjusted, the happy individual as the desideratum. We strive to develop the efficiently functioning individual as the ideal.

Herskovits also discusses a study that Spiro undertook on the Micronesian island of Ifaluk. According to Herskovits, Spiro found that the inhabitants exhibited neither aggression nor competition. Herskovits postulates that the lack of these characteristics may have been related to Spiro's further observations on the general absence of creative artistic ability and the extreme fearfulness of the ghosts of evil people.

> One cannot but ask, then, is utopian behavior the thing we should strive for? Oughtn't we to look at the hidden premise in our assumption? Should we not ask ourselves what sort of human being we feel desirable? Should we not ask the individual to attain enough adjustment to get along in his culture, but not expect him to solve all his problems and perhaps thus lose much of the source of stimulation that eventuates in socially desirable behavior?

It should be noted that Herskovits is drawing his conclusions on the basis of Western standards, which tend to value certain characteristics, such as adjustment, more than others.

Hsu (1961) hopes to have overcome the limitations of Western standards in his criteria for determining the normality of individuals in any culture. Hsu claims that "psychological anthropology" has suffered considerably from an inability to differentiate precisely between the normal and the abnormal. He believes that, despite this failing, there is evidence indicating that a "core difference exists between the two, above and beyond any cultural variations."

Hsu (1962) designates areas in which normal behavior can be evaluated pragmatically by emphasizing the importance of man's ability to relate to his fellow man. A positive relationship, namely, going toward others and not withdrawing, distinguishes the normal man from the abnormal one. Since the needs for food and sex are shared by men and animals, only the following "three S's" are exclusively motivated by human behavior:

1. Sociability.
2. Security.
3. Status.

He believes that in the Western culture one should add another factor:

4. Creative urge, or the desire for new experiences.

Because of the instability of human relationships, Hsu advocates that only those who cannot maintain *any* relationships *anywhere* should be considered abnormal. Hsu's theory overcomes the risk of equating abnormality with deviance from cultural values. Since deviants and the various antisocial characters have their own need for sociability, security, and status, they will not be labeled "abnormal" merely because of their differences from the conformer. Inasmuch as the vast majority of the population is psychologically elastic, only a few people will be defined as abnormal.

A detailed analysis of mental illness from a biocultural point of view has been presented by Wallace (1961). In his view, a behavior system is disturbed when an independent variable, organic in nature, passes certain boundary values. Thus, Wallace postulates for mental health and illness universal criteria that are based on the biological functions of the human organism. Only the particular defenses against the altered physiological processes (such as mental illness) are culturally determined. Wallace stresses that a biocultural approach is one that considers the specific nature of the interaction between biological and cultural variables with a true interdisciplinary spirit. Wallace defines mental health as "a state in which the person is performing to his own and others' satisfaction the roles appropriate to his situation in society." Each person maintains cognitive "maps" in which he interprets the world as he perceives it. These maps give meaning to individual experience and help the person to act appropriately. When the "status" of the maps is altered by a biological process, "transfer mechanisms" are in action that effect certain changes in the person's map and institute a "program of illness." It is important to note that Wallace reaches his conclusions through deductive processes different from those of other anthropologists presented in this section.

Criticisms

Wegrocki (1939) distinguishes two approaches that most anthropologists accept in viewing normality. First, the statistico-relative approach assesses normal behavior relative to the culture in which it is performed. Symptoms that are abnormal in one particular culture are not necessarily indicative of abnormality in another. The hallucinations of the Plains Indians are not abnormal, even though they resemble the hallucinations of schizophrenics. The mechanism is similar, but the function is different. The behavior of the Indian is analogous but not homologous to that of the schizophrenic.

The second approach, functionalism, evaluates the function of behavior within the total economy of the personality while accepting the premise that behavior is in part culturally determined. Wegrocki believes that it is necessary to examine the pre-morbid personality of the person in order to decide if the choice of behavior is in line with his past functioning. In other words, is the behavior ego-determined or ego-alien? Wegrocki writes (1939, p. 166):

> We could state the quintessence of abnormality as the *tendency to choose a type of reaction which represents an escape from conflict-producing situations instead of a facing of the problem.*

The only way we can understand behavior, then, is by delving into its individual meaning.

Devereux (1956), who is both an anthropologist and a psychoanalyst, completely rejects the authenticity of the first approach outlined by Wegrocki (1939), because he does not accept the possibility of determining normality on the basis of cultural values. Contrary to most anthropologists, he relates mental illness primarily to internal structures of psychological abnormalities. In Devereux's opinion, the shaman, although conforming to the standards of his culture, should be considered mentally ill.

More than any other discipline, anthropology has emphasized the culture-bound determinants of behavior. If one visualizes a seven-point scale ranging from extreme cultural relativity on one end, to be marked by a score of seven (7), and the universality of psychopathology on the other, to be marked by a score of one (1), the majority of cultural anthropologists will cluster on the relativist side by a score of five or six (5–6).

Sociology

Paucity of Interest in the Concept of Normality

Investigators in the field of sociology reveal scant interest in developing their own definitions of normality or health. For the most part, sociologists are interested in studying the *act of becoming deviant;* they ask not "what is normality?" but rather "what kind of sociological structure leads to certain groups of people being labeled abnormal by other observers?" Some sociologists consider the question of whether a person is correctly labeled "deviant" to be the domain of the psychiatrist and/or the psychologist, whereas others would not give the psychologist or psychiatrist exclusive domain in this area (Strauss, 1963). Bucher (1963) has stated that a sociologist who becomes concerned with defining terms like "normality" or "health" may be turning into an amateur psychiatrist. To the sociologist, these terms imply value judgments that would be necessary only if it were his place to treat rather than study the society. According to Zald (1964), one of the reasons sociologists are not concerned with individual deviance is related to their wish to treat biological and psychological factors as essentially constant. Zald points out that the scientific logic behind this point of view is that "a tight hypothetico-deductive model works *within* a level of conceptual abstraction." For the sociologist, then, the social relation is the key unit, not personality factors or intrapsychic processes.

Some sociologists have excluded the psychiatric syndromes from their definitions of deviance. A. K. Cohen (1959, p. 462), for example, states:

> First, we here define "deviant" behavior in terms of the relationships of action to institutionalized expectations, not in terms of its relationship to personality structure. Behavior which is psychotic, neurotic, maladjusted, or otherwise pathological from a psychiatric or mental-hygiene point of view is defined in terms of its dependence upon or consequence for personality structure. Therefore, the pathology of personality is not, as such, subject matter for the sociology of deviant behavior.

Cohen's definition of deviancy differs from those emphasizing the intrapsychic antecedents and consequences of deviancy. His focus is upon the interpretability of individual actions by societal standards. In contrast to some of his colleagues, Cohen does not demonstrate an interest in bridging the two conceptual models. A number of sociologists have attempted to develop techniques of integrating institutional-structural role functioning and individual behavior (Goffman, 1961; Strauss et al., 1964; Srole et al., 1962; Stanton & Schwartz, 1954; and, in another context, Parsons, 1964). It is notable that these bridging studies rarely include theoretical models of normal behavior from the hierarchy of levels, including intrapersonal elements.

Deviancy and Normality

Merton (1949, pp. 125–149) is one of the few sociologists who delineate the issues of deviancy and normality from a sociological point of view.[3] He writes:

> Today, as a decade ago, we have still much to learn about the processes through which social structure generates the circumstances in which infringement of social codes constitutes a normal (that is to say an expectable) response. . . . The framework set out in this essay is designed to provide one systematic approach to the analysis of social and cultural services of deviant behavior. Our primary aim is to discover how some *social structures exert a definite pressure upon certain persons in the society to engage in nonconformist* rather than conformist conduct. If we can locate groups peculiarly subject to such pressures, we should expect to find fairly high rates of deviant behavior in these groups not because human beings comprising them are compounded of distinctive biological tendencies but because they are responding normally to the social situation in which they find themselves. Our perspective is sociological. We look at variations in the *rates* of deviant behavior, not at its

[3] See Appendix under Robert K. Merton.

incidence. Should our guess be at all successful, some forms of deviant behavior will be found to be as psychologically normal as conformist behavior, and the equation of deviation and abnormality will be put in question.

Merton proceeds to state that the variability in the incidence of individual deviant-behavior patterns can be attributed to the role of biological and personality differences, but that the structure of our society is responsible for the occurrence of deviancy as such. When looking at aberrant behavior from a sociological point of view, Merton states that his central hypothesis is that deviancy is a "symptom of dissociation between culturally prescribed aspirations and socially structured avenues for realizing these aspirations."

Once a sociologist has understood the culturally prescribed aspirations and the structuralized vehicles to achieve these aims, he should be able to predict the rates of deviant and non-deviant behavior for this particular society.[4]

Merton's emphasis on social structure leading to deviancy is viewed from a different angle by Coser (1962), who assigns deviancy the role of enlightening us about the very society that, according to Merton, is causing the deviancy.

Coser discusses "functions" of deviancy that ordinarily are not perceived by those working with individual cases of deviancy. He points out that deviancy helps in redefining "normal" behavior for the community in which it takes place. It can do this in many different ways and it is at times unsuccessful, but the process of sharpening the boundaries between normality and abnormality is based upon experience with

[4] Moore (1964) has discussed the problem of "Predicting Discontinuities in Social Change." Although he is cautiously optimistic about the future of prediction in the social sciences, he does state that: "For sequential relations, however, and thus for real prediction of historic future, our aspirations are ahead of our achievements."

actual deviants. It is of interest to note that Coser uses an ethical analogy when he wants to clarify his position. He states that good makes no sense by itself except in relation to bad. Similarly, normalcy can hardly be perceived except against the background of deviance. Hence, normality is inextricably tied to deviancy. It is necessary in each group to define the behavior of some of its members—usually a small minority—as deviant in order to clarify what is normal for the remainder of the group. The deviant can thus serve a very useful function, instead of being dysfunctional to society at large. K. T. Erikson (1960) has stated it in the following way:

> Each time the community brings sanctions against a detail of behavior . . . it sharpens the authority of the violated norm and redefines the boundaries within which the norm exercises its special jurisdiction.

Merton, Coser, and Erikson link together the concepts of deviancy and normality because of their roles in leading to or clarifying each other; yet, the two concepts remain opposites. Other sociologists emphasize even tighter interrelationship between deviancy and normality. To them, normality can exist within deviancy. In other words, the member of a deviant group can be labeled "normal" if his actions coincide with the deviance of the group.

In order to illustrate that "deviants" as such have their own codes and "social norms," Becker (1963) compares the jazz musicians and the marijuana smokers. The behavior of neither group is "abnormal" or "bizarre" if understood in its social frame of reference. Following Becker's thesis, to be normal is to learn the norms of the group, be it a "criminal" group, like marijuana smokers, or a group often viewed as eccentric, like jazz musicians, in which the individual participates. Becker and other sociologists believe that the process that sociologists should study is: who names whom as deviant and how the conscious comes about or fails to be achieved.

Social Structure and Normality

Parsons (1958, 1959) speaks less of deviancy than of the positive states of health and normality, which he then attempts to differentiate. Health refers to a capacity; whereas normality relates to the actions of an individual within a particular action system. In defining health, Parsons (1958) states that we must look to social structures to determine their significance in producing the individual's optimum social capacity.[5] According to Parsons, each individual is socialized to develop a capacity for effective performance of specific roles and tasks. Individuals vary qualitatively in their capacities. Health is equated with a state of optimum capacity for undertaking a particular task. In the following quote, Parsons (1958, p. 176) makes an important distinction between capacity and commitment.

> Finally, let me repeat that I am defining health as concerned with capacity, not with commitment to *particular* roles, tasks, norms, or even values as such. The question of whether a man wants to remain with his wife or likes his particular job or ever feels committed to refrain from highway robbery is not *as such* a health problem; though a health problem may underlie and be interwoven with problems of this sort.

So, too, will the health problem be interwoven with classifications of normality and abnormality. The capacity of health will be a determinant of the ability to be normal. Parsons (1959, p. 643) writes about his conception of normality in the following:

[5] See Appendix under Talcott Parsons.

> Finally, a word about the problem of normality and pathology. We have stressed that there is *always* a normative aspect in the analysis of process in systems of action (we believe this to be the case with all physiological processes as well). This was brought out most clearly in the case of the concept of communication; if the conventions of the sign meaning system are violated, communication is disturbed. We connect this normative reference with the property of boundary maintenance which we impute to systems of action. Boundary maintenance means maintenance of a distinctive intrasystem pattern which is not assimilated to the patterning of the extrasystem situation. In this theoretical setting, the question of "how well" or "successfully" the system is maintaining the pattern is unavoidable on any comprehensive level of theoretical analysis, though for special purposes it can be avoided. Furthermore, the question cannot be localized in any specific aspect of system functioning; it applies to the system as a whole in relation to the situation as a whole. In a relative sense, the functioning of systems must be evaluated: they are more or less well adapted to their situations, more or less well integrated, and so forth. A conceptual scheme which makes values a central category cannot evade this consequence, and should not attempt to. But evaluation of the functioning of a particular system in a particular situation is a very different thing from a judgment of the value of that system and its results in some wider frame of reference. Our theory makes no particular assumptions on the latter level.

It should be noted that Parsons (1959) distinguishes the functioning of a particular system in its particular context from a "wider frame of reference." Within each system, normative references are possible and, furthermore, it is possible to make value judgments regarding the functioning of the particular system. It is more complicated to make value judgments while utilizing the broader perspective. In Parsons' terminology, the activities of distinctive groups would constitute an action system. A group of middle-class adolescents in a particular high school, or the inhabitants of a primitive South Sea island, or one segment of a professional group would be involved in a system of action whenever there exists an adequate "boundary maintenance" or, in other words, a reasonably clear-cut distinctiveness about the groups.

Parsons thus is saying that one may talk of normative function within such groups, and it is our assumption that he would determine the "conventions of the sign meaning system" by a straightforward statistical analysis. It would be possible, however, in his scheme to make judgments regarding each person's functioning according to the degree of his adaptation or integration within the system. But Parsons adds that it would be very difficult to generalize about adaptation or integration beyond the system and situation under focus.

In this chapter, we cited investigators who believe that a normal variation of individual behavior has to be studied and understood in relation to the culture in which it occurs. Different techniques are used to arrive at the modal or basic personality of people in a culture. The range of psychological types is somewhat limited in a particular culture but varies to a much larger extent cross-culturally. Normality is seen as relative to the culture in which it occurs, although the possibility of discovering universally valid criteria for normality has also been raised.

Within a particular culture or society, the deviant has also been described as adaptive. Social norms have to be established in order to study the deviant, but defining a group as deviant does not mean that persons within this group have to manifest psychopathological symptoms. If one understands the meaning of deviancy within the social context in which it takes place, one should be able to outline the social structure that is correlated with the occurrence of this particular type of deviance and ultimately, via prediction, validate the hypothesis concerning the particular social structure.

Lastly, we would like to state that the cross-sectional studies of cultures and societies are important not only in one particular generation but also temporally and throughout history as well. They may give us yet another glimpse into the changing patterns of norms and normal behavior and highlight the intrinsic similarities as well as some basic differences between cultures and societies.

5

The Structural Perspective in the Biological Sciences

> We are gradually learning that in biology the only permanent thing is change—change requiring ever new adaptive responses on the part of organisms, races and species to serve their need to survive. —STEWART WOLF (1961)

To state that behavior is related to underlying organic structure is to state a truism that is meaningless unless the details of the relationship are specified. Clearly, however, structure does force certain broad restrictions on the behavior that a particular organism can potentially portray. It is the extent and nature of these restrictions that biologists are investigating. In his search for criteria of normal behavior, the biologist examines not the cultural surroundings of the organism or its subjective experiences; rather, he examines structural formations and their functions. Since behavior is viewed from this perspective as based upon existent structural formations, any biological definition of normal behavior must either refer to one specific point in time or incorporate the element of change throughout time. The definition of normality will depend upon the same laws that apply to biological organisms in general. As living organisms undergo the effects of evolution, older concepts of normality will have to be discarded or reapplied as a result of changing evidence. It would be an oversimplification to assume that the principle of the survival of the fittest indicates that the range of existent behavior continually would encompass more and better mental and corporal abilities. Darwin (1859) contends not that a constant biological betterment of mankind will take place, but that "natural selection . . . only takes advantage of such variations as arise and are beneficial to each creature under its complex relations of life." Behavioral ranges will change concomitantly with these variations, although the laws governing the changes are quite complex and not clearly understood.

Change in the Potential Range of Normal Behavior: Evolution

In recent biological studies, the thematic accent is upon structural diversity. The biologist would not label any one act of behavior "normal" and exclude all others from this category. In the brain alone, according to Lashley (1947), "individuals start life with brains differing enormously in structure, unlike in number, size and arrangement of neurons as well as in gross features." It is likely that biologic scientists would strongly resist any definition that pinpointed one particular way of functioning and declared it "normal" because it alone most exemplified ideal behavior. Only if a definition of normal behavior were to describe a pattern that would allow for individual diversities and change over time could such an investigator be willing to accept it as a working definition.

The theory of behavior expounded by Child (1924) accounts for both diversities and temporal changes.[1] Child regards behavior as a whole unit being standardized by the accidents of nature throughout time and yet covering a broad

[1] See Appendix under Charles M. Child.

enough adaptive range to allow for variations. According to Child, the main force responsible for the standardization of behavior from a physiological point of view is the particular developmental path that evolution has taken. Normal behavior is the result of an interplay between the genetic and environmental forces that compel the organism to behave or adapt in a specific way. Since evolution is a dynamic process continuing indefinitely, the best analysis of any bit of behavior at one particular point in time is fragmentary. Thus, it becomes almost impossible to arrive at a precise definition or description of normal behavior. The normal in biology (including normal behavior), according to Child, represents the potential range of patterns of the protoplasmic system and hence must be defined in evolutionary terms.

These terms must describe conditions resulting both from genetic and environmental circumstances. The next step is to investigate the weight of each of these in determining the evolutionary changes or standardizations that will be classified as "normal." Herrick (1956, pp. 16, 21) minimizes the degree of environmental influence upon the behavioral pattern that will evolve.[2] He credits personal genetic predisposition within each organism with being the primary determiner of behavioral patterns. His substantiation is based on the theory that all behavior is goal-directed; that is, all normal behavior is based on goal-directed action. Herrick makes goal–directiveness the most important single force in causing evolutionary changes and, consequently, paramount in determining normality. Lack of a positive directiveness indicates a behavioral breakdown. Herrick describes his point of view in the following way:

> People and all other animals sometimes do things that are not good for them, but what they do must in the aggregate be bene-

[2] See Appendix under C. Judson Herrick.

ficial or they perish. Although behavior is normally goal-directed, situations sometimes arise which frustrate the satisfaction sought. If the frustration is not overcome by trial and error or otherwise, the normal course of behavior is disrupted, with results that may lead to catastrophic disorder and eventually to a pathological neurosis. Such abnormalities of conduct can be avoided or remedied only if the causes of the frustration are recognized and corrected. Whatever name we choose to apply to it, the directive quality of normal behavior is fundamental. This quality gives us the only basis we have for predicting the behavior of other creatures, and, especially of other people, and so gives some promise of control of behavior, which is what we are after in the upshot.

Herrick differs from those who define the directedness as synonymous with conscious anticipation of the end-goals, since his concept includes animal as well as human behavior. In subhuman species we cannot determine if the animal is aware of the purpose of his actions. Accepting this limitation, Herrick nonetheless emphasizes the ontogenetic development of individual patterns of normal goal-directed behavior, limited, of course, by the varying potentialities of the particular species.

In discussing the "individuality" of man, Loeb (1945) maintains that each man is engaged not only in a struggle for survival with nature, but also in an individual social struggle with other human beings. He states that the further the organism advances along evolutionary lines, the more it succeeds in its struggles and the more integrated its parts will become. However, the organism never becomes one totally connected whole, since its individual adaptation is never sufficient to avoid eventual deterioration and death. A hypothesis concerning the role that man's social adaptation may play upon his biological evolution is presented by Freedman and Roe (1958). They suggest that much of man's maladaptive behavior is a byproduct of the present stage of his progressive evolutionary development. Biological evolution has made man unable to withstand the stress of existence without showing severe psychopathological strains. It is social evolution that has prevented the maladaptive behaviorism from being fatal. And what is more, Freedman and Roe suggest that it is just the values of man's social evolution that makes him "the animal most likely to survive in spite of severe maladaptive behavior." This has resulted in a wider range of human variabilities, whose existence serves a positive function in the society. Feibleman (1961) also believes that maladaptive behavior has a special function in the human society. Among animals, maladaptive behavior usually undergoes phyletic extinction. Only in human society do we "bring the victims along." In that way we can both help the patients and learn from the manifestation of pathology, in its broadest term, "how healthier specimens may better adapt and so survive."

Stability in the Range of Normal Behavior: Genetics

In studies of the inheritance of characteristics, two theories are employed in modern genetics. They are the classical and the balance theories (see Dobzhansky, 1962, for details). We will use these theories as our basic frame of reference in discussing the genetic theories concerning the inheritance of behavioral characteristics. According to the classical theory, normal people carry mostly normal genes, and these genes are for the most part homozygous. In other words, only a small number of genes have two or more alleles each; in the other or others, one of the alleles will be normal and the others abnormal. Within the human species the adaptive norm will consist, therefore, of individuals who carry almost completely normal genes. By definition, then, abnormal people carry abnormal genes. In other words, every behavioral abnormality has "behind" it an abnormal gene.

Kallmann (1959) and Lenz (1961) are among the geneticists who favor the classical theory. They think that in the future genetics will be able to explain patterns of normal functioning based on the inheritance of behavioral characteristics. Kallmann states (p. 175) that even at present genetics can make a contribution in that direction.

> In line with an elementary genetic principle, the occurrence of a mutational change is sufficient evidence for the existence of a normal allele (the corresponding member of a pair of genes located at a definable point of a chromosome). The normal gene, even if its biochemical equivalents have yet to be identified, can be assumed to make a vital contribution toward maintaining adequate health and normal behavior.
>
> One of the corollaries of modern genetic theory, therefore, is that such phenomena as personality integration, emotional balance, and mental health are more than the result of chance circumstance reflecting only mild cultural pressures, or a fortuitous absence of disturbing experiences in childhood. More appropriately, the given phenomena are viewed as end products of a multitude of genetically potentialized properties and functions that are continuously molded by "ethnoplastic" forces—"the myriad elements constituting the life cycle of a human organism."

According to the balance theory, matters are more complex, because genes can be represented in the population by many alleles. Dobzhansky (1962, p. 126) states:[3]

> For such genes, no allele is necessarily normal, and good health and high fitness occur mainly in heterozygotes for pairs of differ-

[3] See Appendix under Theodosius Dobzhansky.

> ent alleles. The homozygotes would easily be less fit. The upshot is, then, that there are not only many but also many kinds of normal, healthy, and highly fit people. The adaptive norm is a great array of genotypes, not just one or a few genetic complexes. Medicine had better be versatile, for not all patients will respond alike to its ministrations.

Vogel (1963), too, believes that the balance theory correctly represents our present-day knowledge about genetics. He says that there is a great range of variability in behavior and that, though it is theoretically possible to conceptualize an optimal genotype, he doubts whether such a structure could exist. As an example, he cites the introvert and the extrovert. Both serve an important function in our social organization, and it would be difficult to determine which one carries an optimal genotype. The two theories have in common the recognition that the boundary between the genetically normal and the genetically handicapped is not sharp. In both of these theories, normal behavior will be correlated with the nature of the genotype. The adaptive norm, in both instances, can consist of a mixture of normal and abnormal genes, although a greater array of genotypes is possible, according to the balance theory. One of the main differences between the theories lies in their conceptualization of the specific genetic mechanisms involved in the inheritance of normal characteristics. According to the classical theory, only one allele can be normal in the genes that contain many alleles; according to the balance theory, there can be different alleles for certain genes, so that we can have more than one normal allele, thus "allowing" for diversification of normal behavior.

Whatever the theoretical position assumed by a geneticist, he would argue, nonetheless, that there is a close connection between heredity and behavior. Genetic factors not only influence the structural configuration, but also profoundly affect the organism's range of functioning, including its behavior. The function or behavior of an organism is not only influenced by its genetically derived structure, but also depends to a great extent on its experience—yes, on its environment.[4] To illustrate, let us take a single structural characteristic, for example, brain size. The size could be labeled "normal" in the statistical sense when it falls within the mean. As mentioned, this statistical mean would be the exact average only for the point of time in which the data to be calculated were collected. The existence of abnormal structure in the statistical sense does not necessarily mean malfunctioning, however. Thus, normal functioning or behavior, at least in the present stage of biological knowledge, cannot be directly correlated with structural norms. To use another example, the normal and seemingly necessary internal iliac artery can be absent from a human body and cause no apparent malfunctioning. A body structure without an internal iliac artery would be abnormal, in a statistical sense, though functioning would not be impeded. Consequently, as much as function may depend on structure, the attempt to characterize functioning as "abnormal" requires knowledge in addition to the facts of the statistical abnormality said to cause the malfunctioning.

Possible Links between Structure and Normal Behavior: Biochemistry

Much research has been done since the mid-1950's on the biochemistry and physiology of the brain. Although our knowledge has expanded, it is doubtful whether normal behavior can

[4] The nature–nurture controversy reflects an either-or dichotomy that has been abandoned by most serious investigators; it is not heredity versus the environment, but rather the relative importance of each within a dynamic field. (See, for example, the work of Rosenthal, 1963.)

ever be defined in terms of chemical interactions in the brain. Many substances have been found to play an important and, at times, crucial role in brain metabolism and occasionally have been directly correlated with behavior (for example, Adrenalin, Serotonin, and L.S.D.). The question of a possible future chemical definition of normal behavior or mental health has been raised by Abood (1959, p. 132), who states:

> Mental health is probably a condition involving certain concentrations of each of these substances in particular areas of the brain, and an imbalance presumably results in some kind of an aberration. . . . Mental aberrations presumably result when the chemical system is no longer stable or self-sustained, a condition which could be induced by a variety of factors. Ultimately, however, the imbalance should reflect itself in the basic structural unit of the nervous system and would, thereby, lend itself to experimental study.

This statement is prototypic of a classical position in biologic theory, but as has been pointed out repeatedly, it has two major weaknesses.[6] First, it attempts to reduce the mental directly into the physical without consideration of the great number of significant intervening variables or qualitative differences. Second, it runs into difficulties because of the vast diversities that exist. This in itself could make the task of developing a definition of mental health based on "certain concentrations" of substances formidable, if not impossible.

The recent studies of R. Williams (1956, 1957, 1958) reveal some of the difficulties involved in any attempt to overlook what he terms "biochemical individuality." [7] In his Sigma Xi National Lecture (1956–1957), Williams states:

[6] See, for example, the debate between Gerard & Emerson and Novikoff (1945).

[7] See Appendix under Roger J. Williams.

> If we imagine the human population to consist of individuals who are in the average range with respect to the various items which enter into their make-up, we are misleading ourselves to such a degree that sound human understanding is impossible. . . .
>
> It may surprise the reader to know that there is only about one chance in 6,500 that he individually has a medium size stomach, a heart with medium pumping capacity, a thyroid gland of medium activity, a medium number of islets of Langerhans in his pancreas, a medium calcium requirement and a medium vitamin A requirement. If we make the number of categories larger, and even if we enlarge the median group to include much more than the middle one-third, the chance that any individual will be in the median group in all respects is so small as to be negligible.

Williams (1956) made extensive studies of the biochemical make-up of a group of "normal" individuals. He demonstrated that well functioning persons may exhibit many biochemical abnormalities (by having either abnormally high or low values on a specific biochemical examination). Williams (1957) has also shown that although normal young men of the same height and weight may resemble one another in the basal metabolic rate, they nevertheless may have considerable variation in their individual chemical reactions. Williams thinks that the reason for this may be differences in enzyme levels and efficiencies among people, as well as differences in endocrine patterns and secretions. He also discusses variations in the physical characteristics of people as well as biological body systems. Diversities exist because each living biological unit creates its own balance of metabolism. This phenomenon is intricately related to its physical constitution, growth and development, and immediate environmental availabilities.

In this chapter, we concentrated on the broad applications of biological theories in considering norms and variations. Although specific behavior patterns vary greatly and individuation takes place, there are over-all patterns that transcend each living unit. The process of growth, the attainment of maturity, and organic deterioration and death form part of an integrated biological pattern. The entirety of man's behavior cannot be studied in detail, but studies like those of the biologist Coghill (1949) on the total behavior pattern of the amblystoma can be conducted. A documentation of the relationship between structure and function in the lower organisms might reveal certain principles that govern behavior not only in these organisms but also in all living systems. Hence, our understanding of the constitution of normal behavior in man might be extended. We have to ask, as does Williams, to what extent are the variations normal and when can a particular structure be called abnormal? Measurements must be quantified, so that normal behavior can be more precisely defined. It is not enough to view all biological functions as basic to the ultimate adaptation of the organism to its environment. Likewise, unsuccessful adaptations do not necessarily lead to gradual destruction of the organism. Differentiations must be made between physiological reactions, based on specific genetic traits, which help the organism in its fight for survival, and those, if any, that hinder its chances.

The concept of biological normality cannot be pinpointed or described statistically in terms of particular existing behavioral patterns without a consideration of the importance of phylogenetic time. Biological normality is relative to evolutionary stages. Since the concept of evolution cannot be separated from that of change, new classifications will not be devised and new subtypes will not be discovered and specified until new biological data are observed and synthesized. The normal is applied to so many changing ranges of structural varieties that only gross malformations can be labeled abnormal. Ultimately, biologists will find more sophisticated correlations between the structural varieties and adequate functioning, enabling us to define more precisely the biological conception of normal behavior.

PART TWO

The Emerging Trends

6

The Four Perspectives of Normality: A Synthesis

> The two forms of examination, whether they stem from the sick or healthy man, set up a standard of normality, and it is exactly here, before starting with our main theme, that our difficulties begin. We do not know what normal is, and what an exact definition of normality consists of. Our conceptualizations of normality differ considerably, depending on our orientation, be it cultural, social, psychological or medical.
>
> —WALTER HIRSCH (1962)

Each of the disciplines surveyed in the previous chapters has its own unique history, its own style of conceptualizing problems, and its own language. Despite these cross-disciplinary differences, the reader will have noticed that definitions of normality have striking similarities that link investigators from diverse backgrounds, and may point to a joint ancestry. Much of our motivation in preparing this book stemmed from observations of the commonalities or "functional perspectives" underlying discussions of normal behavior. In our opinion, there are four distinctive approaches encompassing all of the complex definitions presented previously. These are: (1) *Normality as Health*; (2) *Normality as Utopia*; (3) *Normality as Average*; (4) *Normality as Transactional Systems*. In this chapter, we delineate each of these perspectives. It will be apparent that some overlapping occurs, but they can be distinguished, nevertheless, by underlying major principles. This functional classification is useful in providing a map for the complex maze and seeming infinitude of definitions contained in much of Part One. Since most discussions pertinent to normality do not explicitly acknowledge that there are discrepancies in functional perspective, we hope that our division will help the reader to evaluate the literature concerned with this subject.

There have been other attempts to classify this field, but, to our knowledge, these have never been extensive. Wolff (1950) organized the various perspectives in a manner quite similar to our own when he defined normality as a construct that can have three different meanings: (1) the statistical average; (2) the normative, which guides therapeutic ideals and is based on moral principles; and (3) the clinical, which defines the normal as being able to function adequately in his own environment.[1] Wolff's use of the "normative" is analogous to our "Normality as Utopia." Although he does not specifically discuss "Normality as Process," it is implied within the other definitions. To cite an additional, similar attempt at definition, Ruesch and Bateson (1951) have discussed three implicit principles underlying the psychiatric concept of pathology: (1) the statistical concept, connoting deviation from the norm; (2) the optimal functioning concept, derived from medicine; and (3) the diagnostic categorization of pathology determined according to known and established criteria. Furthermore, they state that the psychiatrist "tends to construct a hypothetical norm by averaging the exact opposite of those features he sees in his patients." An attempt is made, through therapy, to change the patient's pathology and bring him back to the "normal state." Our classification has certain similarities to that of Ruesch and Bateson but

[1] See also Edwards (1935), who distinguishes between four different types of individuals: the average; the normal; the adjusted; and the effective.

stems somewhat less from a traditional psychiatric interest in pathology and somewhat more from an interest in normality as such.

The functional perspectives described in this chapter are not original with the authors. Each definition has been discussed previously and, as we have indicated, other classifications do indeed approximate our own. Nevertheless, we believe that our categorization of the various approaches is as extensive as any currently available. Undoubtedly, new concepts and new data will emerge that will lead to an even more extensive and inclusive approach to normality. Our purpose is to synthesize the modern perspectives on normality into a coherent and meaningful typology. We hope that such a synthesis will be useful to investigators and will also facilitate the reader's integration of the diverse approaches presented under the rubric of each discipline.

Normality as Health

The first "functional perspective," "Normality as Health," includes the traditional medical-psychiatric approach, which equates normality with health and views health as an almost universal phenomenon. Many investigators have assumed behavior to be within normal limits when no manifest pathology is present. Concentration is then focused upon definitions of pathology, leaving the large residue as "normal" or "healthy." Transposed upon a scale, normality would be the major portion of a continuum and abnormality would be the small remainder. This definition of normality seems to correlate with the activity of the model of the doctor who attempts to free his patients from grossly observable symptoms. To this physician, the lack of unfavorable symptoms indicates health. Health in this context refers to a *reasonable* rather than an *optimal* state of functioning. The psychiatrist subscribing to such an approach is interested in the prevention of disease; for him, prevention implies the treatment of the symptoms that overtly interfere with the adequate functioning of the patient. Barton (1959, p. 233) describes what we have called the traditional medical-psychiatric point of view when he states:

> The phenomenon of a superstate of good mental health, well beyond and above the mere absence of disabling illness, has yet to be scientifically demonstrated. We know little of it beyond occasional subjective, euphoric impressions of the subject that he is "bursting with good health," "feeling grand," or that "all is right with the world," meaning his world.
>
> In contrast, the benefits of disease prevention and control have been tangibly demonstrated in increased ability to work and carry out social obligations, longer life, and individual morale.
>
> Medicine has developed this useful way of looking at health and the normal to the extent that health as the antonym of disease has become a part of the philosophy, or tradition, of physicians.

In its simplest form, this perspective is illustrated by Romano (1950), who states that a healthy person is one who is reasonably free of undue pain, discomfort, and disability.

Psychiatrists are not the only investigators who advocate the "Normality as Health" approach. Alexander (1948), who has been more closely identified with psychoanalysis than with psychiatry as such (see Chapter 2), uses the analogy of a functioning democracy with its checks and balances to describe the normal psyche. Although the functioning may not be ideal, so long as the system is not severely disturbed (for example, turned into a dictatorship), it is normal. This indicates, according to Alexander, that most people will be considered normal, for the vast majority function adequately. Among the anthropologists cited, Hsu (1962; see Chapter 5) most clearly reflects the "Normality as Health" position when he states that there are only a few people who can never, under any circumstances, maintain positive interpersonal relationships, and it is solely these whom Hsu would describe as abnormal. All other people fall under the broad range of normal. Since most people do have some positive interpersonal relationships, most people are relatively normal or healthy. This equation of normality with a generally healthy populace is based on a "Normality as Health" perspective. When Linton (1956) distinguishes between relative and absolute abnormality, stating that only the gross malfunctioning psychotics are absolutely abnormal, he is approximating the same perspective.[2]

In Chapter 5, the "classical" genetic theory was discussed. We have stated that Kallmann (1959) subscribes to this theory. He regards environmental factors as being of little significance in determining a person's primary health status. Kallmann minimizes the importance of "chance circumstances" within the environment that affect psychological functioning of the individual. He states that disease can be caused in the structure primarily by the inheritance of abnormal alleles. In only a few severe psychiatric illnesses, like schizophrenia, has it been shown that a tendency toward the disease can be genetically inherited (Kallmann, 1962). This presupposes that the rest, namely the majority of mankind, are genetically healthy with regard to mental illness.

For psychological studies, there are a number of instruments so constructed that one end of the scale connotes

[2] Dunham (1965) also assumes this perspective when he calls attention to the dangers of an ever-widening definition of mental illness.

pathology (a "negative" value) and the majority of points on the scale connote health ("positive" values). For example, both the Bender Gestalt Test for organicity and the Harrower modification of the Rorschach Test would assign the label of pathology to only a small portion of their sample, whereas the majority of the population would be considered normal, or free of pathology.

The "Normality as Health" perspective remains popular despite frequent attacks upon its definition as an antonym of illness. Prevalent non-scientific assumptions that the majority of a population must be "normal" implicitly influence investigators in the behavioral and social sciences to accept the "Normality as Health" perspective. Furthermore, this approach is considered to have research and conceptual advantages, because disease is thought to be easier to measure than positive states of health.

Normality as Utopia

The second "functional perspective," "Normality as Utopia," which is best typified by psychoanalysts (see Chapter 2), conceives of normality as that harmonious and optimal blending of the diverse elements of the mental apparatus that culminates in optimal functioning, or "self-actualization." Such definitions emerge clearly, although most often implicitly, when psychoanalysts grapple with the complex problem of discussing their criteria of a successful treatment.

Dating from Freud's conception of normality as an ideal fiction, the "Normality as Utopia" view almost has become the trademark of the psychoanalyst. Here is an area where Freudian analysts and neo-Freudian analysts, in their tendency to equate the normal person with the ideal person, speak in similar terms. Definitions of the ideal person differ considerably, but almost all psychoanalysts, either explicitly or implicitly, conceive of normality in terms of ideal functionings.

Typical of the proponents of the "Utopian" concept, Money-Kyrle (1957) would accept neither any conception of normality as relative to a particular society nor the existence of a completely normal person.[3] Money-Kyrle uses clinical impressions to reject the cultural-relativist position, because "some people whom every clinician would class as ill would have to be classed as normal in some societies."[4] He relates normality to self-knowledge, concluding that there "can be no completely normal person," since self-knowledge is always incomplete. Thus, normality is a utopia not to be attained.

It is important to reiterate (see Chapter 2) that those psychoanalysts who either state explicitly that they have no interest in defining normality or totally reject the idea of forming any concept of normality do nevertheless accept an implicit definition that they utilize when treating their patients. Psychoanalysts ask themselves questions similar to these: (1) When has a particular patient benefited optimally from treatment? (2) Has he grown or matured as much as he can? (3) How does this analysis compare to another analysis under similar conditions or to an "ideal" analytic process? The psychiatrist sets his goals of therapy as alleviation of suffering and removal of symptoms. The psychoanalyst, however, seeks to facilitate the patient's development of a healthier character structure. He wants to help the patient to utilize effectively all the resources with which he is endowed. He hopes that the patient will have freer access to his unconscious and also

[3] See Appendix under Roger E. Money-Kyrle.

[4] For example, Ruth Benedict (1934) is an example of an investigator who operationally subscribes to the notion of cultural relativity (for details, see Chapter 4).

become freer of infantile conflicts in order to function optimally. These goals of therapy correspond to the analyst's own conception of the healthy state he wishes his patient to attain. Psychoanalysts realize that these are ideal goals that rarely, if ever, can be attained, but they nevertheless continue to measure their own treatment results in terms of their proximity to "ideal" results.

To clarify the "Normality as Utopia" position, we wish to cite a useful analogy between cardiac functioning and ego structure. A heart, free of any congenital or acquired disease, never functions at its maximum capacity. Inevitable exposures to environmental stresses hamper its functioning. The heart at best can operate only close to what it could have if everything had been "perfect"; the ideal heart remains a fiction. Similarly, according to the structural psychoanalytic theory, the ego of a person, under the average expectable environment (Hartmann, 1958), is only slightly injured by trauma (constitutional, environmental, or circumstantial). In such a situation, only a mild neurosis will develop. If the ego is further damaged, the ego becomes more defective and the person becomes sicker. The important factor to consider here is that, since by definition every ego is subjected to *some* trauma, no perfectly functioning ego can exist.

The "Normality as Utopia" perspective makes the normal man not only a person to be admired but also one who is seldom, if ever, seen in flesh and blood. Such a Platonic ideal tends to be characteristic of a significant segment of psychoanalytic approaches to normality. It is also found among psychotherapists in psychiatry and psychology. When Rogers (1959) describes his model of the "fully functioning person" as "the end point of optimal psychotherapy," he approximates this perspective. Those who utilize the concept of "self-actualization of potential" (Goldstein, 1939; 1959; Maslow,

1954; and Buhler, 1959) also share this point of view. In addition, this position is being adopted increasingly by theorists in preventive medicine, who have enlarged the horizons of illness to its earliest origins and most subtle manifestations. Indubitably, this perspective will become more and more important in the medicine of the future as grosser pathology is steadily decreased.

Normality as Average

The third "functional perspective," "Normality as Average," is commonly employed in normative studies of behavior. This approach is based on the mathematical principle of the Bell-shaped curve and its applicability to physical, psychological, and sociological data. London (1962) states it thus:

> Technically, normal is a term which describes a particular kind of mathematical graph and statistical phenomenon. If certain measurements are made of a very large number of individuals, for example, and half of them fall above and half below a certain point, with most falling very close to it and diminishing numbers falling further and further from that point in precisely equal proportions on both sides of it, then the entire array of measurements is called a normal distribution.

The application of the "normal" Bell-shaped curve to human data contrasts sharply with the other two perspectives described above. These perspectives visualize normality and abnormality primarily as a straight-line continuum. They differ as to where the line should be drawn. The "Normality as Average" perspective conceives of the middle range as normal and *both* extremes as deviant. The normative statistical approach is used to find a way to describe each individual in terms of general assessment and total scores; interindividual variability is explained only within the context of the total group.

In biology and medicine, the adoption of this type of statistical perspective is related to the extensive use that has been made of measurement and classification. Norms have been established and pathology defined according to strict statistical criteria. The more our knowledge advances, the more our norms become refined. In clinical laboratory tests, a person's illness can manifest itself in too high or too low a basal metabolic rate (B.M.R.). Only the middle range is considered normal. Similarly, for a person to have a normal blood count, his red and white blood cells must number within a specific normal range. Deviancy either way means pathology and illness. There are literally thousands of biochemical tests with the same basic principle.

Many psychological tests utilizing questionnaires, rating scales, and projective tests are fundamentally related to the statistical principle of the Bell-shaped curve. The IQ test exemplifies one application of this approach (see Chapter 3) by simply defining the middle range, or one standard deviation from the mean, as the normal or average IQ for a particular society. It means, of course, that the majority of the population falls within the average range, a tendency characterized and criticized by Trotter (1916). Although the majority of the population falls within the average range, this statistical expression does not imply, according to Trotter, that these average individuals are healthy. It is important to stress, says Trotter (1916, p. 55), that:

> in this (i.e., average) type of mind personal satisfaction or adequacy, or, as we may call it, mental comfort, is attained at the cost of an attitude towards experience which greatly affects the value to the species of the activities of minds of this type. This mental stability, then, is to be regarded as, in certain important

directions, a loss . . . and however normal the type may be, it is one which falls far short of the possibilities of the human mind.

The IQ test, which, as mentioned, utilizes the statistical principle of the Bell-shaped curve, describes its results on a continuum ranging from the genius to the mentally retarded. Many psychological tests employ the principle of the Bell-shaped curve in a similar fashion. However, other psychological instruments designate results in the middle range as normative and those at both extremes as connoting pathology. In this approach, two different types of psychopathology become apparent. The subject either has lability or rigidity of affect. He has either too much or too little color response on the Rorschach. He associates too much to a picture or too little. In psychiatry, this approach is seen in Kraepelin's manic-depressive continuum. One striking result of such an application of statistics to behavioral data has been the idealization of the average, or the middle, since both ends of the scale denote pathology.

Two concepts discussed in Chapter 4 that implicitly fall under the "Normality as Average" perspective are Kardiner's (1939, 1945) "basic personality structure" and DuBois's (1944) "modal personality." The former describes people in a culture in terms of the degree of their approximation to its basic personality structure; the latter depicts the range of functioning of an average member of the culture.

Deviant behavior can be the end result of two distinctly different processes (A. K. Cohen, 1959). In one extreme form, the "behavior is psychotic, neurotic, maladjusted, or otherwise pathological from a psychiatric point of view." The other extreme is manifested by "clinically normal individuals" whose deviancy is due primarily to sociological factors. Rates of deviancy (psychiatric and/or sociological) are measured against the bulk of the population, which is considered normal. This is not to imply that these two extremes are the two ends of a simple Bell-shaped curve. There is a complex interaction of forces within a social network. An acceptance of the "Normality as Average" perspective has allowed many sociologists to make the statistical computation that would differentiate the normals from the deviants. A number of sociologists begin with the central values of the society, labeling them "normal," and then judge deviancy by its differentiation from these norms.[5]

Although many disciplines may be included under this perspective, it is of interest to note that we have cited very few psychoanalytic examples. In Chapter 8, we will refer further to the problems and the potentialities of psychoanalysts and psychiatrists employing these statistical concepts in their research.

Normality as Transactional Systems

The fourth "functional perspective," "Normality as Transactional Systems," stresses that normal behavior is the end result of interacting systems that change over time. In contrast to proponents of the other three perspectives, those who advocate this position insist that normality be viewed from a standpoint of temporal progression. Many of these investigators, although believing that temporal changes are essential to any complete definition of normality, may adopt a limited definition as a working hypothesis for the present. Such a limited definition would then fall under the rubric of one of the three other perspectives. Other investigators, whose concepts of

[5] See also Chapter 4, where the function of deviancy in bringing out the norms is discussed.

normality can be classified logically under one of the other three perspectives, often may add a qualifying clause to the effect that their definitions of normality and health are amenable to evolutionary changes. As time passes, the content of statistical averages, the range of health, and the composition of ideal values may all be changed.

In other words, the "Normality as Transactional Systems" perspective stresses changes or processes rather than a cross-sectional definition of normality. Investigators who subscribe to this approach can be found in all the behavioral and social sciences. Most typical is Grinker's (1956 and 1967) thesis of a unified theory of behavior encompassing polarities within a wide range of integration. The recent interest in General System Theory (Von Bertalanffy, 1968; Gray, Duhl, & Rizzo, 1969) has further stressed the applicability of the General System research for psychiatry. "Normality as Transactional Systems" encompasses variables from the biological, psychological, and social fields, all contributing to the functioning of a viable system over time. It is the integration of the variables into the system and the loading (or significance) assigned to each variable that will have to be more thoroughly explored in the future. There have been several attempts to develop a three-dimensional, field-oriented concept of human behavior. Grinker's (1956, p. 370) thesis is an example of a unified concept of behavior that accepts time as a major dimension and yet subordinates it, for the purposes of certain studies, to cross-sectional analyses:

> The reader may be somewhat bewildered by the use of the term "system" applicable to the biological, psychological, cultural, or social aspects of life-in-process. A system is considered to be some whole form in structure of operation, concepts or functions, composed of united and integrated parts. As such it has an extent in time and space, and boundaries. A system has a

past which is partly represented by its parts, for it develops or assembles from something preceding. It has a present, which is its existence as relatively stable or what might be called its resting form, and it has a future, that is, its functional potentialities. In space form, structure and dimensions constitute a framework, which is relatively stable and timeless, yet only relatively so, for its constituents change during time but considerably slower than the novel or more active functions of the system. To view the change of these functions through time, the frame or background may be artificially considered as stable.

The emphasis in the "Normality as Transactional Systems" perspective is placed on change or process, rather than on a cross-sectional definition of normality. Classified under this perspective are the scientists who accentuate the intermediary directional forces that point to more final stages. Such scientists would include the biologist who defines normality in relation to the progression or evolutionary development toward a more perfect biological state. Child (1924) believes that the normal in biology represents a pattern illustrative of the potential of the biological system as seen in the broad evolutionary context. The normal in biology is subject to change over time and further progression along evolutionary lines before its potential can be realized. This broad concept of normality encompasses immeasurable facets of the protoplasmic system that cannot be realized at any one particular point in time.

In *Civilization and Its Discontents*, Freud (1930) speculates on the degree to which evolution influenced culture and normal character traits. In this evaluation of the impact of civilization upon man's nature, Freud approximates the process definition of normal behavior.[6] In discussing man's excessive

[6] Freud also viewed normality as an ideal fiction. For details, see Chapter 2.

vulnerability to psychopathology, Freedman and Roe (1958) relate it directly to the present stage of evolution. Maladaptive behavior, then, is seen as a necessary stage in biological evolution. The assumption is that civilization is evolving toward a higher stage, in which neuroses will not be a by-product. Freedman and Roe accept the function of temporal progression in altering the universality of psychopathology. Feibleman (1961) thinks maladaptation is specifically a function of human society, which needs the maladaptive members at the present stage of its development in order to progress to a higher stage. According to Freedman and Roe, and Feibleman, the course of evolution requires a stage of almost universal psychopathology, wherein neurotic symptoms and psychopathology are part of everyday life.

Central to Erikson's (1959) concept of the epigenesis of personality development is successful mastery of the seven stages of development essential to the attainment of normal adult functioning and maturity. Here Erikson defines normality in terms of the end product in an unfolding process over time. He has emphasized this frame of reference more than those psychoanalysts who, in their discussions of normality, also elaborate successive progressional stages but relegate the epigenesis of normality to one of six metapsychological approaches. For Erikson the process approach is clearly *central* to his thesis.

Parsons (1959) (see Chapter 5) describes a system in which normal functioning can be present without concentrating on current structure. He defines the system in terms of antecedents, motion, and change. In this sense, he, more than other social scientists who have attempted definitions of health and normality, would fall under our "Normality as Transactional Systems" perspective.

We have attempted to demonstrate that the behavioral scientist's conceptualization of normality depends not only on his specific discipline but also on his "functional perspective." Each of the four "functional perspectives" examined in this chapter is utilized by investigators from almost all of the disciplines discussed in our book; hence, each perspective is cross-disciplinary. Each perspective also grapples with different issues and dimensions. The first three perspectives have a two-dimensional approach; the fourth represents a three-dimensional approach.

To a certain extent, each perspective complements the others, so that together they represent the behavioral and social sciences' approach to normality—a total field. We have considered the need to examine concepts of normality and definitions of normal behavior through time, for these concepts change, and understanding how they change will broaden our knowledge of the meaning of the various concepts and definitions.

7

Ethics, Aesthetics, and Normality

Faust: Thou who to farthest bounds
dost tend, all-active spirit,
how close I feel to thee!
Spirit: Thou art like the spirit thou
dost comprehend, not like me!
(*Disappears*)
Faust: (*Crushed*) Not like thee?
Whom then?

—GOETHE (1831)

Scientific formulations of concepts of normality have been influenced by value patterns in the larger cultural surroundings. Through the centuries, value systems, philosophers, historians, and artists have reflected changing attitudes toward the concepts. With a view toward comprehending the roots of the various contemporary scientific approaches to normality, we will refer to certain philosophic and religious influences. Then, using the arts as an example, we will indicate how some concepts of normality have been affected by social attitudes. Finally, an examination will be made of the extent to which the term "normality" can be incorporated and utilized as a scientific tool within the behavioral sciences. Here, the science of psychiatry will serve as a primary example.

The term "normal" itself was not coined until the time of the ancient Romans.[1] The growth of this concept, however,

[1] The word "normal" comes from the Latin *normalis*, which means "made

had already begun in Greek antiquity, when efforts to redefine concepts of health became central philosophical issues. To many Greek thinkers, health appeared to be synonymous with happiness. Happiness, in turn, was viewed from ethical and political perspectives. Plato and Aristotle were, perhaps, the theoreticians most responsible for the development of these perspectives.

Select Philosophical Precedents

Plato developed the concept of health as both a moral and a natural ideal toward which all men strive. The attainment of this ideal is difficult for the masses, who are led astray by the glitter of false suns. In the following selection from Plato's *Phaedrus* (Jowett, 1937), the perfect harmony of mental structure and function that is necessary for the attainment of happiness is presented:

> As I said at the beginning of this tale, I divided each soul into three—two horses and a charioteer; and one of the horses was good and the other bad: the division may remain, but I have not yet explained in what the goodness or badness of either consists, and to that I will proceed. The right hand is upright and cleanly made; he has a lofty neck and an aquiline nose; his color is white, and his eyes dark, he is a lover of honour and modesty and temperance, is guided by word and admonition only. The other is a crooked lumbering animal, put together anyhow; he has a short thick neck; he is flat faced and of a dark color, with grey eyes and blood-red complexion; the mate of insolence and pride, shag-eared and deaf, hardly yielding to whip and spur. Now when the charioteer beholds the vision of love and has his

---

according to rule." It also means "conforming to the standard or the common type; regular, usual, natural" (Webster, 1951).

> whole soul warmed through sense, and is full of the prickings and ticklings of desire, the obedient steed, then as always under the government of shame, refrains from leaping on the beloved; but the other, heedless of the pricks and of the blows of the whip, plunges and runs away, giving all manner of trouble to his companion and the charioteer, whom he forces to approach the beloved and to remember the joys of love.
>
> After this their happiness depends upon their self-control; if the better elements of the mind which lead to order and philosophy prevail, then they pass their life there in happiness and harmony—master of themselves and orderly—enslaving the vicious and emancipating the virtuous elements of the soul and when the end comes, they are light and winged for flight, having conquered in one of the three heavenly or truly Olympian victories; nor can human discipline or divine inspiration confer any greater blessing on man than this. If, on the other hand, they leave philosophy and lead the lower life of ambition, then probably, after wine or in some other careless hour, the two wanton animals take the two souls when off their guard and bring them together, and they accomplish that desire of their hearts which to the many is bliss; and this having once enjoyed they continue to enjoy, yet rarely because they have not the approval of the whole soul.

In his horse and charioteer analogy, Plato has set the stage for the psychoanalytic description of the balance of internal forces formulated many centuries later. In the latter, normality or health is seen in the flexibility and harmony among the various parts of the psychic apparatus. The Platonic concept that only the philosopher-kings may approach the attainment of the ideal has served at least in part as a prototype for current concepts of self-actualization of the few. According to Plato, the philosopher alone could climb the ladder of knowledge, while the average man remained chained by ignorance and "ignoble" desires.

Moral ascendancy, according to Plato's *Gorgias,* should be the proper qualification for political ascendancy. Just as the physician's knowledge qualifies him to attend to the health or right ordering of the body, so should the philosopher, with his thorough knowledge of the healthy soul, be the person to prescribe medications to society. The philosopher, rather than the people themselves, should be entrusted with diverting their actions, irrespective of their particular desires. Hence, to the extent that doctors govern the sale of drugs and determine certain sanitary rules, so, according to Plato, should philosophers (or the modern physician, including the psychiatrist?) be allowed to establish the laws for the running of society.

The attainment of knowledge implied the right ordering of one's own soul as well as the ability to govern others. If this line of reasoning is valid, must it logically follow that the present-day psychiatrist, who has been trained in the "ordering of the mind," and the psychoanalyst, who has undergone personal psychoanalysis, should consider it their moral duty to direct the mental health of the populace? Did not Plato pave the way for the psychiatrist to inquire humbly into his god-like qualifications? When the concept of normality was born, it had already inherited from its fellow term "health" a sense of the ideal and consequent reverence due to it.

In Plato's writings, the question of "normal for whom?" is asked in a pre-Roman vocabulary. If only the few could attain true health, then the masses must settle for lesser degrees of health, toward which their more limited perspectives could be oriented most successfully. Thus was designed Plato's *Republic,* where one best suited by temperament to being a carpenter should be a carpenter. Here, health for the many meant adequate adjustment. The decision of what was healthy for whom was a political one.

In his *Ethics,* Aristotle, too, defines a superior type of happiness and lesser types of happiness applicable to less gifted persons. He designates types of happiness for which different groups yearn. First, the common people, who identify happiness with sensual pleasure; second, the superior people, who equate happiness with honor or political life; and third, the only truly happy people, those who lead a contemplative life. In the contemplative life, man does not completely suppress all emotions but rather trains his emotions by reason. These divisions manifest Aristotle's unbelief in an absolute golden rule for happiness for all men. Concepts of happiness are being compartmentalized. Terms such as "suitable" and "adequate" will share with "ideal" as assumed modifiers of normality in many of its later usages.

Aristotle proceeds, in his *Ethics,* to discuss several components of happiness. The desirable characteristics are ranges of moderation between two extremes. Nonetheless, one extreme will often be judged less desirable than its opposite; thus, the mean for happiness will not be a statistical middle point between two poles. The degree of virtue that each man must perfect within himself for his own happiness is relative to each individual, his intellect, and his social position.

Aristotle has postulated no single Platonic ideal of goodness of which all lesser goods partake, but many relative goods determined by practical wisdom. Aristotle singles out one good that is significantly different from all other goods. Not all ends (goods) are final ends, but this chief good, the principle of rationality, is always desirable for itself. God's virtue consists of his total exercise of the power of thought. While no man, being a political animal, can ever lead a life of pure contemplation, it is his duty to live according to the highest in him, that which he shares with God (see Guthrie, 1960).

Although happiness may be regarded as other than an absolute ideal, Aristotle was not the forerunner of our "Normality as Average" perspective. "Now the mass of mankind are evidently quite slavish in their tastes, preferring a life suitable to beasts. . ." (Ross, 1942). With criteria such as "courage," "temperance," "proper pride," and "proper ambition," Aristotle anticipated the conception of normality as a state of health lacking any great sins of extremism. While differing with Plato's philosophical bases, Aristotle reinforced the "happiness as an ideal" concept. The present-day relevance of these theories is evident by comparisons of Aristotle's teaching with the thinking of the past few centuries within the behavioral sciences. Replacing the word "happiness" with the word "normality" in Aristotle's writings leads not to the experimental conclusions of today but to the germs of today's theoretical knowledge. Basically, however, these earlier incorporations of modern findings allow for much more sophistication and particularization.

While ethical and political precedents were being established by these great rational thinkers, the forces of religion and mysticism were fostering moral conceptions of the "abnormal" of which our society still finds residues and recurrences. On the one hand, "normality" is regarded as happiness and good fortune. On the other hand, "normality" is often considered as mediocrity. Ethical approval and disapproval both contribute to the ambiguity of the term. Throughout history, examples of the exaltation of abnormality are prevalent. In the old Grecian and Hebraic eras, the delusional person was regarded as one possessed by supernatural, godlike powers. He was often seen as a prophet or a messenger from God. As Socrates says in *Phaedrus* (Jowett, 1937):

> It might be so if madness were simply an evil; but there is also a madness which is a divine gift, and the source of the chiefest blessing granted to men. For prophecy is a madness, and the prophetess at Delphi and the priestess at Dodona when out of

> their senses have conferred great benefits on Hellas, both in public and private life, but when in their senses few or none.

We see that even in ancient times there was a tendency to consider mental illness in light of its adaptation within the existing society; abnormality was given a value meaning based upon its context. "Abnormal," when not equated with "holy," was associated with the opposite quality and seen as the incarnation of all evil. Demonic powers were attributed to the psychotic individual. Even those who rationally disagreed with a particular, prevalent philosophy were frequently accused of being marked by evil spirits (Bromberg, 1959). Both they and the disruptive psychotics were considered abnormal, not medically, but religiously. According to Veith (1958, p. 9), medieval dogmatism viewed all behavior deviant from its rigid structures as a religious offense:

> The problem was met with exorcism, intended to bring about recantation of an unholy alliance, and frequently, if the patient's type of dementia did not lend itself to a public disavowal, he was, for the good of his own soul, tortured to death or burned outright.

The Artistic Connotations

Despite efforts to eliminate ethical judgments from scientific language, the scientist often accepts these same judgments before he begins to select criteria for defining normality. He must decide whether his "normality" is a prized or a disdained one.[2] He must also decide whether he can establish criteria

[2] An example of the latter is masterfully illustrated in the following quotation from Dostoyevsky's *Notes from the Underground* (1961): "In my view, such a spontaneous man—the real, normal man—is the fulfillment of the wishes of his tender mother, Nature, who so lovingly created him

for an eternal type of definition of normality or whether he must take account of the cultural changes in attitude whereby the normal for today is the abnormal of yesterday and vice versa. In making these decisions, the scientist can profitably turn to the field of aesthetics, because the arts most strikingly portray the relations between connotations of normality and changing value systems. Our discussion of aesthetics in this section is intended to clarify such relationships as they pertain to the various scientific disciplines involved in the definitions of normal or healthy behavior.

In the arts, the bizarre, the unusual, of a generation might later be called the average or normal of the same generation that had rejected it. Although this conception of change is common to many fields, the artist stands in the particular position of bringing to our eyes that which, he believes, relates to the essence of life without need of absolute proofs. He need not be objective; he can immerse himself in subjectivity. As is true in philosophy, the artist will bring to the fore ideas that, if valid, will lend themselves to development within other specialties. Thus, from the artist comes a subjective view of man as he is and man as he ideally might be.

How does art reveal the normal actions and emotions of man? Each artist portrays his conceptions of what man is or

---

on this earth. I envy that man. I'm bilious with envy. He's stupid, I won't dispute that, but then, maybe a normal man is supposed to be stupid; what makes you think he isn't? Perhaps that's the great beauty of it. And what makes me even more inclined to suspect this is that if we take the antithesis of a normal man, the man of heightened consciousness, who is a test-tube product rather than a child of nature (this is almost mysticism, my friends, but I have a feeling that it is so), we find that this test-tube man is so subdued by his antithesis that he views himself—heightened consciousness and all—as a mouse rather than a man. So, even if he's a mouse with a heightened consciousness, he's still nothing but a mouse, whereas the other is a man. So there. And, what's more, he regards himself as a mouse; no one asks him to do so. This is a very important point."

of how he, as a man, views the universe. He tries to capture those criteria that are most important to him in expressing man's essential being. The criteria cover a wide range. Some artists describe man as an ideal conception, others portray his average functioning from day to day, and still others attempt to find some universal characteristics of man. In other words, an artist often illustrates through his work that which he considers essential or significant in man. The following examples illustrate our point.

Rembrandt can be seen through his paintings as having conceived of man as a spirit radiating through the bodily frame. Edgar Degas stresses the gawkiness that is part of man. Beethoven's music implies strength and shows the force of man's hopes and inspirations. Wolfgang Mozart's music has an angelic quality that conveys a legendary aura of fantasy and beauty in the abstract. Thomas Mann's *Buddenbrooks* illustrates man's desire for carrying on family tradition and conforming to his social environment in his everyday life. Of course, these artists' creations are tremendously more complex than our capsule characterizations suggest, but even such gross oversimplifications convey that the genius of the great artist reflects his personal view of man.

As his work becomes known, the artist's revelations may be accepted as descriptions of man in his relation to the universe. Whose works, though, can be said to represent the normal (in the sense of any of our four perspectives) at any given time? If a contradiction exists, shall we go to the most popular or greatest artists of the time for a true picture of a particular period in history? Though Johann Sebastian Bach was highly thought of as an organist during his lifetime and made a comfortable living as a musician, he was not considered a great composer. It was his son, Karl Philipp Emanuel Bach, who was known during his lifetime as "the great

Bach." J. S. Bach was forgotten after his death. Eighty to one hundred years later, an interest in J. S. Bach's music was revived, notably by Felix Mendelssohn. It took another eighty to one hundred years before J. S. Bach's music became a part of the established repertoire of the great music of the Western world.

The effect of the passage of time can be illustrated by still another example from the history of music. Gustav Mahler is quoted (Reik, 1960) as saying that his teacher and friend, Hans Von Bülow, who was both a distinguished conductor and a leading music critic of the nineteenth century, told him: "If this (Mahler's second symphony) is still music, then I do not understand anything of music anymore."

When there is a distinction between popular art and great art, the concept of normality will be affected by both types of art. That which is depicted most frequently will indicate the generally accepted patterns of normality at a particular time. The insights of the great artist not only will operate upon the concepts of normality for a more extended period of time, but also possibly will penetrate areas of scientific endeavor. Great creations may reflect, however, something innate and characteristic of man, while the majority of artists of the same period are depicting surface judgments more acceptable to society. The new ideas brought to light by the great artist might be frightening to the populace with its preconceptions of what ought to be. Thus, the passage of time is often necessary before people can incorporate the artist's revelations into their ordinary, average, or ideal perspectives on normality. According to Sterba (1960):

> The real artist who expressed the *Zeitgeist* of his era is never fully appreciated in his time because his higher sensitivity to the currents of his period and to the directions of the spiritual movements of his time enables him to express them in his crea-

> tions long before the general public becomes aware of them . . . the true artist deals with the fundamental problems of life and in his creations expresses the spirit of the time.

An acceptance of great artistic creations as reflectors of psychological changes may cause qualities formerly considered as deviant to be re-categorized. For example, through the force of subjective artistic portrayals, loneliness, rigidity, or brashness could become considered as characteristic of a particular period or of the human condition.

The legend of the artist himself, as a deviant living on the periphery of society, has supported the association between abnormality and superiority. In reality, many highly creative artists work quietly and effectively within their own social milieu. Nonetheless, creativity and genius are frequently seen as being enriched by social deviances or neuroses.[3] It may be that society wishes to alienate itself from its artists so that it will not have to view artistic creations seriously.

Society's intense ambivalence toward its artists can be likened to the attitude of the Greeks toward Philoctetes, the expert archer. In *Philoctetes,* by Sophocles, the hero is bitten by a snake while performing a public sacrifice. His groans and the horrible smell emanating from the wound so disturb his companions that he is banished to a neighboring island and not recalled until ten years later upon the advice of a Trojan soothsayer. Upon his return, a physician healed the disturbing wound. Likewise, when artists condemn aspects of their own society, its instruments often are activated to expel them as deviants. This is reminiscent of the insistence of some so-

[3] For a possible relationship between neurosis and creativity, see, for example, Freud, 1910, 1928; Rank, 1932; Kris, 1952; Phillips et al., 1957; Kubie, 1958; Eissler, 1962, 1963. We believe with Kubie (1958) that, although highly creative people are sometimes emotionally disturbed, they are creative despite their neuroses rather than because of them.

ciologists that society rejects delinquents because delinquents point to certain weaknesses within the social system. Both artists and delinquents, by the nature of their misdemeanors, depict as deviants a part of the functioning of the environment.

The label "deviant" as applied to the artist and/or his works encourages negative reactions to normalcy. Normality as average or healthy becomes normality as conformist or earthly. Disdain for normality becomes associated with the concept. On the other hand, revelations of a norm, in the sense of an unprecedented insight into the average, healthy, ideal, or process conception of man, are highly valued. Normality in this context is associated with basic truths. To be normal is to share a communality with the artistic portrayal. The negative and the positive values of normality flow from the image that is projected by the artist and his creative works. Further, the fluidity of the term "normality" is emphasized. Changing attitudes toward the revelations of the artist highlight the transitoriness of descriptions of man and his environment. To the extent that normality relates to that which exists or is thought to be most advantageous, changing descriptions of man will cause re-evaluations of the boundaries of normality.

The Intrusion of Values

The philosophic, religious, and aesthetic standards of normality are illustrative of the many forces that have shaped the term. Can the behavioral scientist study normality without being burdened by ethical commentaries? Throughout history the term "normality" has steadily become more significant scientifically despite its quasi-religious and even mystical connotations. When, for example, the ancient Greeks regarded the epileptic as a holy man, they obviously would not have considered therapy for him. Hippocrates challenged the ethical supremacy of the epileptic. His observations of epileptic behavior led him to establish scientific procedures unwarranted by existing religious judgments. Hippocrates, in "On the Sacred Disease" (Thatcher, 1907), refers to epilepsy as an affliction caused by a brain disorder. Examples of such courageous thinking are infrequent. Not until the middle of the sixteenth century did belief in witchcraft begin to diminish. The Belgian physician Johann Weyer, with great clinical insight, was one of the first to demonstrate the fallacies of demonology (Zilboorg & Henry, 1941; Bromberg, 1959). Paradoxically, however, Weyer, unable to ascribe natural causes to his patients' symptoms, attributed them to the influence of the devil on individuals weaker than others (Mora, 1963). Despite his own internal struggle with the concept of demonology, Weyer's predominantly naturalistic explanation was a second major achievement in defining unconventional behavior as ethically neutral phenomena. Two and a half centuries later, the French physician Philippe Pinel's removal of the chains of the mentally ill dramatically demonstrated the necessity of medical treatment rather than punishment.

These efforts to isolate the behavioral sciences from social concepts of morality have not been altogether successful. The professional judgments of the behavioral scientist are still influenced by currently accepted social values and centuries of past ethical associations. The psychotherapist, perhaps more often than any other behavioral scientist, is criticized for incorporating his own or his group's ethical prejudices into his professional judgments. Since the major function of the therapist is to correct personality defects, he must be fully qualified to act with scientific objectivity. In a young field with many areas yet to be investigated and only a minimal amount of objectively verifiable data, the judgment of the therapist is already suspect. In addition, given the influence of personal values upon therapy, to what extent can the psychotherapist be an authority on the behavior of others? Most other non-medical behavioral scientists are interested primarily in diagraming and understanding. Altering existing conditions is only secondary. Thus, an intermingling of subjective values with professional skills in these fields is not subject to a corresponding degree of attack.

This controversy is intensified when the mental-health worker extends his services to the community. Must a belief that psychiatric concepts can explain the composition of normality in its ideal or healthy sense logically lead to a belief that psychotherapists should be given full power to care for the mental health of mankind? The therapist would be to mental health what other physicians are to physical health. In discussing philosophic implications of this issue, Wolff states that the psychiatrist's position vis à vis his patients must logically support an analogous position vis à vis the individuals who have not expressed their desire for psychiatric treatment. In referring to current psychiatry, Wolff (1963) states:

> Modern day psychiatrists don't realize the immensely powerful implications of their theory of mental health, whereas Plato *did* realize the implications of his analogous theories. Both Plato and psychiatrists feel confident in telling a person that he is not really happy, even though he thinks he is. And this is done on the basis of observable phenomena which can be confirmed by repeated examinations of patients. . . .
>
> If mental health is a reality, then psychiatrists should be the judges of matters pertaining thereto, for they are the most knowledgeable people in this area. In fact, just such a trend has

developed. With regard to juvenile delinquency, certain forms of adult crime, aspects of education, and so forth, we have begun to treat the issues as amenable to expert judgment, like questions of fluoridation, inoculation, and so forth.

Psychiatry, as described by Wolff, would transcend the fields of law, politics, and economics, on the one hand, and ethics, religion, and philosophy on the other. Although philosophy was a combination of all the above at certain times in the past (for example, Aristotle), most psychiatrists and psychoanalysts do not see themselves as a present-day incarnation of the Greek philosopher. Rather, they limit themselves to the behavioral sciences, where their specific knowledge of human psychopathology and psychotherapy gives them a basis to help those who ask for guidance. If the psychiatrist were to act as judge of the mores of society, his scientific judgment would have to be comparatively free of the current standards of society. Whether or not such scientific objectivity is possible in areas of human behavior is debatable. It could be contended that, instead of acting as a judge and being above the mores, the psychotherapist actually is part of the mores and, thereby, creates conformist standards for society.

There are certain psychiatrists, psychoanalysts, and psychologists who have, however, attempted to broaden the implication of, for example, the findings of psychoanalytic psychology and would accept this role, which, according to Wolff, is the logical conclusion of their theories. Following in a Platonic tradition, Fromm (1960) and Meerloo (1962) do try to establish certain rules for "The Sane Society" based on their expert knowledge of psychopathology and their notion of normal or healthy psychology. On the other hand, Szasz (1963) cautions against what he calls excessive and unwarranted "social engineering." He warns society at large of the implications of giving the psychiatrist just the kind of "expertness" that we have described above. Szasz feels that the knowledge of the psychiatrist is not necessarily the knowledge requisite to the good functioning of society. The psychiatrist can help the individual make peace with himself but cannot, and should not, determine the order of peace within society at large.

Szasz (1956, 1961) finds a fallacy in the parallels drawn between the medical physician and the psychiatrist. According to his theories, psychiatry is culture-bound, whereas medicine is universal. He claims that psychiatrists use the verbiage of medicine only as a cover-up for essentially unscientific value-laden judgments: "In organic medicine, we have certain criteria by which many people of widely varying backgrounds and beliefs can agree on what constitutes health and disease." According to Szasz, such criteria are specifically missing in psychiatry.[4]

Must we then abandon efforts to define normality scientifically? Instead of asserting the scientific supremacy of psychiatric judgments of human behavior, perhaps we should reassert the interrelatedness and interdependence of psychiatry with prevailing ethical and social values. Accordingly, Hoffman (1960) emphasizes the power of the social environment upon all definitions of health.

> Our attempt to define "health" in psychiatry has not really produced satisfactory results, *and* we always have to define "health" within a specific cultural context of *values*. It would

[4] This statement is highly over-simplified. Differences of opinion among physicians in organic medicine do not differ markedly from those among psychiatrists when similar types of cases are compared. A consideration of the less serious physical illnesses will lead to as wide a range of opinion as would studies of neuroses. Similarly, criteria for diagnoses of severe mental illness (for example, psychosis or severe depression) seldom vary more than do severe physical illness criteria (for example, see Beck, 1962, and Beck et al., 1962).

seem that our difficulty in defining "mental health" is due precisely to the fact that it is not properly a scientific term. In fact, it can only be meaningful when ultimate values have already been postulated by some extra-scientific (for example, religious, cultural) means. It may be doubted whether any two theorists in the field will ever agree on the same order of ultimate values. Consequently, we shall never have a "true" definition of "health" within legitimate scientific definition of "justice."

Perhaps, as Hoffman suggests, an ideal definition of health can never be attained, just as an ideally healthy man can never be brought into existence. This should not, however, impede efforts to perfect the use of the concept of normality by further defining it. The cultural connotations of normality can be retained so long as there is an awareness of the influence of non-scientific values and an ability to distinguish the moral from the scientific. Hippocrates, Weyer, and Pinel made their contributions with an understanding of these influences in their proper perspective. According to London (1962):

> Science and morality have generally been confounded in psychotherapy—willy nilly, by the unwitting imposition of value and fact upon each other, by the causal assumption that there exist norms which suit values when the former have not been measured and the latter not defined, by the failure to weigh means (technique) against ends (goals) and both against fact.

In order to avoid this "willy nilly" confusion, definitions of terms and evaluations of the scientific worth of the definitions are needed. In this direction, Grinker suggests the following as values to which the psychiatrist in our society appears to subscribe:

> Upward mobility regardless of intellectual, aptitudinal or social fit, doing and becoming which is operationally goal-changing

rather than goal-seeking, permissiveness rather than boundary fixing of behavior, work, strict religious belief, and discipline; and child-rearing according to the latest fact based on current theory.

Obviously, the impact of values upon psychiatry and the behavioral sciences in general has been considerable.

In order to study people separate from his own social and cultural milieu, an investigator needs to be aware of his own values and those of the people whom he studies. Only then will he approach what is necessary for a reasonably objective investigator. Similarly, a psychotherapist needs to be aware of his patients' values and when they conflict with his own, before open communication can be established.

It is apparent that any definition of normality will be affected by values influenced by philosophic and aesthetic theories. The scientist's original choice of one of the four perspectives of normality may be motivated by his past conditioning. Correspondingly, the behavioral scientist's criteria of normality, which he proceeds to establish experimentally or clinically, may not differ greatly from the criteria he has absorbed from the philosophic, religious, or aesthetic values of his culture. The non-scientific use of the term "normality" has not invalidated its use in the behavioral sciences. Social judgments on the boundaries of normality have merely made the concept a more complex one. It becomes even more important to have clear definitions of normality.

In Chapter 8, we attempt to explain how the various concepts of normality have been utilized by the various disciplines in psychiatric research. We also attempt to demonstrate how the divergent perspectives have, at times, confused interdisciplinary communication and why in the interpretation of research findings one should consider the investigator's own perspective on normality together with his findings.

8

Empirical Research On Normality: A New Look

> Disease and health are relative terms: In order to understand the nature of health and disease we must decide on just how we are to approach the study of the human organism. . . .
>
> —WILLIAM A. WHITE (1926)

In behavioral-science research the term "normal" is used to describe two different types of persons. In the first, which is the more traditional context, the "normal" is used to describe the individual who is part of a control population being compared with a particular group of "sick" people; in the second, the "normal" individual is the one who is the research subject as such. In presenting these two contexts we first discuss issues associated with selecting a meaningful control group. We then focus upon the research on so-called normal populations being studied for their own sake. The illustrative research strategies to be discussed are primarily those that have been carried out since 1955 and are limited to empirical studies. In emphasizing more recent studies, we wish to accentuate the growing awareness on the part of many investigators that one "normal" population in any given study can be markedly different from a "normal" population in another study. An examination of the methods of selecting and studying "normal" populations will also accentuate the need for more than superficial study of the so-called normal as an individual.

The Use of "Normal" Controls in Research

The use of "normal" controls for the purpose of research is standard procedure in the behavioral sciences. Standard procedure in this case does not necessarily indicate scientifically valid procedure. Psychiatrists, for example, will often begin the study of a patient population by first selecting a "normal" control group. The psychiatrist then compares and contrasts this group with the patient group, without feeling compelled to analyze the assumptions that underlie his selection of the control group.

The *Report of the Group for the Advancement of Psychiatry* (1959), which studied the role and the use of controls in psychiatric research, stated that the problem of the "normal" control in such research is an especially "thorny one." In part, this is due to the fact that by "normal" controls psychiatrists ordinarily refer to persons who are not grossly disturbed and who have not been in psychiatric treatment.

In the behavioral sciences, there is considerable variance in the specific choices of "normal" controls. The following four groups have often served as controls: (1) populations of student nurses and laboratory personnel at hospitals (for example, see Veech et al., 1960); (2) medical and surgical patients at a general hospital (for example, see Taylor et al., 1963); (3) several small religious or ethnic groups (for example, the National Institute of Mental Health used pacifists—Dastur et al., 1963); and finally (4) the most commonly used control group of all, college students (for example, see Levitt, Persky, & Brady, 1964). These examples, taken at random from the mental health literature, illustrate that for most investigators a "normal" control subject will fulfill his function if he does not possess the specific ailment for which he serves as a control.

When an investigator chooses a "normal" control group for research purposes and defines "normal" controls as "individuals who are not under psychiatric treatment or not grossly disturbed," he employs explicitly or implicitly what we have called the criterion of "Normality as Health." He apparently believes that most people are essentially functioning on an adequate level and that only the extremes cannot be used for the purpose of a "normal" control.

Recently, there have been a number of studies that concentrated on understanding the nature of the groups utilized as "normal" controls.

Certain researchers are not content to call their control group a totally "normal" group. They dissect the "normal" controls, pointing out percentages of abnormalities. Esecover et al. (1961) found a high degree of psychopathology in "normal" control volunteers for hallucinogen drug studies.[1] Forty-six per cent of their group received positive psychiatric diagnoses and 41 per cent were estimated as needing psychiatric treatment. Another study, that of Perlin et al. (1958), at the National Institute of Mental Health, reported a similar high percentage of disturbed persons in two groups of "normal" volunteers, one with the median age of twenty-one and the other with a median age of seventy-two. There have been other reports (for example, that of Lasagna & von Felsinger, 1954) indicating a higher degree of psychopathology in a

[1] An illustrative incident happened to one of us. A borderline patient, who was a college student in one of the universities near Chicago, had been in treatment for many months. He read that another university, seeking "normal" controls for one of its drug studies, was offering $25.00 to volunteers. Because he needed money, he volunteered for the experiment and denied that he had been in therapy. He "passed" all the tests. We had some reservations when we read the results of that study, which compared the effects of hallucinogen drugs on "psychiatric patients and a 'normal' control group."

group of student volunteers than would be expected in an unselected college population.

In addition, the mere fact of being a volunteer subject may in itself affect the type of personality under study. Motivational reasons for volunteering will vary from one individual to the next (Butler, 1963). Such covert motivations as underlying desires for therapy imply the further necessity of discerning how those who volunteer constitute a special population.

How then are we to solve the problem of the "normal" control group? Should we abandon any attempt to develop psychological criteria? Or should we have stricter criteria that may be more practical? Perlin et al. (1958, p. 80) state that "in finding controls, an initial psychiatric evaluation of large populations may be impractical as well as introducing its own bias. Physiological or biochemical screening of a mass population may be a more efficient initial procedure." Although Perlin and his group believed it was difficult if not impossible to conceptualize a psychiatric description of "normal" controls for large studies, we believe that a normative perspective can be adopted for such purposes. The M.M.P.I., for example, can be effective as a psychological test for mass screening of groups.[2]

There are other possibilities. In another section of this chapter we will describe our own normative, psychiatric method of selecting a modal group from a much larger sample. This method is practical, and allows us theoretically to tap a group that has coherence.

We contend that it is essential to select a *meaningful* "normal" control group for studies within the behavioral sciences.[3]

[2] As an example, see Ostfeld (1965) and Shekelle & Ostfeld (1965).

[3] For an excellent discussion of an example of the difficulties involved in

Otherwise, in our judgment, there is considerable risk of entering into a blind alley. In order to make selection of "normal" control groups plausible, "normal" must be understood in its relation to total populations. To learn about disease, control groups are necessary, but the criterion for normality in larger populations must be investigated in order to select these control groups.

We further believe that the use of "normal" controls is often ambiguous and occasionally meaningless. Let us consider a theoretical example. A behavioral scientist wishes to study a group of twenty hyperthyroid patients purported to have psychosomatic illness. He would like to determine whether they differ significantly in psychological make-up and functioning from a group of "normal" controls. With this purpose in mind he selects a group of patients with a different illness (for example, gallstones) or writes a memorandum to his staff asking for volunteers. The groups are then matched for the variables of age, sex, education, socio-economic status, religion, race, weight, and height, and if the investigator is very zealous, he controls even for variables such as ordinal position in the family. If fifteen out of twenty (75 per cent) of his hyperthyroid patients have a basically hysterical character and only five (25 per cent) of this group are obsessive-compulsives, while in the control group 75 per cent possess obsessive-compulsive tendencies (much more likely among workers in the medical and behavioral sciences!), the investigator is then studying two groups who differ in essential psychological make-up. Under these circumstances it is highly likely that the comparative analysis will lead to differences. The results can be significant only if a *truly random* sample is chosen in the con-

selecting a proper group of controls in behavioral-science research, see Rosenthal & Kety (1968).

trol group. However, although it is practical to choose hospital personnel as a control group, they nonetheless do not comprise a random sample and as such may give skewed results.[4] In medical (drug) studies, basic psychological responses are often ignored when one undertakes a double-blind study. We know that people react differently to stress and that stress affects not only behavior but also the complex internal homeostasis. It seems necessary, therefore, that in order to control for individual variations the characterological make-up of the subjects, together with their basic pattern of responses, should be carefully studied and incorporated in the two populations under comparison. In other words, for a proper use of controls for psychological aspects of the pharmacotherapy, it is not sufficient to control for the ingestion of the drug nor is it sufficient to control for investigator bias.

We know that subjects differ in respect to their affective responses. This fact alone may cause the investigators to obtain significant results where the difference may be due to other causes.[5]

To restate our position, we believe that a more specific utilization should be made of controls. An investigator should know as precisely as possible what he is controlling for and include psychological variables in his general schemata. Only then can he use controls in a meaningful way. If, to use our earlier example, an investigator is studying the psychosomatic

[4] A discussion of the difficulty in finding controls in psychological research can be found in Levitt, Persky, & Brady (1964). They point out that controls should differ from the population studied with respect to the *dependent variable*. They also discuss the various differences between volunteers and non-volunteers, stressing that for some researchers the difference may be crucial, while for others it is insignificant.

[5] For example, Oken (1960) described three sub-categories of anger response: (1) direct expression of anger in behavior and motor activity; (2) verbally reported, subjectively experienced anger; and (3) indications of anger in verbal and other linguistic behavior.

aspects of hyperthyroids, he has to control, of course, for the disease and he will seek, as controls, patients without hyperthyroidism. He will also control for the various independent variables, such as age, sex, race, religion, height, weight, socioeconomic status, vocation and ordinal position. We believe that certain psychological aspects must also be controlled. For example, if the focus of the study is the emotional response of the hyperthyroids to stress interviews, the investigator will need to control for other factors, such as the basic character trait. He should have, for example, as many obsessive-compulsive characters in his control group as are present in the relevant general population. On the other hand, if one is interested in the psychological make-up of the group of hyperthyroids, which includes their basic character trait, one will need to know the epidemiology of character types within the general population: What is the percentage of obsessive-compulsive characters and of hysterical characters within the general population?[6] One will need to know these facts in order to use the term "control" in a meaningful way. If the investigator finds, then, that 75 per cent of his patients with hyperthyroidism have a hysterical character, the result will be meaningful only if the distribution of hysterics within the general population is significantly different (for example, 40 per cent). We are, of course, aware that this kind of data is as yet not widely available, but it is our hope that current and future epidemiological studies, using in part a psychiatric frame of reference, will ultimately provide us with the necessary baseline data.

[6] We are fully aware of the fact that the boundaries between the different basic characters and typologies are often not distinct. We do not mean to suggest a simplified solution to this complex matter, but we do believe that more careful thinking has to be given to this very vital part of behavioral-science research.

Empirical Research on "Normal" Populations

The Problem

The investigator who launches a study on "normal" subjects in an attempt to delineate carefully a particular behavioral or psychological trait first has to decide how he is going to select his population. After he decides what population he wants to study (for example, college students), the researcher must understand that the method he employs in selecting his "healthy" students will directly affect his results, because if he takes, for instance, only volunteers, he may bias his results in a very special way.

In evaluating the research on "normal" populations, we are facing, then, a problem similar to the problem that confronts the investigator in search of a "normal" control population. The ramifications of this problem have been discussed in the first part of this chapter. We now examine problems confronting the researcher who attempts to study carefully the behavioral characteristics of a group of "normal" people. In accomplishing this task, we do not present an exhaustive review but focus on three major questions: How did various investigators cope with the problem? Can one population of "normal" individuals be adequately compared with another population of "normals"? Finally, and most importantly for us, how does research on "normal" populations relate to the theoretical conceptualizations of normality?

Research on normal or non-patient populations is not exclusively of recent origin. Anthropologists have been observing cultures other than their own for over a century. Social psychologists and child psychologists have worked with people in experimental and testing situations ever since psychology developed as a scientific discipline. Psychoanalysts, although primarily studying patients who come to see them for psychoanalytic psychotherapy, have extended their theories to include concepts applicable to the personality development of normal children and adults. What has been lacking, in our opinion, are the systematic studies via longitudinal or follow-up investigations of normal populations. There is a distinct need to integrate the clinician's experience and abilities with the researcher's tools and methods (Offer, Freedman, & Offer, 1972). We shall review the findings from the clinical studies on normal populations which have been undertaken during this time frame. It is gratifying to note that during the past decade there has been a steady increase in studies of normal populations.

The two most influential clinical works on normal populations published after World War II were Grinker and Spiegel's *Men Under Stress* (1948) and White's *Lives in Progress* (1952). Both concentrated on coping mechanisms of nonpatient, or normal, populations. Grinker and Spiegel studied the behavior and psychological functioning of soldiers under combat conditions. White followed the lives of a selected group of college students with interviews. He assessed their success or failure in adaptation to their internal and external environment and their over-all psychological competence. Like other brilliant innovative work, both of these pioneering studies raised a host of methodological questions, but they laid the groundwork for the more detailed empirical work that followed.

The understanding of normal personality functioning and development has to come from studies of normal, or nonpatient, populations. For too long, theories of normal development have been extrapolated from studies of patients or deviant populations. Examining the literature, one can conceptualize four different levels of investigations into the psychological functioning and development of healthy or normal people: *cross-sectional, follow-ups, longitudinal,* and *predictive.* In examining these levels it is not yet possible to state that one approach is "better" than another; rather, our aim is to stress the methodological differences in studies on normal populations. The postulated four perspectives of normality are relevant to our understanding of these studies because the selection of subjects and the methodology and the instruments used will depend to a large extent on the orientation of the investigators. Just as the methods for collecting the data vary from study to study, so does the perspective of normality of the individual investigator. Thus, we have cross-sectional studies where the investigator subscribes to the "Normality as Transactional Systems" perspective, and we have longitudinal studies which are based on the "Normality as Health" perspective. In other words, the four different kinds of empirical studies of healthy development or normal personality functioning do not correspond directly to the four perspectives of normality. It would simplify matters if investigators state explicitly which of the four perspectives of normality they are using for a specific project. It would be easier to compare and contrast different studies once the value orientation of the researcher has been made more explicit. As things stand now, the reader must discern an implicit value orientation. Any attempt to identify the underlying perspective of normality of the various investigators could undoubtedly lead to numerous errors. We have, therefore, not done so unless normality was explicitly defined.

CROSS-SECTIONAL STUDIES These investigations involve the assessment of individual psychological functioning at one point in time. The methods of investigators vary considerably. They include survey technique, questionnaires, psychological tests, and in-depth psychiatric interviews.

Relatively more investigators use the cross-sectional approach than any other method. Among the more important studies are those by Grinker (1962), Heath (1965), Holmstrom (1972), King (1971), Smith (1972), and Westley & Epstein (1970). Two studies, one by Grinker (1962) and another by Holmstrom (1972), typify the methods and findings obtained from cross-sectional studies.

Grinker (1962) selected a group of freshman males from a mid-western college sponsored by the Y.M.C.A. His purpose was to obtain "subjects with a health range located around high and low poles of a stability-lability axis." To study this population, Grinker used the methods of observation, description, and statistical analysis. His techniques included interviews, questionnaires, and a behavior rating scale.[7] Grinker's[8] studies of volunteers from a small junior college were summarized by Offer, Offer, & Freedman (1972, p. 275) in the following way:

> In general, the subjects called by Grinker: "Homoclites"[9] were action oriented. Their world was conceived of as being external and calling for action; they were not introspective youths. One does something about problems. The response to affect was to "kick it off." When the students did feel depressed, they coped with the affect by (1) muscular action, (2) denial ("it doesn't matter"), and (3) isolation through withdrawal, sleep, fantasy, or concentration on music. Anxiety referred primarily to fear of failure in school or athletics. Likewise, school work and athletics were primary foci of interest.
>
> These students were not in conflict with their families. They

[7] The studies included a semi-structured interview, the Taylor's Manifest Anxiety Scale, Barron's Ego Strength Scale, Nowlis' Adjective Check List, and Mandler's Perception of Feeling.

[8] See Appendix under Roy R. Grinker, Sr.

[9] The Homoclite Study which was originally conceptualized as a cross-sectional study turned into a Follow-up Study fourteen years later.

had had good affectionate relationships with their parents. Discipline in their homes had been firm and consistent. The boys felt closer emotionally to their mothers, while identifying strongly with their fathers and, subsequently, father figures. With few exceptions, passage through puberty and adolescence had been smooth and devoid of turbulence.

The subjects' present interpersonal relationships revealed good capacities for adequate human relationships. Heterosexual experimentation was minimal.

The homoclites exhibited mild dependency. The capacity for leadership was obtained by virtue of the strength they received from identifying with a cause greater than themselves. They had developed strong feelings of self-worth which would not easily be thwarted because there was little discrepancy between goal-setting and action. The behavior of these students revealed goal-seeking rather than goal-changing ambitions.

Another study from a different culture that basically confirms Grinker's findings was undertaken a decade later by Holmstrom (1972) who studied a group of Finnish college students. According to the psychiatrist's ratings, the students were divided into three groups: the mentally healthy, the ordinary or average, and the mentally ill. The monograph is devoted to careful analysis of the psychosocial variables that contribute to the assessment of the mentally healthy students; the other two groups are used as controls.

Both Grinker and Holmstrom claim that their data clearly demonstrate that non-patient populations of this type are functioning psychologically on a different behavioral and affective level than patients. By comparing their findings to their clinical experience with patients, these authors claim that their normal samples have fewer identity problems and that these individuals move slowly and cautiously in the direction of independence and maturity. While these are significant findings, one major limitation of cross-sectional studies is the difficulty in obtaining reliable and valid data regarding background factors leading to these findings, and one wonders whether these non-patients will stay healthy in the future. To answer these two major questions, follow-up studies and/or longitudinal studies are imperative.

FOLLOW-UP STUDIES By definition, these investigations cover two different points in time. The methods vary as in the cross-sectional studies. Follow-up studies usually have a specific aim in mind, and they are employed in studies of normal as well as disturbed groups. For example, in Garber's (1972) follow-up study of hospitalized adolescents, he wanted to determine why some adolescents do well after discharge and others do not. He compared the functioning of adolescents in the hospital and their functioning years later. The only limit to the number of years between an original study and the follow-up study is the life span of the subject; indeed, some have spanned thirty years. The studies can also turn into longitudinal investigations if the subjects are systematically followed beyond the second point in time. A number of follow-up studies on normal populations have been undertaken in the recent past (e.g., Silber et al., 1961; Symonds, 1961; Cox, 1970; Block, 1971; Vaillant, 1971; and Masterson, 1967).

Silber et al. (1961) delineated the coping mechanism that adolescents use in the transition from high school to college. The students were studied during their senior year in high school. Predictions were made, based on the defensive structure of the ego, as to who would do well in the first year in college and who would not. The investigators found that a good sense of reality, willingness to compete, and a rehearsal of fantasy of possible future events were crucial for a smooth transition from high school to college.

Vaillant (1971) and Vaillant and McArthur (1972) undertook a follow-up study of individuals who went to Harvard

College in the late 1930's. In his thirty-year follow-up study he delineated the psychological characteristics which were found to be essential for mental health in this group. He described the defense mechanisms of the healthy as well as those of the psychopathologic group. One major finding involved the apparent long-term continuity of defensive processes employed by both the healthy and the psychopathologic component. Vaillant divided his study population into two sub-groups: those who needed and sought psychiatric care and those who did not. The group who did not seek psychotherapy were characterized by the following criteria: (1) stable marriages, (2) active participation in sports, (3) church attendance, (4) physical health. There was no correlation between turmoil during the adolescent years and later healthy development in the adult years.

Block (1971) has also stressed that the key finding in his follow-up study was continuity and stability in psychological functioning over the years. He studied subjects who were followed in the *Berkeley Guidance Study* and the *Oakland Growth Study* over a period of forty years. These individuals were chosen initially because of the investigator's interest in studying normal personality development. The studies began when the subjects were children. Once the children were selected, parents were asked to cooperate with the investigation. With the help of the Q-sort method, Block compared the psychological functioning and personality attributes of the subjects during their adolescent years and during middle adulthood. The striking finding was that psychological continuity rather than change characterized this population during the years that separated the two data-collection periods. The subjects could be differentiated according to their ego strength, adaptation to their environment, success, and happiness. After classifying the adults into five groups, Block found that functioning during the adolescent years could be employed to predict in which of the five groups the subjects would belong as an adult.

These follow-up studies provide significant support for the hypothesis that continuity does exist in the realm of psychological functioning. In many ways the stability of psycho-social findings reported in the follow-up studies confirm the validity of the cross-sectional studies. They leave unanswered the question: How is the continuity maintained? More specific micro-psychological analysis of behavior and feeling states of individuals across time is necessary before we can begin to answer this perplexing question. Longitudinal studies bring behavioral scientists one step closer to answering this last question, although the answers they tend to provide are not necessarily definitive.

LONGITUDINAL STUDIES In these investigations the subjects are studied over time by appropriate methods. The purpose of these studies is usually to determine the factors that influence the functioning and adjustment of individuals over time. The subjects are studied on at least three occasions. Some longitudinal studies have gone on for thirty or forty years. One advantage of multiple observations is that they tend to eliminate errors induced by less frequent contact.

There are only a few published longitudinal studies on the functioning and psychological development of normal individuals: Kagen and Moss' (1962) studies of children from birth to the age of sixteen, the California studies by Block (1971), King's (1971) studies of college students, and Offer's (1973) and Offer & Offer's (1975) studies of adolescents and young adults.

King (1971) and his associates have studied the psychological functioning and coping abilities of students throughout the four years of college. Four patterns of personality change were reported by these authors. They are:

1. *Progressive Maturation.* Here King found continuity between past and present. The subjects had good object relationships. They increased their self-esteem during college, maintained good impulse control, and developed their vocational and general interests. Their mood became stabilized and, in general, their behavior was goal-directed.

2. *Delayed Maturation.* This group showed some discontinuity between their past and present functioning. The students were confused about themselves and lacked a solid identity. They had a capacity to adapt, and they were depressed at times. On the whole they did not cope with the same degree of consistency as did the students belonging to the first group.

3. *Crisis and Reintegration.* This group showed definite psychiatric symptoms. Their coping abilities were limited; their self-images were negative. They had problems with anger. They were loners, and, in general, had poor interpersonal relationships. The longitudinal study was significant in demonstrating the pattern of periodic crises, followed by temporary reintegration.

4. *Deterioration* (5 per cent of the total sample). This group showed serious disturbances in their emotional and cognitive functioning. This finding should not come as a surprise; when one selects a random population for study, one is apt to discover disturbed individuals within it.

We agree with King that the crisis model of development is not appropriate for all members of the adolescent population. King recommends instead a more generalized acceptance of a continuity model of development. The latter could be better used to describe the bulk of King's sample.

PREDICTIVE STUDIES Predictive studies are conceptually difficult to organize because one rarely knows what the right questions or variables are at the inception of the study. Furthermore, such studies are empirically difficult to undertake because of the expense, commitment, and time involved. Such studies are also difficult to start because it is almost impossible to know which intervening variables will have the most influence on the functioning of individuals in the future. At times the intervening variables are not even in existence when the study begins (e.g., the impact of the Woman's Liberation movement on the behavior and psychology of the young adult woman: Chesler, 1972). Predictive studies will indeed be impressive if the precisely formulated predictions are borne out despite the difficulties. Although there are no predictive studies that fulfill all the author's scientific criteria, short-term predictive studies on populations at risk have been made (e.g., parents of leukemic children: Futterman & Hoffman, 1973). These successful predictions were made on selected individual cases. There are also successful predictions on groups (e.g., the likelihood of a child developing schizophrenia if both parents are schizophrenics is much better than chance: Rosenthal & Kety, 1968).

These studies bring behavioral scientists a step closer to penultimate predictive studies where we will be able to predict how individuals will cope under a variety of life situations including those that are not necessarily stressful. For example, after studying a group of one hundred children at the ages of seven and eight one could attempt to predict which children will do well at puberty and which will not. Or after studying a group of one hundred newly married couples, one could predict which couple will still be married five or ten years later, and, more importantly, who will be happy and well adjusted and who will not. The fact that many intra-psychic, inter-personal, and environmental factors and their interrelationships are involved makes it exceedingly difficult to undertake such a project. At times, one can utilize retrospective studies by deciphering crucial from non-crucial variables and by attempting to identify those variables with potential predictive power.

These empirical studies help behavioral scientists to understand the complexities of the psychology and behavior of non-patients. Such studies shift the focus away from medical interest and concern with disease, maladaptation, and psychopathology. They show that in order to know more about "problems in living" one needs to study well-adjusted individuals in depth to understand better what went right. However, a few words of caution. All of the studies reported in this chapter were done on middle-class, if not upper-middle-class, populations. There are few published studies on the normal coping processes demonstrated in minority group populations. Also, the majority of the subjects studied were males. The danger is obvious. There may be a tendency to use the middle-class white male as a model. There is an urgent need to study other non-patient populations in order to broaden the understanding of the vicissitudes of normality and health.

The Modal Adolescent Project: A Prototypic Clinical Study

Within the field of adolescent research, definitions of normality are particularly difficult to formulate. Emotional conflicts seen as normal adolescent turmoil by one investigator may be regarded as psychopathological process by another. Clinical descriptions of the functioning of an adolescent described as "healthy" are often couched in the same terms as are diagnoses of psychiatric patients regarded as "sick" by their therapists. Studies of adolescence illustrate the use of all of the perspectives on normality described in Chapter 7. Certain of the difficulties can be attributed to the variance in perspective. If an investigator defines only severe disturbance, such as dementia praecox, in adolescence as psychopathology, he accepts our "Normality as Health" perspective. On the other hand, some investigators believe that to be "normal" during the adolescent years is an impossibility; since adolescents must go through a period of turmoil, an adolescent cannot be categorized as characterologically normal. These investigators subscribe to the "Normality as Utopia" perspective. Investigators who stress stage of development, defining normal behavior as an end product in an unfolding process over time, accept the "Normality as Transactional Systems" perspective. Finally, investigators who define normal as a range on a Bell-shaped curve employ the "Normality as Average" perspective. In our opinion, this statistical approach is especially effective in screening modal or average groups from larger samples. It has been employed in the past for studying the adolescent in terms of general assessment and total scores. In the following section, we describe the use of "Normality as Average" perspective for the selection process in our research. We also share with the reader some results from our eight-year longitudinal study. The findings are described in detail in Offer (1973) and Offer & Offer (1975).

THE SELECTION PROCESS In the fall of 1962, we began a longitudinal study on a group of non-patient boys in two Chicago suburbs (see Offer, 1969). We administered the Offer Self-Image Questionnaire to 326 freshman boys in the two suburban high schools (Offer & Howard, 1972). The self-image questionnaire was designed to evaluate the adolescent functioning in multiple areas. On the basis of their scores, eighty-four subjects were selected in the beginning of high school. A typical or normal student was defined as one whose answers, on our self-image questionnaire, fell within one standard deviation from the mean in nine out of ten scales which described various aspects of adolescent functioning. A group of teen-agers whose adaptation to their environment was not seen as deviant by parents, teachers, or our initial selection instruments was selected. The high-school studies were completed on seventy-three of the eighty-four subjects selected.

Throughout the high-school years, two psychiatrists[10] interviewed the seventy-three males selected. During this part of the study each subject was interviewed once every four months. Parents were interviewed by a research colleague. High-school teachers completed rating scales on the adjustment of the students. For the follow-up study, we have data on sixty-one out of the seventy-three high-school subjects. After their high-school graduation, each subject was interviewed once a year for a two-to-three-hour interview. In addition, the subjects received a yearly adjustment questionnaire. Parents were asked to rate the adjustment of their children at the end of the first post-high-school year. The subjects were given psychological testing twice, at ages sixteen and twenty-one.

THE LONGITUDINAL STUDY: NORMALITY AS TRANSACTIONAL SYSTEMS Once the subjects had been selected, the perspective on normality shifted. "Normality as Average" was no longer to be the major mode of evaluating this group. For a further in-depth personality study one need not rely on the kind of behavioral data that often must be utilized in numerically larger studies. We had the facilities, the time, and the cooperation of the subjects so that we could now concentrate more on differing patterns of meaning for each individual's set of responses. The "Normality as Transactional Systems" approach was utilized for describing the population that was being studied. Within this approach, changes or processes are

[10] Dr. D. Offer interviewed 85 per cent of the subjects and Dr. D. Marcus interviewed the other 15 per cent.

the crucial variants of normality; cross-sectional static definitions of normality are useful only as they play a role within the broader field approach. The "Normality as Transactional Systems" approach provided the general direction for the data analysis, which began with the establishment of variable counts and proceeded to the study of the interrelationships between groups of variables.

SELECTED RESULTS The group as a whole is characterized by above average IQ (115) and good physical health. During the course of the study, few subjects manifested gross psychopathology or severe physical illness. Most of these subjects demonstrated an ability to experience affects flexibly and actively bring their conflicts to a reasonable resolution. In general, the subjects coped well with anxiety, depression, shame, guilt, and anger. They had relatively good peer relationships as well as a capacity to relate to and identify with adults.

For the majority of students who were studied, independence could be achieved without a significant devaluation of parents. Generally, these adolescents did not reject important parental values. During early adolescence the struggle for emotional disengagement was enacted in areas which are often viewed as trivial by adults. When the parent could keep the issue in perspective, by and large the adolescent would achieve the victory needed for his sense of self-esteem. These "battles" could be won without the adolescent having to jeopardize parental support. Even the issues chosen for the arguments often were dependent on parental preferences, but in a negative way. This has been conceptualized by Baittle & Offer (1971, p. 145):

> When the adolescent rebels, he often expresses his intentions in a manner resembling negation. He defines what he does in

> terms of what his parents do not want him to do. If his parents want him to turn off the radio and study, this is the precise time he keeps the radio on and claims he cannot study. If they want him to buy new clothes, the old ones are good enough. In periods like this, it becomes obvious that the adolescent's decisions are in reality based on the negative of the parents' wishes, rather than on his own positive desires. What they do, and the judgment they make, are, in fact, dependent on the parents' opinions and suggestions, but in a negative way. This may be termed a stage of "negative dependence." Thus, while the oppositional behavior and protest against the parents are indeed a manifestation of rebellion and in the service of emancipation from the parents, at the same time it reveals that the passive dependent longings are still in force. The adolescent is in conflict over desires to emancipate, and the rebellious behavior is a compromise formation which supports his efforts to give up the parental object and, at the same time, gratifies his dependent longings on them.

During high school, most subjects described their fathers as reliable and their mothers as understanding; generally, these adolescents felt closer emotionally to their mothers. The typical subject wanted to be accepted by his parents and admitted into their way of life, but he wanted to do this with a feeling that he was acting as his own free agent. After high school the relationship with the parents changed: most of the male subjects developed more positive identifications with their fathers. The relationship with the mothers, on the other hand, often became more conflictual as the subjects shifted some of this emotional investment to girlfriends.

The normal adolescent sample usually managed to cope with even severe stresses through their particular individual defensive structures and their action orientation. When an unusual situation occurred, such as the death of a father, the adolescent would first deny the full emotional impact of the event. Then, he would cope with the stressful situation, as well as the affect aroused by it, through doing something. The adolescent would involve himself in time-consuming activities; often these activities were ones which would be necessitated by practical realities. Only gradually would he let himself experience the loss and mourn.

The stresses produced by the changes in body, in body image, and in emotional states were managed by these adolescents with little evidence of total personality upheavals or ascetic renunciations of all bodily desires. The male adolescent experienced the most difficulty with controlling his impulses during early adolescence. In mid-adolescence the involvement in sports, in cars, in hobbies, or in debating teams channeled his energies quite effectively. In late adolescence, the subjects as a group became slightly more introspective. Sports were not as available anymore as an easy outlet, and these adolescents spent more time questioning themselves and their goals than speaking of their accomplishments. Particularly in the first post-high-school year many subjects described loneliness and a diffuse depressive reaction.

Most of the subjects had a realistic self-image. Their overall pattern of behavior was goal-directed, toward a future which they could envision and for which they were making mental time schedules. Although they had questions concerning their vocational choices, most of these adolescents have been following their plans with only minor shifts.

The cardinal finding concerning adolescent sexuality was that there is a discrepancy of several years between the time our adolescent subject was biologically mature and the time he engaged in intensive heterosexual activities. In this sense, the male adolescent subject was "slow" in becoming involved sexually with a female, at least by standards widely reported in the 1970's. Ten per cent of the study population had sexual intercourse by the end of the junior year of high school. By the end of the first post-high-school year, 30 per cent of the total group had had sexual intercourse at least once. The rate rises to 50 per cent by the end of the third post-high-school year.

The adolescent male in early and mid-adolescence was not worried about his participation, or lack of participation, in heterosexual activities. For the male, his own attention was focused on learning to curb his aggressive impulses rather than learning to handle his sexual impulses. When he acts out, it is most often aggressively, in delinquent or otherwise violent behavior. Especially during the high-school years, sexuality remained an emotional taboo as well as an environmental one.

Although the teen-ager was uncomfortable when he talked about his own sexual feelings and impulses, he liked to appear "liberal" when talking about such issues as premarital sex. The high-school student generally thought that sexual intercourse was "okay" after high school.

After high school many subjects gave the availability or lack of availability of a room or a car as the reason for their virginity or lack of it. They did not want to take full responsibility themselves but preferred to delegate it to environmental circumstances.

The typical subject was an average, white, suburban, Protestant, male adolescent. It was, therefore, of great interest that when the data were analyzed, by factor and typal analysis, three sub-groups of adolescents, each manifesting a different emotional constellation, were discovered. The sub-groups were called "routes" in order to stress their developmental aspects. Each route makes clinical as well as statistical sense, and no one route is preferable or superior to the others. A complex interaction of bio-psycho-social variables such as child-rearing practices, genetic background, experiential factors, cultural and social surrounding, and the inner psychological world of the individual determines the course of the development of each person. The three groups[11] have been labeled by the most prominent differentiating growth pattern that they have demonstrated throughout the eight-year course of the study.

1. Continuous growth (23 % of the total group).
2. Surgent growth (35 % of the total group).
3. Tumultuous growth (21 % of the total group).

THE THREE ROUTES THROUGH ADOLESCENCE

1. *Continuous Growth.* By and large the individuals in this group had strong egos and were able to cope well with internal and external environments. They had an active fantasy life and an ability to postpone gratification. They accepted general cultural norms. Throughout the eight years of the study there was mutual respect, trust, and affection between the generations. They had no serious super-ego problems and developed meaningful ego ideals. When an external stress occurred, they used the defenses of denial and isolation to cope with the initial affect. By and large, their techniques of coping with situational stresses, such as leaving home after graduating from high school, were handled without significant external signs of turmoil.

2. *Surgent Growth.* Most of this group were not able to cope smoothly with unexpected stress. There was a slight tendency to use the defenses of projection, anger, and depression when things did not turn out as they had been planned. They were not as action-oriented as the first group. In general they were less introspective than either the first or the third group. Relationships with parents were not smooth. The mothers had

[11] Twenty-one per cent of the subjects could not be classified—they had mixed scores and did not fit into any of the sub-groups (as explained above).

difficulty in separating from their children. Neither the continuous growth group nor the surgent growth group had observable identity crises in the usual Eriksonian sense, although they may have experienced a "silent identity crisis" (Erikson, 1968). One of the main differences between this group and the third group was that the periods of regression were circumscribed, both temporarily and psychologically in the second group.

3. *Tumultuous Growth.* Some subjects reacted to internal and/or external stresses as if they were a major tragic event. These individuals had a greater tendency to display the affects of anxiety, depression, and emotional turmoil. They were, in general, mistrustful of others. They were highly sensitive and introspective individuals. One-third of this group had received psychotherapy or counseling during the course of the study. Some members of this group were neurotic adolescents identical with the ones treated in outpatient clinics. Separation was painful to the parents, who were unsure of their own value systems.

Many investigators and theoreticians in the field of youth have stressed the importance of the "turmoil" concept for all adolescents. Based on the behavioral criteria which have been observed in normal populations, adolescence may or may not be a manifestly tumultuous period. But, what of the notion that if one would only delve deeper, more turmoil would be uncovered in the seemingly content subjects? In one sense, one might agree with this theoretical conceptualization because the turmoil of adolescents has been accepted as a given of adolescence, and through these expectations the culture has helped look for it and, thus, make it more manifest. Then, it would follow, by definition, that a healthy adolescent will undergo periods of disruptive behavior. But, one cannot say that because one expects it, finds it, and cherishes it, it is a defining characteristic of a healthy adolescent unless one finds it to be more prominent in adolescents than in other groups where it might also be respected and cherished—such as, for example, artists or geniuses. One does not know to what extent the tolerance for the turmoil helps to allow it to surface, and for which individuals of the group it will surface.

The existence of at least three psychological routes from childhood to adulthood has been documented. One cannot say which group is the healthiest, because one would have to add, "Healthiest for what?" For the individual's self-contentment? For the future of the culture? For a better and changing world? The response remains an unanswered philosophical question, dependent on the investigator's as well as on the subject's value system.

While the above examples focus on adolescent and young adult growth and development, longitudinal studies can obviously be undertaken at any stage of the life cycle. As has been emphasized, the major findings suggest that stability rather than change characterizes successive adaptation throughout the life cycle. This is not to state that people do not change as they grow older. It is our hypothesis, however, that the coping styles and psychological reactions in the different stages of the life cycle are similar. For example, if an individual had a tumultuous adolescence, she would be more likely to have a tumultuous menopause than others who reacted differently.

Current studies which differentiate between groups of adolescents should help us to identify the various healthy coping mechanisms and learn to what extent they, as well as age-specific tasks, characterize adolescence as a stage apart. Then we can look at the patient who needs help with a more precise conceptualization of the possibilities of adolescent development. Or, if the patient belongs in the tumultuous development category, we will be able to isolate his problems more specifically, along his own developmental lines rather than along the necessities of his age.

For the adolescent in general, we should know that his rebellion against society is not to be programmed into our plans for him. And if he does not change our world as he grows older, perhaps it is because he never really wanted to. Our assessment of the young and our goals for a better world to come should not lead to disappointment in the young who will not lead us there, or to a crushing of their independence because we fear they may be leading us astray. The fears and the hopes are probably theirs as well as ours, because we have so bred them.

In another context, we (Offer, Freedman, & Offer, 1972) have stated that in no areas of psychiatry is the integration of the clinician's experience and abilities with the researcher's tools and methods more important than in the area of clinical research. An integration of the two through the "Normality as Transactional Systems" perspective would do much to enhance the furtherance of knowledge in the field of psychiatry. This is the aim toward which many of us in psychiatry are striving.

Summary and Conclusion

In this chapter it has been shown that people from many different populations are used as "normal" control subjects by psychiatric investigators. Control subjects exhibit a diversity of characteristics, and some are reported to show a high degree of psychopathology. Systematic and specific screening is needed for the "normal" control, if he is to be truly a control subject. The screening method must be based on as clear an understanding of normality as is possible, and, hence, the most appropriate "normal" population may be selected for the specific research questions

Different "functional perspectives," preconceptions, fields of interest, and methods of selection are accepted by the different investigators studying normal populations. How can these varied criteria be employed? Theoretically, there are three possibilities:

1. The compilation of all the criteria and extraction of certain commonly occurring items that could be regarded as the core of normality.
2. The compilation of all these studies and the considerations of each as exemplifying a different aspect of one holistic definition of normality.
3. The separate consideration of each definition of normality as valid within the circumstances that were particular to its derivation.

The first of the possibilities would indeed represent an ideal state in terms of formulations of working hypotheses but, thus far, is the least possible scientifically. With the exception of "the lack of overt psychopathology," no criterion has been found to occur commonly enough throughout the research findings presented to be accepted as a characteristic of normality. Devoid of explanatory notes, criteria like "autonomy" and "ability to cope" would make too flimsy a substructure to provide significant advantage for future research. To date, the possibility of formulating a core for clinical conceptualizations of normality has not been substantiated by research.

A study of the projects completed lends greater plausibility to the second possibility. Meaningful combinations of the studies might be arranged to begin the formation of a total picture of normality. If we could visualize one vast compilation of all possible behavior, could we formulate one array of criteria, including all intra-psychic and inter-personal relationships? Do we have enough evidence to believe that the results of behavioral-science research on normal populations might function as pieces of a larger picture? The answer must await further research, although results stemming from research described in this chapter are beginning to show promise.

According to the third possibility, neither common denominator nor holistic definitions can be constructed because the many existent definitions of normality cannot be considered apart from highly specific referential material. Criteria for normality are often value-laden to the extent that they can be postulated only for particular environmental situations. It is possible that definitions of normality will never serve us in such a way as to make "normality" a singular rather than a plural term (see next chapter).

The research to date cannot definitively justify any of these three approaches. A combination of further empirical research and a clarification of procedural processes is needed. The social- and behavioral-sciences approach to normality is still a wide-open research arena.

9

Toward an Increased Understanding of Normality and Mental Health

Future research among *many kinds* of populations will be necessary to delineate *other kinds* of health or normality. Combining the results of many such studies may enable us to develop suitable abstractions and theories which contain more than words and generalities. —ROY R. GRINKER (1962)

The statement that it is difficult to define mental health and normality has become a cliché. The difficulties have been pointed out since antiquity, but the awareness of the significance of this problem has increased steadily during the past decade. Indeed, references to the theoretical and practical difficulties attest to the growing interest on the part of many investigators in the field of normality and health. Throughout this book the complexities and difficulties encountered in studies of normality and mental health have been discussed. Our assumption, however, has always been that it is possible to define the problem, and, thus, in the long run we will better understand the different kinds of mental health and normality. As the interest in studying normality by behavioral scientists increases, we have also identified forces among the mental health professionals, as well as in the community, that resist these studies. The antagonism, in part, stems from fear—the fear that behavioral scientists might set up normative standards for behavior that will interfere with individual freedom. The resistance also stems from the belief of some behavioral scientists that it is not possible to conceptualize normality or mental health, and therefore why engage in a fruitless exercise. Nonetheless, a significant group of social and behavioral scientists believe that it is essential to meet these challenging arguments and, hopefully, overcome the problems.

Why has the empirical study of normality and health been a relative newcomer in behavioral-science investigations? One obvious reason is that it is a result of training, in that training produces not only a set of skills but also what Kaplan (1967) calls a "trained incapacity." Trained to recognize the abnormal, the behavioral scientist and his teacher have had difficulty with recognizing, let alone conceptualizing, the normal. In part it is important to study normality because it serves as a baseline for all behavior whether pathological or not.

The Prevalence of Disturbance in Normal Populations

The traditional medical public health approach to prevalence and incidence is closely tied to case finding and clinical symptomatology. The well-known studies of Eaton & Weil (1954), Leighton (1959), and Srole (1962) all describe the incidence of mental illness or psychopathology in a random, non-selected population. The authors ask not, What is normal behavior? but rather, How much mental illness can be found in the sample? Leighton's (1959, p. 250) description of mental health is typical, and would be classified under our "Normality as Health" perspective:

> In this book it [mental health] has been defined as the absence of known pathology. Such a definition is, of course, unsatisfactory for many purposes, since it provides no content for a conception of health. Its main virtue lies in that it persistently raises the question as to what health is.

Beiser's (1971) follow-up study of Leighton's original sample still concentrated in the main on case finding and prevalence of mental illness.

Masterson's (1967) study, although selecting and studying a group of patients, compared the results obtained from the patients with a randomly selected group of non-patients. He was interested in answering the following questions:

1. How much and what kind of symptomatology is present in a group of adolescents who have never been seen for psychiatric consultation?
2. How do the symptoms in this group of adolescents compare with the symptoms found in a patient group?
3. What are some of the major factors that determine whether or not an adolescent seeks treatment?

Another example is Harris (1959), who in his book *Normal Children and Mothers* follows the principle of studying a "normal" group and describing the degree of psychopathology that he found in it. He studied fifty-four boys and girls, aged nine and ten, and their mothers. The children were referred by the public schools and were rated by the teachers as "normal." The children and their mothers were then subjected to the same diagnostic study that would be employed commonly in a child-guidance clinic, namely, psychiatric interviews, psychological testing, and social work history. Harris does not clearly define "normality" for the purposes of selecting his population, though operationally, as noted, his sample was referred by teachers who rated the children as "normal." Voluminous, descriptive, psychiatric data have led Harris to state that each child reveals an admixture of "normal" and "abnormal" behavior. On the basis of his ratings, he reported that only 25 per cent of the group met what he termed "the rough criterion of optimum normality," by which he meant that they were well adjusted in all facets of life, at present and in the past, and had no symptoms. There was no definition, however, of specific positive attributes possessed by this optimal group.

The public health approach to normality encompasses a vast number of studies, and many could be cited in this section. The point to be emphasized, however, is that epidemiological studies of mental illness have not, on the whole, begun to ask the question: What is the prevalence of coping behavior and healthy adaptation? One of the reasons that we note such wide discrepancies in prevalence and incidence rates of psychiatric illness across subcultural and geographic boundaries, is determined, at least in part, by variations in the operational definitions of normality. We believe that the time has come when one needs to develop an epidemiology of coping behavior and normality. Such data would be of vital importance in permitting behavioral scientists to evaluate preventive and treatment programs much more objectively and with a higher degree of precision.

Coping and Adaptation

Normality and health have often been associated with terms such as "adaptation," "competence," and, most recently, "coping." We have to keep in mind that these concepts, like normality and health, are complex theoretical constructs which have not been adequately explained on the basis of any past or present single theory or hypothesis. One of the major problems that has plagued investigators in the behavioral sciences has been the great difficulty of making successful predictions about the long-term future behavior of an individual, or even of a majority within a group. Current research endeavors in the behavioral sciences have, therefore, tended to identify, operationally, clusters of traits and behavior which describe the variety of healthy or normal populations (see Chapter 8).

The interest of behavioral scientists in studies of coping and adaptation has increased rapidly during the past decade. Several of these studies have been brought to our attention by Sells (1967) through his report of a conference on the measurement of mental health. A variety of definitions of coping have been offered in the literature. Hamburg and Adams (1967) define coping as "seeking and utilizing of information under stressful conditions." Heath (1965) defines adaptation as "to so regulate behavior as to optimize simultaneously both the stability of the self structures and their accommodation to environmental requirements." Coping is defined by Lazarus et al. (1974) as consisting of problem-solving efforts made by an individual when the demands he faces have potential outcome of a high degree of relevance for his welfare (i.e., a situation of great jeopardy or promise), and particularly when these demands tax heavily his adaptive resources. Competence, according to White (1960), means "the competence of an organism . . . its fitness or ability to carry on those transactions with the environment which result in its maintaining itself, growing or flourishing."

Ability to cope is another way of assessing the type of character structure and the defenses utilized by individuals; the "healthier" the defenses the better the coping abilities (see, for example, Grinker, 1962, and Valliant, 1971). A recent review by Weinshel (1970) includes a discussion of the direct correlations between ego strength and mental health and normality. Here again the stronger (or healthier) the ego, the easier it is for the individual to adapt to his internal as well as to his external environments.

From a physiological point of view, studies of coping mechanisms tended to agree that "it is not the stimulus that is specific, but rather the response. This response specificity is clearly based on phenotypic patterns derived from combinations of genic and experiential factors" (Grinker, 1974, p. xii). Recognizing the importance of response specificity, the most significant investigations of coping behavior have involved analysis of variations in responses to stressful situations. The responses to a large variety of stimuli from either the external or the internal environment (e.g., affects such as anxiety, anger, fear, or depression) have a common physiological pathway. This has made it easier to study the somatic responses to stress. It has not, however, made it any easier to study coping behavior from a psychological point of view. The individualized response is based on constitutional, experiential, familial, social, and cultural factors. Individuals cope with stress in a variety of ways rather than a uniform pattern of "response specificity." Thus, what causes one person to be unable to cope *at a particular time* will not necessarily cause the same response at a different developmental state. A knowledge of the individual's background can tell us what defense mechanism (or coping behavior) an individual will choose to combat a particular stress. However, behavioral scientists have only achieved limited success in the past in predicting who will cope successfully under stressful conditions.

Until recently, the dominant assumption has been that the royal route to studying psychosocial coping is through deviancy, be it psychopathology (Jones, 1961) or stressful situations (Hamburg & Adams, 1967; Grinker & Spiegel, 1948; Lazarus, 1974; and Janis, 1974).

To many investigators the term "coping" implies that there is something negative to which one has to attend. This view of coping is conceptually similar to the psychoanalytic theory of defense mechanisms—the defenses are erected to protect the person against the resurgence of powerful aggressive and sexual instinctual demands from within and from undue pressure from without. From this perspective the best way to study coping is by observing populations which are experiencing stressful reactions in highly conflictual situations.

In a recent publication which resulted from a conference on coping and adaptation, Hamburg, Coelho, and Adams (1974) stressed that we need to know more about the range of strategies employed in the general population for meeting stressful situations. They are concerned with the statements made in the present chapter that longitudinal studies are particularly well suited for observing coping behavior by non-patients from a developmental point of view. There also is a need to develop assessment techniques which reliably define coping variables.

Erikson (1968, p. 91) presents human growth from the point of view of conflict, crisis, and stress: "For man, in order to remain psychologically alive, constantly re-resolves these conflicts just as his body unceasingly combats the encroachment of physical deterioration." He postulates that during the eight specific crisis periods one can study the human condition better because both the potential for growth and the emergence of pathological defense mechanisms are more evident during the crisis periods. It remains unclear whether Erikson extends the crisis periods to include all sub-stages or phases of the eight crisis periods. The concepts which define the beginning and end of each crisis period have not, as yet, been operationally defined. Erikson assumes that crisis like stress elicits emergency defenses; hence the study of crisis serves as a way to decipher how well a person is able to cope.

An alternative perspective to sequential life crises is one that assumes periods of relative equilibrium and disequilibrium. The modal adolescent (studied by Offer, 1973) described above (Chapter 8) goes through adolescence without reacting to it in toto as a stressful situation or even as a series of *major* crises. Coping can, therefore, be studied in this context by observing quantitatively different phenomena, for example, the most ordinary life situation of one group of teen-agers. We need new terminology which will describe the nuances in coping behavior and which will take into account the tremendous variability in reactions of individuals to stress and crisis. It will allow us to view a continuum of stressful situations from most stressful to least stressful with crisis being at one end of the continuum and everyday tasks at the other end.

We believe that there are a number of adaptational routes[1] open to individuals. Based on a complex interaction of biopsychosocial variables in a system which we call an individual, a person will have developed a coping style unique to him early in life. It is our opinion that in a majority of individuals the psychological system which an individual erects in order to cope with crisis, stress, and everyday life will by and large remain relatively constant through life, since the repertoire of adaptive mechanisms, including defenses, appears to be relatively fixed in early childhood. Some individuals will undergo "Sturm and Drang" at every major crossroad through the life cycle. Others will go through life with little turmoil. We post-

[1] See Chapter 8 where three developmental routes of normal adolescents are discussed: (1) Continuous Growth, (2) Surgent Growth, and (3) Tumultuous Growth (Offer & Offer, 1975).

ulate that the healthier individuals will have a variety of coping techniques available to them, will have a larger array of defenses at their disposal, will utilize the more adaptive and object-seeking defenses,[2] and will show more flexibility in dealing with internal as well as external events. Whether those who show less overt (behavioral) turmoil are the ones who are optimally healthier cannot be determined without intimate knowledge of the biopsychosocial variables which contribute to the behavior.

Normality, Values, and the Behavioral Sciences

Studies of adaptation and coping could optimally enable us to formulate more precise understanding of what Jahoda (1959) called "positive aspects of mental health." While psychiatrists and behavioral scientists have always been quick to extrapolate from psychopathology to normative theory, it has not been simple for them to focus on the adaptive aspects of human behavior. One reason for this, as discussed in Chapter 7, is the value dilemma. The problem of normal behavior is so saturated with value-laden concepts that it does indeed make it difficult to separate normative from pathological behavior (Hoffman, 1960; London, 1962; Smith, 1961). The four perspectives of normality have been presented (Chapter 6) so that individual investigators might be in a better position to choose which perspective of normality suits their interests, beliefs, or scientific postures better. It is not assumed that one perspective is "better" or closer to "the truth" than the other. This is particularly pertinent since one always should

[2] Better inter-personal relationships.

add the caveat to the concept of normality—"for whom," "under what circumstances," and "for what purposes."

However, some behavioral scientists believe that one perspective is indeed superior to the others, or they reject all of the perspectives and employ a single unifying alternative approach. For example, White (1973) has concluded that mental health practitioners are in the "value business"; and he further declared that, therefore, mental health is a meaningless concept. White recommends that we replace the term "mental health" with "maturity." In our opinion this does not solve the inherent problem, as it may in fact substitute one complex term with another.

The rapid increase in the clinician's interest in studying nonpatient populations, which was documented in Chapter 8, has not brought forth ready-made answers as to what constitutes the normal. The multiple perspectives of the individual investigators made it even more imperative that we clarify for each other what we mean by mental health and normality.

Smith (1972) has indirectly answered White. He states that we should be concerned with normality and mental health for three reasons:

1. Any conception of the abnormal or deviant requires, at least implicitly, an understanding of the normal. If the view remains implicit, it may be based on error and/or covert values and is less likely to be subjected to empirical corrections.
2. The clinician needs a clear concept of normality in order to help him clarify his therapeutic goals.
3. Primarily under the influence of long-term medical precepts including, for example, the development of psychoanalytic theory, we believe that our understanding of the normal can be greatly advanced by a close look at the pathological or deviant. Productive as this approach has been, it can also be potentially misleading. Normal behavior deserves scrutiny in its own right.

The problems arising from the imposition of values on scientific attempts and from the inability to formulate accepted definitions of mental illness further impede the search for criteria of normality (Scott, 1958; Ward et al., 1962; Beck, 1962). This is particularly true in the cases where "lack of overt psychopathology" is used as the only or the prime criterion for mental health. It is particularly in the area of neurosis and character disorder that accurate definitions, designating clear boundary lines, are lacking.

If the theory of the universality of neuroses (see Chapter 2) is accepted, then either the normal man must be non-existent or his normality must consist of certain degrees of neuroses. If normality is composed of varying shades of neuroses, the opposition of normality versus disease cannot be maintained. Correspondingly, many of the investigators cited have concentrated on measuring degrees of neuroses in the normal man. They believe that abnormality existent in the normal man cannot be studied from therapist-patient relationships alone. This belief is contrary to that of psychoanalysts who claim that their patients do not differ dramatically from people who have not undergone treatment.[3] The claim that the population of patients in psychoanalysis is a random sample is refuted by certain circumstances and practices related to psychoanalytic treatment. First, the psychoanalyst treats patients having only circumscribed types of psychological conflicts. Persons manifesting conflicts not amenable to psychoanalysis are often excluded from his patient population. Second, social and cultural factors are of prime importance in influencing people to seek psychoanalytic treatment. Individuals from populations alien to or indifferent to psychoanalysis are less likely to become patients. Thus, the psychoanalyst can gain

[3] An opposite opinion often has been voiced, namely, that most persons seen in psychoanalytic office practices are "superior individuals." (See, for example, Saul & Pulver, 1965.) As such, they are also far from a random sample.

an understanding of the totality of normality via analysis of his patients only if the population at large is also studied and if the hypothesis of randomness in the patient population is validated.

Psychoanalysts, however, are not exclusively interested in learning about the normal from patient populations. In the twentieth century, psychoanalysts have been responsible for a great upsurge of interest in normal psychology. Freud's theories distinctly were not limited to psychopathology but were an attempt to provide a contribution to "normal" psychology. (See Chapter 2 for details.) Subsequent generations of psychoanalysts have in their practice and research elaborated on "normal" psychology, but as the century progressed, psychoanalysis tended to concentrate its efforts on particular clinical problems and particular segments of the populations. It has been somewhat limited in its facilitation of research on specific catchment areas that include populations not previously studied by psychoanalysts.

In our opinion, the works of Kardiner (1939, 1945), Hartmann (1964), Erikson (1950, 1959), Kohut (1971), and Gedo and Goldberg (1973) best exemplify the potential of bridge-building between psychoanalysis, on the one side, and other disciplines within the behavioral sciences, on the other. That psychoanalysis increasingly is becoming a world-wide specialty represents another important development. As psychoanalysts practice in multiple parts of the world, it seems plausible to predict that cross-cultural comparisons will become more frequent in the ensuing decades (for example, see Doi, 1973). It is also predictable that psychoanalysts will become more involved in the public health aspects of medicine, as described in our discussion of changes within psychiatry. Another trend worth noting relevant to psychoanalytic interest in this problem relates to the growth of child psychoanalysis. Although opinion is not uniform, it is nevertheless possible to state that a significant number of psychoanalysts have been engaged in normative studies of children and adolescents (Murphy, 1962; Escalona & Heider, 1959; A. Freud, 1963, 1965; Spitz, 1957). The increased willingness to participate in such investigations is a reflection of the need to confirm some of the major psychoanalytic hypotheses by empirical studies on so-called normal populations. It is our prediction that this trend will continue and converge with the other trends previously mentioned.

In our discussion of psychology, we pointed out that clinical psychology has developed rapidly since World War II. Clinical psychology and psychiatry are overlapping considerably; while psychiatrists move toward greater participation in normative studies, psychologists move toward increased contact with emotionally disturbed individuals. This coalescence has a number of theoretical and practical advantages. One consequence germane to our discussion is the fact that an increasing number of psychologists will combine their more traditional interests in statistical normative studies with clinical considerations. This should lead to studies of normal populations, studies with increasing depth and scope, in contrast to purely statistical normative analyses. Sociologists and anthropologists also show greater interest and involvement in studies of mental health and illness (for example, Becker, 1963). Although, as we have pointed out, sociologists tend to avoid initiating definitions of deviancy, more of them probably will attempt socio-psychological studies relevant to the fields of health and normality. Parsons (1958, 1959, 1972) has given leadership in this direction, as we have indicated. Others with special interest in the mental health field should also take leadership in bridging the areas involved for such studies. The field of culture and personality has undergone several cycles in recent decades, but there is good reason to predict a revival of interest in this area too (Hsu, 1961). Leadership indubitably will be exercised by those who are well trained in psychological as well as in more traditional anthropological subjects. As transcultural and cross-cultural data become increasingly accessible, this trend should be strengthened. An excellent recent example of a serious attempt to bridge the fields of psychology, anthropology, and psychoanalysis is the work of LeVine (1973).

In the field of biological research in mental health, there are also hopeful integrating signs. Though we have pointed to the tendency in some quarters to attempt to reduce behavior to its underlying neurophysiological and anatomical foundations, we have highlighted reverse trends also. Interest in over-all central-nervous-system organization and integrating systems is also proceeding rapidly. We believe that here, too, scientists will emerge who can provide better syntheses (Grinker, 1956; Leiderman & Shapiro, 1963; Knapp, 1963; and more recently, Offer & Freedman, 1972) of underlying biological mechanisms with psychological and social phenomena. We do not wish to underestimate the difficulties inherent in such syntheses, but at the same time we want to call attention to the willingness of many investigators to essay this task.

There is every reason to expect that workers in the field of ethics and aesthetics will conduct collaborative investigations with the behavioral scientists. It is our firm conviction that these collaborative efforts will proceed without jeopardy to society's basic need for artists and philosophers who can transcend current values and retain the exceedingly important role of reflecting fundamental as well as superficial patterns of the time. Philosophers of science interested in questions of aesthetics and epistemology have also become interested in the mental health field. It is our hope and expectation that they will collaborate with social and behavioral scientists on studies of the relationship of value systems to concepts of normality and health. Indeed, if normality and health emerge as a field for inquiry, as anticipated in this volume, we foresee the active involvement of philosophers of science.[4] To move toward a new definition of normality is thus not only a complex task for the current generation of mental health professionals but also one requiring transcending of these disciplines. This task cannot be avoided if the social and behavioral sciences seriously intend to understand and deal with the full range of human behavior.

Normality and Emergent Social Movements

The recommendations made in the previous sections have implications which transcend specific research issues in the study of healthy populations. These implications bring into focus major criticisms of psychiatry (Robinson, 1973), including those enunciated during the past decade (Ennis, 1972; Chu & Trotter, 1973). In our judgment several of these critiques are pertinent to the concepts of normality in psychiatry, and they are included in this chapter to illustrate areas which require further clarification.

Recently, the women's movement in the United States has criticized psychiatry and the mental health profession frequently for the portrayal of the normal psychology of women. Indeed the statement is often made that psychiatry's characterizations of feminine behavior have been derived from a male perspective and are decidedly sexist in nature (Chesler,

[4] Kaplan's recent monograph, *The Conduct of Inquiry* (1964), can be seen as a step in this direction.

1972). Whatever changes take place in the socio-political sphere, these criticisms raise serious questions about the impact of values and other social variables on our perspective of normality and health. To what extent are concepts of female sexuality based on culturally determined expectations of feminine role behavior? The often quoted statement of Deutsch (1944) that women are by nature passive-receptive and masochistic illustrates a point of view that provoked the recent criticism by several women writers. It follows, from this concept, that if a woman is competitive, aggressive, and interested in a professional career, that she is suffering from "penis envy," is neurotic and, therefore, by definition, not normal. Analogously, do role expectations shape our concepts of women's "normal" developmental processes? In both cases there is much recent evidence to question our prior hypotheses and concepts. In reality women appear to be less vulnerable, less fragile psychologically, and more able to cope with developmental and situational vicissitudes than many of our concepts seem to acknowledge (Bart, 1971a, 1971b).

In a similar manner there has been frequent criticism of psychiatry's tendency to emphasize psychopathology in minority groups (Sabshin et al., 1970). Our portrayal of psychological issues related to blacks has appeared especially tinged with an overemphasis on pathology as compared to adaptability and coping. The psychiatric literature is saturated with statements focusing on the purported frequent absence of black fathers or the so-called primitive character structure in blacks. Without sound empirical evidence, there has been a tendency to assume that societal forces have rendered black men incapable of the mature object relationship necessary for sustained marital responsibility and parenthood. We have tended to overlook the evidence indicating that black men do cope with marital and family problems with heterogeneous patterns of adaptation. In attempting to be "sympathetic" to the plight of blacks, we have often failed to note the myriad and diversified ways by which black people really attempt to deal with both societal constraints and opportunities. In addition, as has been pointed out by one of the co-authors, institutional racism has pervaded psychiatry in many ways and has influenced our concept of normality in blacks as well as in other minorities (Sabshin et al., 1970).

Much of the criticism raised against psychiatry and the mental health profession by blacks and by women illustrates a strong reaction against stereotyping. Psychiatrists have also been accused of stereotyping by age (e.g., our concepts of normal behavior in people over seventy tend to emphasize enfeeblement and to ignore adaptive capacities), by social class (e.g., we have tended to avoid psychotherapeutic work with blue-collar populations and indeed with poverty stricken people), and by geography (e.g., psychiatry in rural America is less well developed than in selective parts of urban America).

Does psychotherapy or psychoanalysis prevent creativity in the potential genius? It has been assumed by many scientists, humanists, artists, and just plain people that psychiatry has a Procrustean therapeutic couch on which it places its "victims." If Einstein, Goethe, Mozart, or Picasso had been in psychotherapy, would their creativity have decreased? Does the psychotherapist impose his own middle-class values on the patient who consults him? It is not the purpose of this book to discuss these thorny issues in depth, although they have been touched on in Chapter 7 and in this chapter. It is our contention that helping a person deal with neurotic or psychotic symptoms, with his object relations, and with his feelings does not *necessarily* interfere with his creative process. It might possibly interfere with the creative process; or it might also help the person's creativity. Since we do not know the results of our interventions before we try them, it is imperative that it be left up to the individual himself to decide when he or she can use professional help. The systems from which (a) mental problems arise and (b) creativity stems are, in our opinion, only loosely connected. A change in one does not, ipso facto, initiate a change in the other to the same degree in the same direction, or in the opposite direction. We need to know more about the psychology of the creative process. We know even less about the "normal genius," than we know about the "normal man or woman."

Summary and Conclusion

Part One of this volume focused on a discussion and a survey of the impact of the multiple perspectives. We have pointed out how investigators from a wide array of disciplines have tended to approach the problems of normality and health from their own traditions and vantage points. It would be understandable if a reader who had read only Part One reached the conclusion that the divergent perspectives constitute an almost insurmountable problem and that an integrated approach to normality and health is not possible at this time. Indeed, there is support for such a pessimistic outlook among a number of behavioral scientists. In our opinion, however, recent developments afford considerable hope for an approach to the dimensions of health from an empirical and also a more integrated basis. Part Two of this book illustrates how the various disciplines are converging toward a new definition of normality and health, and the authors' efforts are dedicated to such a convergence.

Our aim in writing this book has been to offer an "analytic" approach to the problem of normality. We demonstrated the various definitions of normality used by investigators, the nature of the reasoning behind the definitions, and the meaning of the different concepts. We examined the basic inconsistencies between definitions and traced these disagreements to their scientific origins. We have not offered a "substantive" definition of normality. We believe that the process of definition is currently the responsibility of the individual investigator who, understanding the array of possible definitions, can employ knowledge rather than arbitrary ignorance to formulate his own definition. Ultimately, this utilization of increasingly precise knowledge will lead to a more unified theory that transcends but also integrates the various dimensions, perspectives, and disciplines.

Do we see a profile emerging which reliably and validly describes the "normal man or woman"? Definitely not. The more we study normal populations the more we become aware that healthy functioning is at least as complex and varied as our psychopathological entities. Normality and mental health cannot be understood in the abstract; rather they depend on the cultural norms, society's expectations and values, professionals' biases, individual differences, and the political climate of the time (e.g., tolerance for deviance).

It has often been stated that the normal person is devoid of imagination, conforms to his environment without attempting to change it, and is psychologically inflexible (see Golden et al., 1962, 1963; Grinker, 1962; Smith, 1972). This view of normality can possibly be explained by our "Normality as Average" perspective. Some persons in any culture at a given point in time will carry the so-called cultural and behavioral norms. However, it needs to be stressed again that there are other perspectives of normality. There are also other kinds of normal people whose psychological make-up is quite different. The burden of the labeling process is squarely on the shoulders of the behavioral scientist. Awareness of his own values, ideals, and philosophy of life will help minimize distortions and will aid in our further understanding of the different typologies of normality.

The four perspectives of normality enable us to differentiate among different kinds of normality. During the past decade, increased studies of normal populations, using a variety of psycho-social and clinical methods, indicate that we have indeed taken an important step in the right direction.

It is our belief that continued empirical investigations will lead us to a better understanding of the complexity of healthy development. We are presently shifting from deduction and theorizing about normal development to empirical investigations of the relationship among the multiplicity of variables which contribute to the healthy, or normal, development of individuals. Greater efforts in studies of coping and adaptation will prove to be useful in elucidating the theoretical perspectives of normality and mental health. The empirical data being collected from follow-up and longitudinal studies on normal populations will enable us to conceptualize normal behavior with more precision. In addition, the development of community mental health programs affords an excellent opportunity to begin a series of investigations of normative behavior not heretofore possible. While the image of communities as laboratories for research has brought about resistance as well as consternation in some areas, there is reason to believe that the efforts to conduct investigations *with* communities will, after some hesitation, supplant our tendency to do research *on* communities. Evidence already exists indicating the advantage to communities of increased understanding of its population's behavior as compared to stereotyping and attendant distortions. Furthermore, communities will be interested in evaluation of intervention programs within their borders, and they will cooperate with investigations which facilitate such evaluation. Finally, the clinician will also benefit from the availability of a set of standards of what is considered normal behavior in a specific group or community at a particular point in time. Therapeutic goals might then be less arbitrary and more in keeping with the patients' needs and expectations.

Appendix*

FRANZ ALEXANDER

A healthy ego can best be compared to a democratic state which recognizes private needs of all kinds, gives them a hearing, and meets the conflicting interests by mediation and compromise. This insures a stable but fluid state of affairs. The neurotic personality is comparable to an autocratic government which suppresses all opinions and aspirations that do not conform to its ruling principles. As long as rebellious opinions and demands can be controlled by an iron rule, unity prevails. It is built, however, on a volcanic foundation. Whenever the autocracy is weakened the outlawed rebels break through and destroy the whole system. The energy spent in keeping unruly desires in check is diverted from constructive use. Fear and coercion are the only motives operative, as the cultural sterility and lack of creativeness in totalitarian systems prove.

A neurotic personality is comparable to such an autocratic country impoverished in initiative, governed by anxiety and coercion. The analogy should not, however, be carried too far, and we now turn to the specific facts of the human personality. The central dynamic factor in neurosis is repression and those defense meas-

* In this section, the interested reader will find detailed definitions and opinions of a select group of investigators referred to in the book. These quotations are presented as a supplement to concepts of normal behavior included in the text.

ures by which the ego attempts to keep all the unacceptable impulses out of its territory.

As we have seen, repression is normal in a child but undesirable in an adult. Of course, even a healthy person takes recourse to repression to some degree. Only an ideally efficient ego would function without it. The ego develops gradually with growth. It does not belong to our hereditary equipment but is a product of learning. Needs and impulses such as hunger, sex, and raw aggression, however, are present from the beginning. To co-ordinate these impulses and their derivatives and to satisfy them consistently with conditions in nature and society is the ego's task. It must learn how to exercise this complex executive function. In young children only the dynamic building stones, the primitive impulses, exist, from which the socially adjusted person must be constructed.

The impulses which the child represses because his ego cannot manage them become a problem in his later life. Their pressure is felt from time to time, and he will have to take defensive measures to keep them out of consciousness. These repressed, unconscious impulses are preserved in their original form as in an icebox and emerge in dreams in strange and unintelligible images, the language of the infantile mind, in waking life in neurotic symptoms, irrational anxieties, obsessions, and impulsive behavior.

Our first question, then, is, why does not everyone develop a neurosis? Everyone has similar infantile experiences, everyone has to repress some of his early impulses because his infantile ego was weak and could not assimilate, control, and modify them.

First of all, we must remember that neurosis and normality are not wholly different. The psychology of neurosis and normality is the same in quality; the differences are merely quantitative. We have seen that repression is not an efficient method of adjusting needs to life's requirements. It does not permit the modification of unadjusted impulses. What is repressed is no longer amenable to education, since this is the function of the unconscious mind. It is true that the unity of the ego is preserved by excluding everything disturbing to its unity, but this is accomplished at a great price. The repressed energy is lost for outward-directed activity, and the ego is impoverished. Moreover, since repressed impulses continue to exist, the need for constant defense against them consumes the available energies. This not only means further impoverishment but also constitutes a threat. It is obvious, then, that the less the child has to repress and the more his adjustment is based upon efficient control, the sounder will be his development.

We have compared the healthy ego to democratic government which permits expression of private particularistic needs. Naturally, all aspirations cannot be fulfilled in their original form. The parliamentary system, however, allows free expression and negotiation leading to compromises inclusive of all interests as far as possible.

From *Fundamentals of Psychoanalysis* (New York: W. W. Norton & Co. Inc., 1948), p. 194; (London: George Allen and Unwin, Ltd.).

WALTER E. BARTON

All of us can benefit, however, from attempts to define and measure good health, whether psychological or physical, and should welcome heterodox efforts to do so. Perhaps, through the mind of social science, unencumbered by medical tradition, research may be designed that will eventually quantify the psychological content of mental health. The phenomenon of a superstate of good mental health, well beyond and above the *mere absence* of disabling illness, has yet to be scientifically demonstrated. We know little of it beyond occasional subjective, euphoric impressions of the subject that he is "bursting with good health," "feeling grand," or that "all is right with the world," meaning *his* world.

In contrast, the benefits of disease prevention and control have been tangibly demonstrated in increased ability to work and carry out social obligations, longer life, and individual morale.

Medicine has developed this useful way of looking at health

and the normal to the extent that health as the antonym of disease has become a part of the philosophy, or tradition, of physicians.

The idea first was propounded by Hippocrates, who held health to be a state of universal harmony, and the role of the physician to be that of restoring equilibrium between the various components of the body and the whole of Nature. This approach was encompassed by Walter Cannon in his principle of homeostatis, meaning a tendency toward uniformity or stability in the normal body states of the organism relating to the fluid balance and, more generally, the so-called "internal environment." By extension, the same idea of equilibrium permeates observation of such matters as "nitrogen balance" and various other physiological or biochemical states.

The inference of good health, or the normal state, as a manifestation of harmony or balance with the external environment can be found in biology as well as physiology. Out of Spencer's idea of evolution as the "survival of the fittest" came the notion of "nature in the raw" and eternal aggression and defense, which influenced the older conception of the germ theory of disease and made us appear victims of a kind of microbial warfare. But Darwin pointed out in *Descent of Man* that commonly in nature "struggle is replaced by co-operation." The concept of "a balance of nature" again emerged as a unifying idea.

In modern microbiology, the older idea of infectious disease as a "fight" against foreign "invasion" has been to a great extent superseded by the concept of man and his bacteria and viruses as habitually living together in various states of symbiosis or germ–host relationships involving infection, with or without apparent disease. Accompanying this has been a strong revival of the multiple-cause theory of disease at the expense of the one-germ–one-disease viewpoint. René J. Dubos, for instance, regards "invasion" or "attack" as less characteristic of the relationship of man's pathogens to man than is "peaceful co-existence."

Subclinical or inapparent infection appears to be the rule, with periodic epidemics or individual imbalances due to lowered resistance of the human organism or heightened virulence of the micro-organism actually occurring as exceptions.

So we see that a unifying concept of health and disease does run through medical thought, founded in biology and physiology as well as in biochemistry and microbiology. The tendency of the organism is to serve its structural, functional, and species purposes and, internally or externally, to strike some kind of balance that will permit it to do so. It is normal for the organism to do this.

Leston L. Havens (1958) has pointed out:

"Usually in medicine we say an organ is healthy if it does its job within the normal range and over the usual time. We do not expect too much, although the usual range is not the range of the average man but of the average healthy man. Statistical norms are useful in this context and should not be dismissed despite the difficulties of agreeing on a normal population in the mental health area. Without such a point of reference, one cannot tell what is a toxic experience and what is normal tolerance. Without norms there is also the danger of unreal goals of treatment. This may be a significant clinical hazard. Ideal or even 'potential' health criteria are too easily spun out of theories or brief glimpses of people at their momentary best."

Both gross and cellular pathology have well-defined concepts of normal and abnormal. The tissue and cell are normal if they exhibit no disturbance of structure as compared to most tissues or cells of like kind. Precisely the same understanding extends from structure to function. Granted, the physician's estimate of what is normal sometimes has been of far too narrow a range, as for example in determining what constitutes abnormal blood pressure.

From "Viewpoint of a Clinician." In Marie Jahoda (Ed.), *Current Concepts of Positive Mental Health* (New York: Basic Books, Inc., 1958), pp. 112–115.

CHARLES M. CHILD

Normal Development and Heredity

It may appear, and in fact has often been asserted that the course of development in its earlier stages is, so far as its "typical" or "normal" features are concerned, independent of external factors and determined by heredity (pp. 215–219). That is to say, up to a certain point at which functional relation to the external world begins, the individual organism represents primarily the working out of a scheme, order, or pattern predetermined by heredity. This typical hereditary course of events may be modified by external factors which transcend the normal range, but within the normal range the external factors play no essential part, except in making possible the continuation of life. This typical or normal course of development unmodified by external factors results in the normal individual and regulation represents the return or approach to normal when modification does occur. According to this preformistic conception, the development of the individual represents primarily the construction of certain mechanisms through internal factors, and only when this construction is completed, or has attained a certain stage, does function begin. Regulation is a sort of repair process, through which the hereditary mechanism obliterates or compensates more or less completely the accidental action of external factors. The biologists of the Roux-Weismann school, and particularly Roux, have made much of this distinction between the typical or normal as predetermined and the regulatory as essentially the result of accident, and have attempted in various ways to reconcile it with facts of developmental physiology.

Actually, however, it becomes more and more evident that life is largely, if not wholly made up of accidents. The constancy and uniformity of normal development in nature, results, as already noted, from the fact that a certain degree of standardization has occurred in the course of evolution as regards the range of such accidents to which the developing individual is likely to be exposed. This has been accomplished in various ways, for example, through position of the gonads, through conditions under which fertilization occurs, through the formation of enveloping membranes, jelly, or capsules about the developing eggs, through the selection of certain localities for egg deposition, through care of the young, viviparity, and so forth. But these various provisions do not eliminate external factors; they merely tend to limit the variation in range, in other words, to standardize their action.

The gamete and the developing embryo are acted upon by, and react to factors external to themselves at all periods of their existence and whatever mechanisms or structures are present at any time are functioning. Material exchange is always going on and we know that excitation by various forms of energy and the transmission of such excitation may occur in these stages as well as in the fully developed individual. We know also that even within the range of the normal many differences between individuals result from differences in external conditions within the standardized range. And finally, we know that when we subject these stages to external conditions outside the standard range, that is, "abnormal" conditions, reaction of some sort, with equilibration leading either to a normal or an abnormal result, or destruction of the system and death may result. In fact, we can find no evidence for the hereditary predetermination of a normal or typical course of development, except in so far as each protoplasm possesses a certain hereditary constitution and as the conditions under which the individual develops are more or less exactly determined or standardized by the hereditary mechanisms of the parent and the species. The hereditary constitution of the protoplasm determines certain possibilities which are realized only in relation to external factors, and the hereditary mechanism of the parent or species, as noted above, determines position of gonads, method of egg deposition, and so forth. So far predetermination occurs, but such predetermination is indirect and physiological, rather than direct, that is, it determines, on the one hand, the possibilities of reaction and on the other, the range of conditions likely to be met.

From *Physiological Foundations of Behavior* (New York: Henry Holt & Co., 1924), pp. 221–222.

THEODOSIUS DOBZHANSKY

We nevertheless speak of good or normal health and ill health, of genetically handicapped people and those free from such handicaps, and finally of normal and abnormal people. The use of the word "normal" poses a semantic problem. No end of misconception and lax thinking is caused by the belief in something called "normal man" or "normal human nature." This phantom is imagined by some to be full of good intentions waiting only for propitious circumstances to manifest themselves and by others a nasty brute bent only on mischief and evil (see Chapters 2 and 3). But trouble is in store whichever preconception is espoused, for either makes you expect people to act alike, whereas they are plainly diverse in their behavior.

A kind of "normal man" idea exists in biology in the classical theory of population structure, which we shall consider further in Chapter 11. The essence of this theory is that normal people carry mostly normal genes, and for most of these genes they are homozygous. Only a minority of the genes are represented in human populations by two or more alleles each, and then one of the alleles is normal and the other abnormal. The adaptive norm of the human species would, according to this view, consist of those who carry mostly or only normal genes, while the unfortunate ones who happen to carry abnormal genes will need the attention of medicine to help them and of eugenics to eliminate them.

According to the balance theory of population structure things may not be so simple (see Chapter 11). This supposes that some genes are represented in populations by two, several, or many alleles. For such genes, no allele is necessarily normal, and good health and high fitness occur mainly in heterozygotes for pairs of different alleles. The homozygotes would usually be less fit. The upshot is, then, that there are not only many but also many kinds of normal, healthy, and highly fit people. The adaptive norm is a great array of genotypes, not just one or a few genetic complexes. Medicine had better be versatile, for not all patients will respond alike to its ministrations. Eugenics must still be more dexterous, for instead of making everybody alike, possessing some one optimal genotype, it will have to engineer a gene pool of the human population that would maximize the frequency of the fit and minimize that of the unfit.

We need not commit ourselves at this stage to a choice between the classical and the balance theories. They have in common the recognition that the boundary between the adaptive norm and the genetically handicapped sector of the population is not sharp. As the standards of fitness are made more rigid, this latter sector seems to expand. One possible definition of the adaptive norm must exclude only those persons who, because of their genetic defects, must be permanently hospitalized or cared for in special institutions; another definition would exclude even those whose genetic handicaps require medical attention or special regimens at any time in their lives.

The concept of the adaptive norm is useful despite the arbitrariness of its delimitation. Rules of sanitation and hygiene, techniques of instruction and education, social services, legislation, and the whole body of custom and usage are tailored to fit the adaptive norm, broadly or narrowly conceived. The evolutionary origin of the adaptive norm and the deviations from it is a major problem which the science of man has to face.

From *Mankind Evolving* (New Haven: Yale University Press, 1962), pp. 126–127.

KURT R. EISSLER

It is worth while to review briefly the place which the term "normality" takes in Freud's work. The two different contexts in which the concept is used may be roughly distinguished as first, methodological, and, second, clinical. Freud (1917) speaks of *normal* prototypes, such as the dream vs. narcissistic mental disorders, or grief vs. melancholia. The concept of normality, here, serves as an operational tool to investigate by its contrast certain psychopathological phenomena, but not as a yardstick or measure of clinical evaluation.[32] This was unmistakably expressed when Freud (1917) wrote: "We are able to learn in various ways how advantageous it is for our researches to institute comparisons with certain states and phenomena which may be conceived of as *normal prototypes* of morbid affections" (p. 137, italics by Freud). The concept of normal for the purpose of gaining insight into contrasting structures does not throw any light on the subject matter of this study.

The clinical application of the concept occurs rather rarely in Freud's writings except in his comprehensive paper on the efficacy and limitations of psychoanalytic therapy (Freud, 1937). The term is used in a variety of meanings which may be briefly outlined:

1. *Descriptive meaning* (normality as a subjective feeling) in order to characterize a patient's feelings after the termination of his analysis; Freud writes that the patient "felt normal" (1937, p. 318). Here the term is used descriptively for a subjective state among other data such as behavior, in order to evaluate the effect of treatment.

2. *Structural meaning* (absolute psychic normality). Freud raised the question whether an analysis could ever result in a condition in which all the patient's repressions had been lifted and every memory gap filled. In such circumstances further therapy would not bring forth any changes. The patient would have reached a level of absolute psychic normality (1937, p. 320).

3. *Economic meaning* (fictitious normality ego).[33] Freud in evaluating the difficulties encountered in the process of analysis established a scale, one end of which was marked by the ego of

[32] The dream remained for Freud psychopathology. "A dream . . . is a psychosis, with all the absurdities, delusions and illusions of a psychosis. No doubt it is a psychosis which has only a short duration, etc." (1938, p. 61).

[33] See Freud (1937, pp. 337 and 342), where his term fiktives Normal-Ich (Ges. W., XVI, p. 185) is translated as "imaginary normal ego."

the psychotic. His ego structure has undergone extensive and intensive modification of such degree as to make a psychoanalytic treatment impossible. On the other end of the scale there would be a fictitious normality ego which follows *all* the necessities of treatment, that is to say, is inexhaustible in its loyalty to the analytic process and therefore is unlimitedly willing to bear displeasure for the sake of its recovery and thus would be apt to execute uncompromisingly the requirements of the psychoanalytic procedure. In psychoanalytic practice, egos approaching to a varying degree the psychotic are encountered.

4. *Dynamic meaning* (harmony of the ego). It is not the goal of a psychoanalytic treatment to enforce the disappearance of a drive the warding off of which had resulted in the patient's neurotic symptomatology. The drive should be brought into the harmony of the ego, that is to say, should be mastered and tamed. However, if the ego is weakened the drive may seek substitute gratification by means of *abnormal* ways (Freud, 1937, p. 327). Hence, this aspect would result in normality pertaining to temporary states of balance between ego and id, states which can be attained by the ego only under particular conditions, since sleep (a "normal" occurrence) would already upset this kind of equilibrium.

5. *Functional meaning* (degrees of normality). The patient's recovery may be obstructed by the analyst's own deficiencies. The analyst should have a high measure of psychic normality. It can be measured by his ability in "discerning his patient's situation correctly and reacting to it in a manner conducive to cure" (Freud, 1937, p. 351).

6. *Social meaning* (schematic normality) (Freud, 1937, p. 354). Depending on society and particular goals, certain concepts of normality may be conceived, such as absence of conflicts or passions in a person. Such definitions certainly have no clinical validity and appear arbitrary from the scientific viewpoint, although the one who conceives of them may try to base them on objective data.

It is impressive to notice how precisely Freud indicated in

which sense he wished the term to be understood whenever he spoke of normality. Further, he points out each time where the data may be obtained which will indicate the distance from or closeness to a normal condition, that is to say, he gives the frame of reference to which the respective meaning of the term belongs whenever the term has a nondescriptive meaning. Further, there seems to be no indication that he thought the *clinical* reality of "normal" to be essentially divorced from the interplay of those forces which are so well observed in the neurotic and the psychotic.

With regard to the question of conflict and adjustment I wish to refer to an allied topic. In reading biographies of indubitably creative masters and in paying special attention to situations in which patients present particular skills in constructive achievements one gains the inescapable impression that these pursuits—which must be considered accomplishments or achievements (*Leistungen*) in contrast to symptoms—are the final outcome of particularly intense conflicts. The psychological circumstances in which the conflict (and its solution) exhausts itself completely in the formation of an autoplastic change such as a symptom are quite different from those in which it leads to the realization of an artistic value in which others can participate. But the two outcomes seem to have in common that they grow out of conflicts. The discovery of what the difference is that leads in the one case to a useless and painful symptom and in another to a highly appreciated structure would be of great value.

Health is a fictitious concept in the psychic stratum; perhaps it has a proper place in the biological. There are defenses which cause displeasure or pleasure and there are defenses which favor the survival of the individual or of the species or lead to the individual's destruction. We need the concept of health for practical purposes and the concept requires redefinition probably with each important historical change and probably with each new developmental phase of the individual. I do not see how the concept can theoretically be defined in a meaningful way and still stay in accordance with the principles of scientific psychology.

This, however, does not negate the need—nor, perhaps, the possibility—of outlining the conditions under which man has the greatest chance to continue functioning even when exposed to the weight of trying excessive stimulation coming from either external or internal sources. While the ability so to function may be made the cornerstone of the concept of health, I wished to demonstrate that such functioning can, and, as I surmise, even must, be bought at the price of unquestionably severe psychopathology. Thus this paper may be taken as an attempt at trying out the operational value of the concept of the psychopathology of normality.

From "The Efficient Soldier." In Warner Muensterburger and Sidney Axelrod (Eds.), *The Psychoanalytic Study of Society* (New York: International Universities Press, 1960), pp. 91–94.

ROY R. GRINKER, SR.

Despite the current attitude of pessimism concerning the possibilities of research on "mental health" because of the entanglement with value systems, considerable knowledge may be obtained about various kinds of mental health using longitudinal-descriptive, psycho-dynamic, behavioral, and sociocultural approaches. The implications of this statement are that in the total "field" should be included: hereditary and constitutional data, an accurate description of physical and emotional experiences during maturation and development, a knowledge of resulting psychodynamics insofar as possible, a study of behavior at whatever and whenever maturity is reached (when growth and progress has ceased or slowed), a study of the sociocultural matrix within which development occurred and those matrices in which the subjects function well and the number of these. Rather than considering value judgments as obstacles to research, they become attributes of the culture and suitable for scientific investigation.

Such a field, large as it may be, furnishes the opportunity for the study of permutations of a large number of variables which may be combined into a lesser number of categories or systems in transaction. This should permit the crystallization of types of "mental health" amidst a spectrum of psychopathology and should lead to the finding and formulation of a number of specific hypotheses, some of which are listed below.

1. Ego functions may be described in clusters of traits representing behavioral types which may be correlated with genetic, psychodynamic, and social conditions.
2. The conditions during maturation and development leading to mental health when accurately described without theoretical biases, disclose a rich variety of parameters.
3. Freedom from serious physical illness in critical periods facilitates the development of mental health.
4. Early deprivation of, or excessive, communications are a factor in the type of later health or illness.
5. The constitutionally given quantity of drive energy and/or the influences leading to the capacity for direct discharge in action is involved in a type of mental health.
6. The capacities for the development of mature and so-called healthy behavior depend on a sequence of positive relations (regardless of techniques employed) with mother and then father.
7. Average intelligence with realistic self-appraisal facilitates the use of ego functions for goal directed behavior, albeit minimum goal-changing behavior.
8. A type of mental health may develop in individuals who pass smoothly from one phase of development to another without intervening or visible "crises."
9. Structurally a type of mental health may be associated with a psychological organization which has little access to unconscious processes in the form of fantasy or regression.
10. The capacity of the individual to maintain goal-seeking functions adequately is dependent upon a degree of compulsivity that is not crippling but at the same time maintains a consistent line of behavior.

11. Mental health is not only associated with balance of internal forces but also with a subjective well-feeling and an objective capacity for adaptation.
12. The prerequisites of such balance are, among others, the experience of satisfactory gratifications in early life without too much frustration, the knowledge of definite limitations or boundaries placed on behavior with reasonable and consistent punishment, and firm sound early religious and ethical training.
13. Mental health is influenced by social and cultural factors, and various types of mental health require for maintenance a necessary environmental fit.
14. One attribute of mental health is a flexibility depending on the number of environments into which the personality type fits comfortably.
15. The number of identifications learned early furnishes a role repertoire suitable for a variety of environments. The capacity for multiple identifications is based on precursors not well defined.
16. Mental health as a definition requires the knowledge of the culturally derived values within subject-patient, observer-investigator, and the culture in which they exist.
17. Subjects comprising a mentally healthy group do not show absolute mental health, which does not exist. It is tempting to view mental health and illness as a continuum using traditional ways of thinking. It is far more sophisticated to analyze the reciprocal and sequential relations among multiple variables to obtain typologies with probabilistic boundaries.

There is no question that our understanding of normal psychodynamics has been faciliated by studies of psychopathology. We, at least, assume that the general and specific aspects of psychoanalytic theory are applicable to the healthy. However, the monotonous reiteration of theory based on the psychoanalysis of one or, at most, a few patients is not conducive to much more progress in our knowledge of health. We need sharply defined hypotheses for scientific observations, descriptions, and experimentation not only to further our knowledge of the abnormal but also of the varieties of normal. We cannot be content to discuss the latter as "only a question of values." Systematic psychodynamic studies in addition to other methods applicable to the entire field should be encouraged to define various kinds of mental health. Especially from the point of view of practical application we need to know who is sick and when and how he becomes well.

From "A Dynamic Story of the 'Homoclite.' " in Jules H. Masserman (Ed.), *Science and Psychoanalysis* (New York: Grune & Stratton, 1963), pp. 131–133. Reprinted by permission.

C. JUDSON HERRICK

Most behavior is obviously directed toward some end. The objective may be something advantageous or satisfying to the individual, or it may be something favorable to the species or group to which he belongs. These two motivating agencies act differently and sometimes they are in conflict. The social factors of behavior will be examined in due course, but attention is first directed to some of the simpler personal aspects.

An animal or a man ordinarily behaves in order to accomplish something that promotes his own welfare, that satisfies a need or desire. If the need is urgent and satisfaction is not achieved, then he tries something else. Behavior that may seem to an observer to be random is not random from the standpoint of the behaving animal. His every action is the result of causes that can be discovered, and these activities are more or less systematically organized.

People and all other animals sometimes do things that are not good for them, but what they do must in the aggregate be beneficial or they perish. Although behavior is normally goal-directed, situations sometimes arise which frustrate the satisfactions sought. If the frustration is not overcome by trial and error or otherwise, the normal course of behavior is disrupted, with results that may lead to catastrophic disorder and eventually to a pathological neurosis. Such abnormalities of conduct can be avoided or remedied only if the causes of the frustration are recognized and corrected.

The goal of normal behavior, we repeat, is satisfaction, which may or may not be consciously recognized as such. This directive behavior is here called "goal-directive," whether or not the goal is consciously recognized. Schneirla (1949, p. 270) would restrict the term to patterns of behavior which "are anticipated in terms of their expected outcomes." I prefer the more inclusive definition, both because we have no reliable criteria for determining whether the animal is aware of the end for which his behavior is adapted, and because consciously purposeful behavior has undoubtedly emerged from biologically adaptive behavior in which no conscious purpose can be recognized.

Whatever name we choose to apply to it, the directive quality of normal behavior is fundamental. This quality gives us the only basis we have for predicting the behavior of other creatures, and especially of other people, and so gives some promise of control of behavior, which is what we are after in the upshot.

From *The Evolution of Human Nature* (Austin: University of Texas Press, 1956), pp. 20–21.

MARIE JAHODA

III. *The Psychological Meaning of Various Criteria for Positive Mental Health.*

So far, three efforts to give psychological meaning to the notion of positive mental health have been examined and found more or less wanting. To regard the absence of mental disease as a criterion has proved to be an insufficient indication in view of the difficulty of defining disease. Normality, in one connotation, is but a synonym for mental health; in another sense it was found to be unspecific and bare of psychological content. Various states of well-being proved unsuitable because they reflect not only individual functioning but also external circumstances.

A survey of the relevant literature reveals a host of other approaches to the subject which seem more promising; at least, at first sight, it appears that the objections raised in the preceding pages do not apply to them. Although no claim can be made that this survey discovered every contribution to the topic, the search was extensive. It is hoped that no major idea in the area has escaped our attention.

SIX APPROACHES TO A CONCEPT From an inspection of the diverse approaches uncovered, six major categories of concepts emerge.

1. There are several proposals suggesting that indicators of positive mental health should be sought in the *attitudes of an individual toward his own self*. Various distinctions in the manner of perceiving oneself are regarded as demonstrating higher or lower degrees of health.
2. Another group of criteria designates the individual's style and degree of *growth, development, or self-actualization* as expressions of mental health. This group of criteria, in contrast to the first, is concerned not with self-perception but with what a person does with his self over a period of time.
3. Various proposals place the emphasis on a central synthesizing psychological function, incorporating some of the suggested criteria defined in (1) and (2) above. This function will here be called integration.

The following three groups of criteria concentrate more exclusively than the preceding ones on the individual's relation to reality.

4. *Autonomy* singles out the individual's degree of independence from social influences as most revealing of the state of his mental health.
5. A number of proposals suggest that mental health is manifested in the adequacy of an individual's *perception of reality*.
6. Finally, there are suggestions that *environmental mastery* be regarded as a criterion for mental health.

All ideas on positive mental health examined can be assigned to one of these six categories with relative ease, even though there is a certain amount of overlap. As will become apparent, many authors have made contributions to several of the categories. And it could be argued that there exists an empirical or theoretical relationship between these groups. But the purpose of this review is to present current thoughts on *criteria* of positive mental health; not—at least, not yet—to inquire into the relationship of these criteria to each other, to an author's other contributions, or to theories.

One consequence of this emphasis on criteria is that similarities may appear where theoretical differences have not led one to expect them. Another is that it will be possible to examine these criteria from the point of view of mental health, rather than of the fruitfulness of the general approach of which they form part.

From *Current Concepts of Positive Mental Health* (New York: Basic Books, Inc., 1958), pp. 22–24.

CARL G. JUNG

29. *Individuation.* The concept of individuation plays a large role in our psychology. In general, it is the process by which individual beings are formed and differentiated; in particular, it is the development of the psychological *individual* (q.v.) as a being distinct from the general, collective psychology. Individuation, therefore, is a process of *differentiation* (q.v.), having for its goal the development of the individual personality.

Individuation is a natural necessity inasmuch as its prevention by a levelling down to collective standards is injurious to the vital activity of the individual. Since *individuality* (q.v.) is a prior psychological and physiological datum, it also expresses itself in psychological ways. Any serious check to individuality, therefore, is an artificial stunting. It is obvious that a social group consisting of stunted individuals cannot be a healthy and viable institution; only a society that can preserve its internal cohesion and collective values, while at the same time granting the individual the greatest possible freedom, has any prospect of enduring vitality. As the individual is not just a single, separate being, but by his very existence presupposes a collective relationship, it follows that the process of individuation must lead to more intense and broader collective relationships and not to isolation.

Individuation is closely connected with the *transcendent function* (v. *Symbol*, par. 828), since this function creates individual lines of development which could never be reached by keeping to the path prescribed by collective norms.

Under no circumstances can individuation be the sole aim of psychological education. Before it can be taken as a goal, the educational aim of adaptation to the necessary minimum of collective norms must first be attained. If a plant is to unfold its specific nature to the full, it must first be able to grow in the soil in which it is planted.

Individuation is always to some extent opposed to collective norms, since it means separation and differentiation from the general and a building up of the particular—not a particularity that is *sought out*, but one that is already ingrained in the psychic constitution. The opposition to the collective norm, however, is only apparent, since closer examination shows that the individual standpoint is not *antagonistic* to it, but only *differently oriented*. The individual way can never be directly opposed to the collective norm, because the opposite of the collective norm could only be another, but contrary, norm. But the individual way can, by definition, never be a norm. A norm is the product of the totality of individual ways, and its justification and beneficial effect are contingent upon the existence of individual ways that need from time to time to orient to a norm. A norm serves no purpose when it possesses absolute validity. A real conflict with the collective norm arises only when an individual way is raised to a norm, which is the actual aim of extreme individualism. Naturally this aim is pathological and inimical to life. It has, accordingly, nothing to do with individuation, which, though it may strike out on an individual bypath, precisely on that account needs the norm for its *orientation* (q.v.) to society and for the vitally necessary relationship of the individual to society. Individuation, therefore, leads to a natural esteem for the collective norm, but if the orientation is exclusively collective the norm becomes increasingly superfluous and morality goes to pieces. The more a man's life is shaped by the collective norm, the greater is his individual immorality.

Individuation is practically the same as the development of consciousness out of the original state of *identity* (q.v.). It is thus an extension of the sphere of consciousness, an enriching of conscious psychological life.

From *The Collected Works of C. G. Jung*, edited by G. Adler, M. Fordham, H. Read, and W. McGuire, trans. by R. F. C. Hull, Bollingen Series XX vol. 6, *Psychological Types* (copyright © 1971 by Princeton University Press): pp. 448–450.

LAWRENCE S. KUBIE

IV. *The Essential Difference Between Health and Neurosis.*

Every human act, thought, feeling, and impulse can under appropriate circumstances be normal or it can be neurotic. What difference, then, can indicate when an act is the one and when it is the other? I emphasize that only after this differentiation can be made with respect to single moments of human behavior will it be possible cautiously to apply the same principle to patterns of general conduct, then to personalities as a whole, and finally perhaps to whole cultures.

Let me repeat what I have previously emphasized. Not one of the qualities popularly associated with the idea of neurosis is an invariable concomitant or cause or result of the neurotic process

(II). One quality however is constant and sets a normal act apart from one that is a manifestation of the neurotic process. This is not a judgment of value, but rather a clinical description of that one attribute of behavior common to every neurotic action and absent from every normal act. If we are to understand the difference between the two, it is essential to keep this characteristic clearly in mind. This clinically derived distinguishing trait centers around the freedom and flexibility to learn through experience, to change, and to adapt to changing external circumstances. Thus the essence of normality is flexibility, in contrast to the freezing of behavior into patterns of unalterability that characterizes every manifestation of the neurotic process, whether in impulses, purposes, acts, thoughts, or feelings. *Whether or not a behavioral event is free to change depends not upon the quality of the act itself, but upon the nature of the constellation of forces that has produced it. No moment of behavior can be looked upon as neurotic unless the processes that have set it in motion predetermine its automatic repetition irrespective of the situation, the utility, or the consequences of the act.* This may be the most basic lesson about human conduct that has been learned from psychoanalysis. Let me repeat: no single psychological act can be looked upon as neurotic unless it is the product of processes that predetermine a tendency to its automatic repetition. Whenever this occurs, under whatever culture or circumstances, the neurotic process will be found at work.[1] This then is my working hypothesis concerning the essential distinction between an act that is healthy and an act that is neurotic. In the unstable equilibrium

[1] Certain organic deformations of the central nervous system can determine automatic repetitiveness (1, 20, 17); furthermore, biochemical processes may contribute to stereotyped repetitions or may release latent repetitive patterns. One can cite the tedious repetitive liturgies of the alcoholic, and the similar actions that occur under the influence of barbiturates and in hypoglycemic states. Such clinical phenomena indicate that automatic repetitiveness is a disturbance of function in which organic and psychological processes converge. This interaction of organic and psychological processes constitutes a crossroads which merits more systematic interdisciplinary investigation than it has ever received.

among the many psychological and physiological processes that determine all psychological functions, what types of disturbance can determine this tendency to stereotyped and automatic repetition?

The answer I suggest is that wherever an alliance of the conscious and preconscious systems predominates in the production of behavior, the resultant behavior will come to rest either when its goal is achieved and satiety is attained, or when the goal is found to be unattainable or ungratifying or both, whereupon the effort ceases. Thus such behavior never becomes either insatiable or stereotyped. It can be altered by the experience of success and failure, of rewards and punishments, of pleasure and pain. It can be used to test reality and it can be tested against reality. It is therefore anchored in reality, yet it remains freely flexible. On the contrary, whenever the unconscious system (or perhaps an alliance between the preconscious and unconscious systems) predominates, the resultant action must be repeated endlessly. This occurs because its goals are predominantly unconscious symbols, and unconscious symbolic goals are never attainable. Since the predominant forces are unconscious, they will not be responsive to the experience of pleasure or of pain, or to rewards and punishments, or to logical argument—neither to the logic of events, nor to any appeals to mind or heart. The behavior that results from a dominance of the unconscious system has the insatiability, the automaticity, and the endless repetitiveness that are the stamp of the neurotic process, whether this expresses itself through overt neurotic symptoms, or through art forms, or through subtle deformations of those general patterns of behavior that constitute the personality.

If we generalize from this to a concept of health in a still broader sense, extrapolating from isolated moments of behavior to patterns and to personalities, we may say that a state of greater health is achieved whenever those areas of life that are dominated by inaccessibly unconscious forces are shrunk, so that a larger area of life is dominated by conscious or preconscious forces, which can come to awareness when necessary. This is a reasonable concept of health and a reasonable formulation of the goal of therapy, leaving ample room for the creative economics of intuitive, preconscious functioning. This conception makes it possible to understand how psychoanalytic therapy may enable the preconscious processes of the artist and scientist to operate freely and creatively, since with successful therapy they will no longer be warped and blocked by forces that emanate from unconscious conflicts. In this way the hypothesis makes clear how unconscious conflicts (that is to say, neurotogenic conflicts) distort both conscious and preconscious functions in all creative processes, whether scientific, literary, artistic, or humorous, and in dreams and psychological illness.

To recapitulate, I should say that on pragmatic grounds we are justified in calling "normal" any act in the determination of which the alliance of conscious and preconscious forces plays the dominant role, that is, forces that are accessible on need; whereas on the same grounds we are justified in calling abnormal or unhealthy or neurotic any act in the determination of which unconscious processes are dominant (whether alone or in an alliance with the preconscious), because such forces will predetermine its automatic repetition irrespective of its suitability to the immediate situation or its immediate or remote consequences. I repeat that this is not to say that the conscious or preconscious process in itself is normal and the unconscious process in itself is abnormal, any more than one can say that a pathogenic bacterium is in itself either normal or abnormal. We deal here with a complex constellation of biological, psychological, and cultural forces, all operating on conscious, preconscious, and unconscious levels, in a state of continuous unstable equilibrium. On different occasions any one act may be precipitated out of this dynamic and unstable equilibrium as the expression of endlessly varied mixtures of forces, which are both cultural and instinctual in origin. It is the composition of the mixture that determines whether the resultant act will meet our pragmatic criterion of health or illness.

From "The Fundamental Nature of the Distinction Between Normality and Neurosis" (*Psychoanalytic Quarterly*, Vol. 23, 1954), pp. 182–185.

RALPH LINTON

It seems to me that the problem for the psychologist . . . is to try to find out *how far the personality norms of various status groups within a society actually correspond to the assumed stereotypes for these*. This is something about which we know very little. I think that we do have indications that, in small homogeneous societies, there exist certain personality norms which differ from one society to another. Presumably these "status personalities," as I have called them, would represent such personality norms plus or minus certain factors related to the status the individual holds. Such a study may seem simple, but is actually exceedingly difficult, because we don't really know much about this field, which deserves more study. The study of age and sex series, in particular, presents interesting problems as does the study of individuals who seem to change their personalities as they move from one status to another in a series. Thus, all societies recognize the sobering effects of having to assume certain types of responsibility. An individual who has been wild may very well change and become a responsible man and a good leader if a suitable task is assigned to him. Again, we have to go back to the problem of how extensive, and particularly how deep running, are the changes in personality which are connected with the changes in overt behavior and also with the changes in the demands which the society makes on the individual. This has a great bearing on the whole problem of normality and abnormality, particularly as regards the problem of how far psychotherapy can modify the basic personality structure of the adult patient.

Under such circumstances the problem of what constitutes normality becomes quite complicated. It seems that one must distinguish between absolute and relative abnormality. All societies provide examples of psychotics, neurotics, and hysterics, who are recognized as such by the members of that society. The symptomatologies associated with these abnormal states differ from society to society in ways which strongly suggest that they are shaped by cultural influences. The methods employed by different societies in dealing with individuals of these different types, including the social utilization of certain forms of psychic abnormality, also differ. However, it seems certain that abnormality of this sort is absolute and probably has a physiological basis. Individuals having the constitutional defects responsible for such abnormalities would be abnormal in any society. At most, particular cultural factors may lead to the manifestation or suppression of symptoms at various levels of defect intensity.

Relative normality, on the other hand, is a matter of the individual's adjustment to the cultural milieu and of the degree to which his personality configuration approaches the basic personality of his society. Tests, supplemented by life histories, analytic studies, and so forth, have shown that, when the individual deviates widely from the basic personality, his early experience has frequently been atypical for his society (15, 19).

The tests of absolute normalcy are the individual's ability to apprehend reality, as understood by his society, to act in terms of this reality, and to be effectively shaped by his society during his developmental period. The test of relative normalcy is the extent to which the individual's experience has given him a personality conforming to the basic personality of his society.

From *Culture and Mental Disorders* (1956), pp. 61–63. Courtesy of Charles C Thomas, Publisher, Springfield, Illinois.

ABRAHAM H. MASLOW
BELA MITTELMANN

The Meaning of "Healthy" ("Normal") and of "Sick" ("Abnormal").

Adjustment of a person may be defined as a characteristic way in which he perceives, reacts to, and solves the main problems of life. For the sake of simplicity, we may classify the main problems of life into three categories: (1) problems set by external reality in its biological and physical aspects (we must get food to eat, and we must have shelter); (2) problems set by the culture in which the person lives—its demands and prohibitions, its habits and taboos, its internal conflicts and inconsistencies; (3) the problems set by internal psychological demands; these in turn may be put under three heads: (a) the need for comfort, gratification, and the avoidance of pain; (b) the need for self-esteem, independence, achievement, and adequacy; (c) the need for security, the love of our fellow men, and a feeling of belongingness.

The words "healthy" and "sick," "normal" and "abnormal," have been used in three senses.

1. The pathological approach: We have mentioned that disturbances and conflicts in the manner of satisfying these needs may produce acute symptoms as well as habitual long-range modes of reaction. The latter we call character disturbances. Such problems as stinginess, the need to produce flawless work, and stubbornness. For example, the patient described in the first chapter worked well as a librarian, but she needed self-aggrandizing attitudes to overcome her feeling of inadequacy and helplessness in the situation. In the history of psychopathology, the extension of the investigation of psychological problems to habitual modes of reaction was a very important enlargement, but it also diminished the sharp delineation between health and sickness, between normal and abnormal. In this respect, even those individuals who did not break down in normal situations of stress, in the face of severe threat had reaction patterns similar to those of the people who did break down. In spite of this, the whole emotional life of the individuals who did not break down could not be understood and fully appreciated without taking into account their habitual modes of reaction. Conversely, the individuals who did not break down showed nevertheless a peculiar rigidity and vulnerability as regards some of the habitual modes of reaction mentioned. The recognition of the similarities in some of the dynamics of sick and healthy individuals is of great psychological importance. It implies, however, in some respects, the definition of pathology as representing only quantita-

tive differences. In other words, an individual may be more or less "sick."

2. The statistical approach: Most psychological traits are assumed to fall into a "normal" distribution, with most of the cases in the middle and a few at the extremes. These extremes, which constitute only a small percentage of the total population, are arbitrarily lopped off and labeled "abnormal" or "pathological" or "deviant," and the far larger percentage clustering around the middle is arbitrarily called "normal" (279). This approach is of value if we recognize its limitations. Much of what lies at the extremes—delusions, anxiety attacks—is pathological; genius is not. Further, many children show an unreasonable fear between the ages of four and seven. Slight fear of harmless animals is common in women. These traits which appear in a great number of individuals are minor "sicknesses," the same way as the common cold is. (See also Morlan (685).)

3. The cultural approach: It is impossible, in many respects, to understand "abnormality" without reference to the cultural background. Some societies expect the individual to show no strong ambition, to refrain from becoming emotionally or physically violent, and to cooperate with other members of the group (Zuñi). Other societies put a premium on boasting, on ambition, on accumulation of wealth, on surpassing and vanquishing others, on certain states of violence, and on killing (Kwakiutl). Each of these two societies strongly disapproves of the "deviant" mode of behavior. It has been suggested that all concepts of normal or abnormal should be considered in terms of conformity to the cultural norms. The facts mentioned pose difficult problems which have not yet been adequately solved, but the following general statements can be made: The "dynamics" of a reaction pattern occurring in a group in which it is accepted has only partial identity with the "dynamics" of the same pattern occurring in individuals living in a society where it is not. This applies even to such phenomena as dream states and hallucinations—including hearing supernatural voices. Occurring in harmony with cultural norms, they may imply, although possibly representing conflict solutions,

a desire to develop in a certain direction and to advance one's career—for example, to become a medicine man. In the group which rejects such phenomena they represent a near-catastrophic solution of conflicts, a state of helplessness—in a word, a state of psychic illness.

In addition, we may add that normality is also relative to social status, age, and sex. Behavior that is healthy in an individual ten years of age may be unquestionably unhealthy in an individual of thirty.

MANIFESTATIONS OF PSYCHOLOGICAL HEALTH ("NORMALITY")

1. *Adequate Feelings of Security.* The feeling that one is safe in contact with fellow beings in the occupational, social, and family settings.
2. *Adequate Self-Evaluation.* This includes (a) adequate self-esteem—a feeling of value proportionate to one's individuality and achievements; (b) an adequate feeling of worth-whileness—feeling morally sound, with the feeling of no severe guilt and the ability to recognize some socially and personally unacceptable common human desires which will always be present as long as one lives in a society.
3. *Adequate Spontaneity and Emotionality.* This involves ability to form strong and lasting emotional ties, such as friendships and love relations; the ability to give adequate expression to resentment without losing control; the ability to understand and to share other people's emotions; the ability to enjoy oneself and laugh. Everyone is unhappy at times, but this must have valid reasons.
4. *Efficient Contact with Reality.* This has at least three aspects: the physical, the social, and the internal world. This implies (a) absence of excessive fantasy; (b) a realistic and broad outlook on the world, with the ability to withstand the ordinary shocks of life, such as illness and reversals; and (c) the ability to change if external circumstances cannot be modified. A good phrase for this is "cooperation with the inevitable."
5. *Adequate Bodily Desires and the Ability to Gratify Them.* This includes (a) a healthy attitude toward bodily functions in terms of

accepting them but not being preoccupied with them; (b) ability to derive pleasure from the physical things in life, such as eating and sleeping, and to recover well from fatigue; (c) sexual adequacy —healthy desire and the ability to gratify it without fear and guilt; (d) ability to perform the excretory functions adequately without shame or conflicts; (e) ability to work; (f) absence of an excessive need to indulge in any of these activities, and the ability to stand, at least temporarily, a fair amount of deprivation.

6. *Adequate Self-Knowledge.* This includes (a) adequate knowledge of one's own major motives, desires, goals, ambitions, inhibitions, compensations, defenses, inferiority feelings, and so forth; (b) realistic appraisal of one's own assets and liabilities. Honest self-appraisal is based on the ability to accept oneself as natural and not to repudiate any important desires or thoughts even if some of them may be socially or personally unacceptable. These will always be present as long as one lives in a society.

7. *Integration and Consistency of Personality.* This means (a) fairly rounded development, versatility, interest in several activities; (b) morals and conscience which are not too inflexible from the group's point of view; (c) ability to concentrate; (d) no major conflicting trends within the personality, and no dissociation of personality.

8. *Adequate Life Goals.* These involve (a) achievable, realistic, and compatible goals; (b) reasonable persistence of efforts to achieve them; (c) goals which involve some good to society.

9. *Ability to Learn from Experience.* The ability to learn from experience includes not only accumulation of knowledge and acquisition of skills through practice, but also an elasticity and receptiveness and therefore absence of rigidity in the approach to handling occupational tasks. Even more important are the ability to learn spontaneously—in the muscles and bones and without the need of elaborate meditation—one's own strength, the dangers of certain situations, the possibility or certainty of success, and the carrying over of this knowledge, which is a knowledge in feeling, action and evaluation into reaction and behavior in the fields of interpersonal relations, the gratification of bodily needs, and pur-

suit of life goals. Equally important is the resultant avoidance of methods that have failed when the risk is not worth taking or better methods are available.

10. *Ability to Satisfy the Requirements of the Group.* The individual must be (a) not too unlike the other members of his group in ways that the group considers important: (b) adequately informed and essentially accepting of the folkways of his group; (c) willing and able to inhibit the drives and desires tabooed by his group; (d) able to show the fundamental strivings expected by his group: ambition, promptness, friendliness, sense of responsibility, loyalty, and so forth; (e) interested in the recreational activities favored by his group.

11. *Adequate Emancipation from the Group or Culture.* This involves (a) at least some originality, individuality, the ability to consider some things good, others bad; (b) some independence of group opinions; (c) the absence of an excessive need for flattery, reassurance, or group approval; (d) some degree of tolerance and appreciation of cultural difference.

> Pages 12–15 of Chapter 2, "The Meaning of 'Healthy' ('Normal') and of 'Sick' ('Abnormal')," *Principles of Abnormal Psychology*, revised edition, by Abraham H. Maslow and Bela Mittelmann.

ROBERT K. MERTON

A decade ago, and all the more so before then, one could speak of a marked tendency in psychological and sociological theory to attribute the faulty operation of social structures to failures of social control over man's imperious biological drives. The imagery of the relations between man and society implied by this doctrine is as clear as it is questionable. In the beginning, there are man's biological impulses which seek full expression. And then, there is the social order, essentially an apparatus for the management of impulses, for the social processing of tensions, for the "renunciation of instinctual gratifications," in the words of Freud. Nonconformity with the demands of a social structure is thus assumed to be anchored in original nature.[1] It is the biologically rooted impulses which from time to time break through social control. And by implication, conformity is the result of an utilitarian calculus or of unreasoned conditioning.

With the more recent advancement of social science, this set of conceptions has undergone basic modification. For one thing, it no longer appears so obvious that man is set against society in an unceasing war between biological impulses and social restraints. The image of man as an untamed bundle of impulses begins to look more like a caricature than a portrait. For another, sociological perspectives have increasingly entered into the analysis of behavior deviating from prescribed patterns of conduct. For whatever the role of biological impulses, there still remains the further question of why it is that the frequency of deviant behavior varies within different social structures and how it happens that the deviations have different shapes and patterns in different social structures. Today, as a decade ago, we have still much to learn about the processes through which social structures generate the circumstances in which infringement of social codes constitutes a "normal" (that is to say, an expectable) response.[2] This paper is an essay seeking clarification of the problem.

The framework set out in this essay is designed to provide one systematic approach to the analysis of social and cultural sources of deviant behavior. Our primary aim is to discover how some *social structures exert a definite pressure upon certain persons in the society to engage in nonconformist rather than conformist conduct.* If we can locate groups peculiarly subject to such pressures, we should expect to find fairly high rates of deviant behavior in these groups, not because the human beings comprising them are compounded of distinctive biological tendencies but because they are responding normally to the social situation in which they find themselves. Our perspective is sociological. We look at variations in the *rates* of deviant behavior, not at its incidence.[3] Should our quest be at all successful, some forms of deviant behavior will be found to be as psychologically normal as conformist behavior, and the equation of deviation and abnormality will be put in question.

ROGER E. MONEY-KYRLE

Anthropology has taught us that any fairly homogeneous people tends to create a society congenial to itself, and that many different kinds of society exist, each of which is "good" to its own members, but "bad" to members of the others. The anthropologist, who himself has a specific character, will naturally prefer some kinds of people and some kinds of society above the rest. But, in the absence of any independent standard against which to measure his own subjective one, he will usually dismiss such judgments as relative and therefore outside the bounds of science. This attitude may be in itself a healthy reaction against a too naïve assumption of superiority by earlier travelers. But it seems to me to be carried much too far in the relativist denial that any independent standard can be found.

The relativist position culminates in the relativist definition of normality, according to which a normal person is one well adapted to the society he lives in. Definitions cannot be false; but they can be ill chosen, or they can fail to fit the pre-existing concept they are endeavoring to express in words. Now the clinical concept of normality may be vague. But it certainly does not depend on adaptation to society; for if it did, some people whom every clinician would class as ill would have to be classed as normal in some societies. A verbal definition or normality that both fits the clinical concept and is absolute in the sense of being independent of the standards of any arbitrarily chosen culture may be difficult to find. But it seems to me to emerge, at least in outline, from the following considerations. What we call illness, whether this is a specific symptom or a "character defect," is something we try to cure, or at least to lessen, by analysis, that is, by helping the patient to achieve a higher degree of insight or self-understanding than he had before. Sometimes the task is beyond our present technicial ability. But this does not lessen our belief that insight, if we could only awaken it, would still effect the cure. In other words, we believe that what we call health is something that can be achieved by insight. Now, if this causal connection between health and insight exists, we can use it to give a verbal definition of normality that does fit the clinical concept and is independent of any arbitrarily chosen cultural standards. We can define a normal—that is, a healthy—mind, as one that knows itself.[1]

Since in reality self-knowledge is always incomplete, it follows from our definition that there can be no completely normal person. But this conclusion, with which no analyst will quarrel, does not lessen the value of a term to denote a limit to which real people approximate in various degrees.

Having reached a definition of a normal mind as one that knows itself, we have next to inquire about its other attributes. These are not included in the definition and can only be discovered empirically. Some of the moral attributes we have already found: they comprise what we called a "humanistic" as opposed to other forms of conscience. Two qualities which Freud used to define normality in a wider sense are certainly attributes of anyone who is approximately normal in the narrow one. These are a well-developed capacity for both work and enjoyment. But, for our present purpose, the most comprehensive and significant attribute is perhaps maturity.

From "Psychoanalysis and Ethics." In *New Directions in Psycho-Analysis* (New York: Basic Books, Inc., 1957), pp. 437–438.

[1] The two expressions: "A mind that knows itself" and "an integrated mind" are I think equivalent. Integration as a criterion of mental health has been stressed by Marjorie Brierley (1947) in her paper "Notes on Psycho-Analysis and Integrative Living," *Int. J. Psycho-Anal.*, Vol. 28, Chapter 6, in *Trends in Psycho-Analysis* (London, 1951).

TALCOTT PARSONS

Health may be defined as the state of optimum *capacity* of an individual for the effective performance of the roles and tasks for which he has been socialized. It is thus defined with reference to the individual's participation in the social system. It is also defined as *relative* to his "status" in the society, that is, to differentiated type of role and corresponding task structure, for example, by sex or age, and by level of education which he has attained and the like. Naturally, also there are qualitative ranges in the differentiation of capacities, within sex groups and at given levels of education. Finally, let me repeat that I am defining health as concerned with capacity, not with commitment to *particular* roles, tasks, norms, or even values as such. The question of whether a man wants to remain with his wife or likes his particular job or even feels committed to refrain from highway robbery is not *as such* a health problem, though a health problem may underlie and be interwoven with problems of this sort.

First, and of course, a very important point, the development of medicine and of health sciences underlying and associated with it, has made possible an entirely new level of control of illness, both preventive and therapeutic, far higher than has ever existed before in history. There is, of course, interdependence. American medicine did not just take over a medical science ready-made, but has developed the European beginnings with an energy and resourcefulness probably matched only in the field of industrial technology. There is, hence, interdependence between the development, on the one hand, of medical science and technology, and on the other, of interest in, and concern for, effective handling of health problems.

Secondly, the order of significance of the problems of social control, starting with commitment to paramount values themselves, running through commitment to norms, then to roles and tasks, is probably, in a very broad sense, of evolutionary significance. This is to say that there is a tendency for a problem area to emerge into salience only when, to a degree, the ones ahead of it in the priority list have in some sense been "solved." This is not to say that any of them ever are definitely solved, but in a relative sense one can speak of solution.

It is not possible to discuss this question here in detail. But it may be suggested that by the mid-nineteenth century, with the very important exception of the problem of the South, a certain national unity had been achieved in terms of values and norms.[17] It can be then further suggested that in the latter half of the nineteenth century there was concentration on the problems of setting up the new industrial system with the institutionalization of the principal role–categories which have to go into that, notably, of course, an occupational role system which was structurally quite different from that of the earlier society of "farmers and mechanics." Not least important in this connection was the institutionalization of the repercussions of these changes on the family, because of the drastic nature of the differentiation of occupational from familial roles. From the point of view of the individual, it may be said that the development of the industrial economy provided, in terms of structural type congruent with American values, a new level of solution of the problem of opportunity.

From this point of view, one might say that after the turn of the century the stage was set for a new level of concern with the problems of education and health, which have indeed figured very prominently in this period, though not by any means to the exclusion of the others. Their importance is, I think, further accentuated by another feature of the development of the society. This is the fact that, with the development of industrialization, urbanism, high technology, mass communications and many other features of our society, there has been a general *upgrading* to higher levels of responsibility. Life has necessarily become more complex and has made greater demands on the typical individual, though different ones at different levels. The sheer problem of capacity to meet these demands has, therefore, become more urgent. The motivation to retreat into ill-health, through mental or psychosomatic channels, has become accentuated and with it the importance of effective mechanisms for coping with those who do so retreat.

Seen in terms of this kind of historical perspective, it makes sense, I think, that *the first major wave of development of the health institutions was in the field of somatic illness and the techniques of dealing with it, and that this has been followed by a wave of interest in problems of mental health.* This is partly, but by no means wholly, because the scientific basis for handling somatic illness has developed earlier and farther. In addition to this, it is well known that the resistances to recognizing the existence of health problems are stronger in the field of mental than of somatic health. Furthermore, a larger component of the phenomena of mental illness presumably operates through motivation and is hence related to the problems and mechanisms of social control. Social changes, however, have not only increased the strain on individuals, thus accentuating the need for mechanisms in this area, but some of the older mechanisms have been destroyed or weakened and a restructuring has been necessary.

For one thing, levels of mental pathology which could be tolerated under pre-industrial conditions have become intolerable under the more stringent pressures of modern life; this probably includes the pushing of many types of personality over the borderline into overt psychosis, who otherwise would have been able to "get along." Furthermore, the family, for example, has undertaken a greatly increased burden in the socialization and personality–management fields, and new institutional arrangements for dealing with the health problems of its members are required. This seems, for example, to be one major factor in the rapid spread of hospitalization.[18]

I may sum up this aspect of the discussion by saying that both by virtue of its value system, and by virtue of the high level of differentiation of its social structure, American society has been one in which it could be expected that the problem of health, and within this more particularly of mental health, would become particularly salient. Its "liberal" cast which militates against highly stringent integration with reference to a system goal tends to emphasize the problem of getting units to "come along." The human individual is the end of the series of units on which the functioning of the society depends, and is hence the "last resort" in this connection. At the same time, the activistic orientation of the society militates against any orientation which would be inclined to let individuals "rest on their oars," but puts very much of a premium on the protection and development of capacity in the sense in which I have discussed it here.

From "Definitions of Health and Illness in the Light of American values and Social Structures." Reprinted with the permission of The Free Press from *Patients, Physicians and Illness,* edited by E. Gartly Jaco. Copyright © 1958 by The Free Press, a Corporation.

FREDRICK C. REDLICH

The problem of normality, as the author sees it, can be put in form of the questions "normal for what?" and "normal for whom?" A moderately inadequate person working in a position of little responsibility in an industrial plant may be a very small problem to anyone except himself. The situation is entirely different if the man with "problems" is an important executive. It is different if psychiatric help is, for geographic, cultural, and psychological reasons, unavailable or if such help can be readily obtained and is considered beneficial in problems of this sort. Actually, only if the latter is the case should we speak of "psychiatric" problems. Otherwise, it would be more appropriate just to speak of "problems." To what extent such problems can be tolerated by the people who suffer from them or whether professional groups—for example, physicians, teachers, lawyers, ministers, welfare personnel, psychiatrists, and so forth—who encounter them are ready to tackle them is another matter. The self-perception of the person with the problem and the role assignment of all actors involved will determine subsequent labeling (normal or abnormal with reference to certain tasks) and subsequent action.

Essentially, I propose to examine the interaction between psychiatrist, patient, and the society in which they function. In doing this there will be focus on the establishment of contact between psychiatrist and patient, on some of the social agreements implied in the treatment process, and on the termination and goals of treatment. It is hoped that these processes will be outlined with particular reference to norms, mores, laws, and social institutions which govern the conduct of the actors involved.

As a preliminary, I shall propose tentatively a dichotomy of the "abnormal" persons into a "severely abnormal" group and a "moderately abnormal" group. It is evident that the first group will not be rigidly delineated from the second group either by symptoms or etiology and course and that the second group will blend equally into the so-called "normal" population. Sometimes a severe disorder may be camouflaged by a seemingly normal surface and the more severe conditions may rapidly or slowly develop out of the mild conditions. Recognition of such phenomena usually will require high diagnostic skill from the expert and often enough challenges the expert beyond his present capacities. Yet I feel that the severe group, which includes all the psychotics and the severe neurotics, can more often be clearly recognized not only by the expert but by lay persons with whom these abnormal persons are in contact. Recognition of the moderately disturbed group is usually much more difficult and in most instances requires the most skillful professional judgment. I propose the above dichotomy because I think that it will aid us in our scrutiny of the social interactions between psychiatrist, patient, and society. Such a scrutiny involves not only an observation of social consequences of mental illness but an attempt to understand action in terms of social theory.

. . .

This discussion of the difference between the severely abnormal and the moderately abnormal patient was based on the application of social theory to clinical experience, not on a systematic investigation. Before these propositions become truly convincing, they will have to rest on solid evidence of well-designed research—evidence that will explain what a case is, its incidence and prevalence, how people become patients, how they change with and without specific intervention, and how treatment is terminated. We expect that conclusions from such research will provide us with more fundamental knowledge about normality.

In summary, we do not possess any general definition of normality and mental health from either a statistical or a clinical viewpoint. Actually, at this time clinicians can barely agree on satisfactory criteria. There is agreement only about extremes, not about the areas of transition or the "cut-off point." Sound epidemiological research on normality is in its infancy. In this chapter an attempt is made to investigate who should be treated psychiatrically rather than to consider the more complex problem of normality. Empirical research into the psychological and social elements of interaction of psychiatrists, patients, and their social environment will contribute to the solution of the problem of mental health; however, it is obvious that criteria of capacity for treatment and of mental illness are not identical. In any case, meaningful propositions on normality can be best made within a specific cultural context, notwithstanding some general propositions denying cultural relativism.

At present, it is true, the no-man's land between mental illness and mental health is ill-defined. Nevertheless, it seems justifiable to divide illness and health into two categories—the first roughly coinciding with psychosis and severe neurosis, the second including mild and transitory mental disturbances.

From "The Concept of Health in Psychiatry." In Alexander H. Leighton, John A. Clausen, and Robert N. Wilson (Eds.), *Explorations in Social Psychiatry* (New York: Basic Books, Inc., 1957), p. 155 & p. 158.

CARL R. ROGERS

This ultimate hypothetical person would be synonymous with "the goal of social evolution," "the end point of optimal psychotherapy," and so forth. We have chosen to term this individual the fully functioning person.

Although it contains nothing not already stated earlier under I and II, it seems worthwhile to spell out this theoretical concept in its own right.

A. The individual has an inherent tendency toward *actualizing* his organism.

B. The individual has the capacity and tendency to *symbolize experiences* accurately in awareness.

   1. A corollary statement is that he has the capacity and tendency to keep his *self-concept* congruent with his *experience.*

C. The individual has a *need for positive regard.*

D. The individual has a *need for positive self-regard.*

E. Tendencies A and B are most fully realized when C and D are met. More specifically, tendencies A and B tend to be most fully realized when

   1. The individual *experiences unconditional positive regard* from significant others.
   2. The pervasiveness of this *unconditional positive regard* is made evident through relationships marked by a complete and communicated *empathic* understanding of the individual's *frame of reference.*

F. If the conditions under E are met to a maximum degree, the individual who experiences these conditions will be a fully functioning person. The fully functioning person will have at least these characteristics:

   1. *He will be open to his experience.*
      a. The corollary statement is that he will exhibit no *defensiveness.*
   2. Hence all *experiences* will be *available to awareness.*
   3. All *symbolizations* will be as accurate as the experiential data will permit.
   4. His *self-structure* will be congruent with his *experience.*
   5. His *self-structure* will be a fluid gestalt, changing flexibly in the process of assimilation of new *experience.*
   6. He will *experience* himself as the *locus of evaluation.*
   7. He will have no *conditions of worth.*
      a. The corollary statement is that he will *experience unconditional self-regard.*

8. He will meet each situation with behavior which is unique and creative adaptation to the newness of that moment.
9. He will find his *organismic valuing* a trustworthy guide to the most satisfying behaviors, because
   a. All available experiential data will be available to *awareness* and used.
   b. No datum of *experience* will be *distorted in, or denied to, awareness.*
   c. The outcomes of behavior in *experience* will be *available to awareness.*
   d. Hence any failure to achieve the maximum possible satisfaction, because of lack of data, will be corrected by this effective reality testing.
10. He will live with others in the maximum possible harmony, because of the rewarding character of reciprocal positive regard.

Comment. It should be evident that the term "fully functioning person" is synonymous with optimal psychological adjustment, optimal psychological maturity, complete congruence, complete openness to experience, complete extensionality, as these terms have been defined.

Since some of these terms sound somewhat static, as though such a person "had arrived," it should be pointed out that all the characteristics of such a person are *process* characteristics. The fully functioning person would be person-in-process, a person continually changing. Thus his specific behaviors cannot in any way be described in advance. The only statement which can be made is that the behaviors would be adequately adaptive to each new situation, and that the person would be continually in process of further self-actualization.

JOHN A. RYLE

For every organ and tissue, and in respect both of its structure and its function, there is a natural range of variability in any population studied and in the species as a whole. Within this range efficient performance and adaptation to common stresses may be recognized. The "normal," in biology and medicine, is better expressed in terms of this variability than as a hypothetical mean or standard.

Temporal variations (perhaps better described as "variants") in the individual, to allow of necessary continuing adaptations, must be distinguished from the species variations which establish "differences between man and man." Both have essential survival value. Adaptability depends on variability.

The study of human variability within the normal range is important (1) as a fundamental biological study; (2) as supplying necessary standards in medicine for the recognition of health and sickness and borderline states; and (3) because the extremes within the normal range of variability in respect of certain functions may help to explain certain innate resistances and predispositions to disease and to place the study of diathesis on a firmer footing.

Preoccupation with sick persons has generally detached the mind of the physician from those investigations of ostensibly healthy populations upon which alone a better understanding of normal variability can be based. Without this better understanding diagnostic precision and therapeutic judgment must be hampered. It is among the functions of those concerned with the advancement of social pathology and hygiology to establish, by their investigations of adequate population samples, acceptable standards of normal variability in man.

Studies of normal variations in the first four quinquennia of life should have special value, for in this formative period the early contributions for good or ill, of nutritional, educational, and other experience are discernible, and the manifold and complex stresses and hazards of adulthood have not yet affixed their mark. At this stage, too, the possibilities of improvement by a change of conditions are greater.

Observed variations must always be considered in relation to environment. Social environment has been shown to have striking effects on mortality and morbidity. It will also be shown to have its effects on physical, mental and emotional equipment and the predispositions to disease (or health) dependent on this equipment. True—for example, inherited—variations—for example, in height, weight, and longevity—may be given a plus or minus bias by environmental opportunity.

Some variations are measurable. Of such are certain external somatic characters, the pulse-rate, the body temperature, the haemoglobin, and the basal metabolic rate, all of which in the study of a group must be recorded under standard conditions and with respect to age and sex. Other variations are immeasurable. Of such are the size and functional state of the tonsils, the state of the thyroid gland, the palpability of the superficial lymph nodes, and certain postural characters. Critical studies of these in appropriate population samples, with a view to determining the incidence of departures from the apparently healthy state, or the relative frequency of states assessed as "healthy," "unhealthy," and "borderline"—given that due attention is also paid to clinical history and the social and nutritional opportunity of the individuals composing the sample—should in time assist clinical judgment and throw much needed light upon certain problems in aetiology. Correlated variations (such as physical and mental associations of duodenal ulcer, eye colour and psoriasis, physical habitus and some mental disorders, and the physique and temperament which accompany vigour, large appetite, and freedom from infection and neurosis in early life but seem later to predispose to heaviness and hyperpiesia) have long had their interest for the physician. They await a more critical investigation.

Variations, increased as they probably are in kind and degree by the racial crossings and other chances of our social evolution, are a fitting subject of inquiry for all students of man, and not least for the physician. In their wider ranges, while consistent with "ordinary well-being," they may predispose to exceptional vigour or a high immunity to infections; they may also invite disease. In their more frequent forms and more moderate degrees, while setting no certain barrier to outstanding performance or to sickness (for these depend partly on the quantity of external influence), they are the essence of biological "normality" and the companions of adaptability and health.

The term health (= "wholeness"), as affecting the individual, should embrace (besides those of sensory well-being and structural integrity) ideas of balance and adaptability; these in turn reflect the coordinated activity of component parts each functioning within its normal range.

Health and disease know no sharp boundary. They could only do so if it were possible for biology to adopt the dictionary definition of normality. But variability, both in time and in the species, is one of the most distinctive and necessary attributes of life, which thus admits no constant and no norm.

From "The Meaning of Normal" (*Lancet*, Vol. 252, 1947), pp. 4–5.

EDWARD JOSEPH SHOBEN, JR.

This model of integrative adjustment as characterized by self-control, personal responsibility, social responsibility, democratic social interest, and ideals must be regarded only in the most tentative fashion. Nevertheless, it does seem to take into account some realistic considerations. It avoids the impossible conception of the normal person as one who is always happy, free from conflict, and without problems. Rather, it suggests that he may often fall short of his ideals; and because of ignorance, the limitations under which an individual lives in a complex world, or the strength of immediate pressures, he may sometimes behave in ways that prove to be short-sighted or self-defeating. Consequently, he knows something of the experience of guilt at times, and because he tries to be fully aware of the risks he takes, he can hardly be entirely free from fear and worry. On the other hand, a person who is congruent to the model is likely to be one who enjoys a relatively consistent and high degree of self-respect and who elicits a predominantly positive and warm reaction from others. Moreover, it is such a person who seems to learn wisdom rather than hostile bitterness or pathologically frightened withdrawal from whatever disappointments or suffering may be his lot. Guilt, for example, becomes a challenge to his honesty, especially with himself but also with others; and it signalizes for him the desirability of modifying his behavior, of greater effort to live up to his ideals, rather than the need to defend himself by such mechanisms as rationalization or projection. Finally, the model permits a wide variation in the actual behaviors in which normal people may engage and even makes allowance for a wide range of disagreements among them. Integrative adjustment does not consist in the individual's fitting a preconceived behavioral mold. It may well consist in the degree to which his efforts fulfill the symbolic and social potentialities that are distinctively human.

From "Toward a Concept of the Normal Personality" (*The American Psychologist,* Vol. 12, 1957), pp. 183–189.

THOMAS S. SZASZ

Mental Illness as a Name for Problems in Living.

The term "mental illness" is widely used to describe something which is very different than a disease of the brain. Many people today take it for granted that living is an arduous process. Its hardship for modern man, moreover, derives not so much from a struggle for biological survival as from the stresses and strains inherent in the social intercourse of complex human personalities. In this context, the notion of mental illness is used to identify or describe some feature of an individual's so-called personality. Mental illness —as a deformity of the personality, so to speak—is then regarded as the *cause* of the human disharmony. It is implicit in this view that social intercourse between people is regarded as something *inherently harmonious*, its disturbance being due solely to the presence of "mental illness" in many people. This is obviously fallacious reasoning, for it makes the abstraction "mental illness" into a *cause*, even though this abstraction was created in the first place to serve only as a shorthand expression for certain types of human behavior. It now becomes necessary to ask: "What kinds of behavior are regarded as indicative of mental illness, and by whom?"

The concept of illness, whether bodily or mental, implies *deviation from some clearly defined norm*. In the case of physical illness, the norm is the structural and functional integrity of the human body. Thus, although the desirability of physical health, as such, is an ethical value, what health *is* can be stated in anatomical and physiological terms. What is the norm deviation from which is regarded as mental illness? This question cannot be easily answered. But whatever this norm might be, we can be certain of only one thing: namely, that it is a norm that must be stated in terms of *psycho-social*, *ethical*, and *legal* concepts. For example, notions such as "excessive repression" or "acting out an unconscious impulse" illustrate the use of psychological concepts for judging (so-called) mental health and illness. The idea that chronic hostility, vengefulness, or divorce are indicative of mental illness would be illustrations of the use of ethical norms (that is, the desirability of love, kindness, and a stable marriage relationship). Finally, the widespread psychiatric opinion that only a mentally ill person would commit homicide illustrates the use of a legal concept as a norm of mental health. The norm from which deviation is measured whenever one speaks of a mental illness is a *psycho-social and ethical one*. Yet, the remedy is sought in terms of *medical* measures which—it is hoped and assumed—are free from wide differences of ethical value. The definition of the disorder and the terms in which its remedy are sought are therefore at serious odds with one another. The practical significance of this covert conflict between the alleged nature of the defect and the remedy can hardly be exaggerated.

Having identified the norms used to measure deviations in cases of mental illness, we will now turn to the question: "Who defines the norms and hence the deviation?" Two basic answers may be offered: (a) It may be the person himself (that is, the patient) who decides that he deviates from a norm. For example, an artist may believe that he suffers from a work inhibition; and he may implement this conclusion by seeking help *for* himself from a psychotherapist. (b) It may be someone other than the patient who decides that the latter is deviant (for example, relatives, physicians, legal authorities, society generally, and so forth). In such a case a psychiatrist may be hired by others to do something *to* the patient in order to correct the deviation.

From "The Myth of Mental Illness" (*The American Psychologist*, Vol. 15, 1960), p. 113.

ROGER J. WILLIAMS

The subject of *variation* with which we are predominantly concerned is, therefore, an old one, and it might be supposed that there would be little new to say. It is our opinion, however, based upon the data presented in this volume, that variability is vastly more important in the biological sciences and in medicine than it is currently assumed to be. And, because of what a study of variability in nutritional needs can do for medicine, such study deserves ten times more direct attention in terms of research time and effort than it is now receiving. The reader must be left to judge for himself whether these opinions are based upon a reasonable interpretation of the facts.

A commonly accepted point of view in the field of biology and related disciplines—physiology, biochemistry, psychology—and in the applied fields of medicine, psychiatry, and social relations appears to be that humanity can be divided into two groups: (1) the vast majority possess attributes which are within the normal range; (2) a small minority possess attributes far enough out of line so that they should be considered deviates. This point of view is more often tacitly assumed than expressed and is illustrated by the fact that when an obstetrician can inform a mother that her new-born child is "normal in every way," everyone is happy; but if the infant must be pronounced abnormal, everyone concerned is distressed.

The most commonly accepted line of demarcation between normal and abnormal in biological work is the 95 per cent level.[4, 5] That is, all values lying outside those possessed by 95 per cent of the population may be regarded as deviant values, and any individual who possesses such deviant values may be regarded as a deviate.

If we consider the possibility that among the numerous measurable attributes that human beings possess there may be many which are not mathematically correlated, we are confronted with an idea which is opposed to the basic dichotomy of normal and abnormal mentioned above. If 0.95 of the population is normal with respect to one measurable item, only 0.902 (0.95^2) would be normal with respect to two measurable items and 0.60 (0.95^{10}) and 0.0059 (0.95^{100}), respectively, would be normal with regard to 10 and 100 uncorrelated items.

The existence in every human being of a vast array of attributes which are potentially measurable (whether by present methods or not), and probably often uncorrelated mathematically, makes quite tenable the hypothesis that *practically every human being is a deviate in some respects.* Some deviations are, of course, more marked and some more important than others. If this hypothesis is valid, new-born children cannot validly be considered as belonging in either one of two groups, normal and abnormal. Substantially all of them are in a sense "abnormal." In the majority, the "abnormalities" may be well enough concealed so that they are not revealed by clinical examination, though they may easily have an important bearing upon the susceptibility of the individual child to disease later in life.

Though this hypothesis may appear perfectly plausible, it has not been tested by experiment so far as we have been able to ascertain. Individual human beings have never been measured in enough different ways in which norms are established so that the data are conclusive.

The question of the validity of this hypothesis is not an academic one. As will be made clear in the later pages of this volume, there is a strong probability that the postulated deviations existing in almost everyone are closely related to the fact that practically every individual born into this world sooner or later gets into distinctive health difficulties of one kind or another. And the number of kinds of such difficulties, like the number of possible deviations, is legion.

To make this discussion more concrete, let us consider briefly some studies on groups of "normal" young men made in our laboratories which tend to support the hypothesis outlined above.[6] In one study five samples (sometimes six) of blood were drawn from each of eleven individuals at weekly intervals under basal conditions; by the use of conventional clinical methods, the samples were carefully analyzed for sugar, lactic acid, urea, creatinine, uric acid, inorganic phosphorus, amylase, lipase, acid phosphatase, alkaline phosphatase, and acetylcholinesterase. In another related investigation a similar group of nine normal young men (eight of whom were individuals included in the other study) was studied by analyzing repeated samples of blood plasma, blood cells, urine, and saliva, for calcium, magnesium, sodium, and potassium and by repeated tests on the same individuals of their taste thresholds for the chlorides of calcium, magnesium, sodium and potassium.

Although for certain items applicable to certain individuals the quantitative values obtained appeared to be a random assortment of values within the "normal" range, this randomness was not universal. One individual, for example, showed consistently a low blood sugar; every one of six determinations yielded values below a commonly accepted normal range. Another individual had high blood uric acid; every value was above the accepted range. A third individual exhibited serum amylase values below the accepted "normal" range. A fourth individual exhibited high alkaline phosphatase values; every one was above the accepted normal range. A fifth individual exhibited high acetylcholinesterase values, every one of which was well above the accepted normal range.

Not only did individuals exhibit high or low blood values, but other distinctive characteristics also appeared in the individual data. One individual, for example, showed a 2-fold spread in his blood creatinine values, with general lack of agreement between values. In contrast, the majority of the individuals showed high consistency with respect to blood creatinine values; one individual yielded *identical* values in six determinations. One individual showed relatively high blood values for sugar, creatinine, urea, uric acid and lactic acid and no low values for any of the items studied. Another individual showed relatively low blood values for acetylcholinesterase, sugar, phosphorus, lipase, and acid phosphatase but a relatively high value for urea.

Among the distinctive differences observed in the mineral analysis study were: (1) nearly a 6-fold difference between two individuals (no overlapping in values) in urinary calcium excretion, (2) nearly a 3-fold variation in plasma magnesium, (3) over a 30 per cent difference (no overlapping of values) in the sodium content of blood cells, (4) a 4-fold variation (with no overlapping values in 21 to 25 samples, respectively) in salivary sodium, (5) a 5-fold variation in salivary magnesium with no overlapping values in 7 to 15 samples, (6) taste threshold values that often differed consistently from individual to individual over a 20-fold range.

It was noted that not only were certain blood values above or below the "normal" range for specific individuals but also that, regardless of the positions in the ranges, each individual exhibited a distinctive pattern. Abundant evidence was obtained from these two studies alone to suggest the importance of studying biochemical individuality and its relationship to susceptibility to a host of diseases. The distinctiveness of these studies lies in the fact that repeated samples from the same well individuals, collected under basal conditions, were analyzed for many different constituents. This procedure is not often followed.

The whole problem of human health and welfare is vastly different if the population, instead of being composed mostly of individuals with normal attributes, is made up of individuals all of whom possess unusual attributes—individuals who deviate from the normal range in several of the numerous possible particulars.

From *Biochemical Individuality* (New York: John Wiley & Sons, Inc., 1956), pp. 2–5.

References

PREFACE

FALSTEIN, EUGENE I., FEINSTEIN, SHERMAN C., OFFER, DANIEL, & FINE, PAUL. Group dynamics: inpatient adolescents engage in an outbreak of vandalism. A.M.A. *Arch. gen. Psychiat.*, 1963, 9, 32–43.

FINE, PAUL, & OFFER, DANIEL. Periodic outbursts of anti-social behavior among adolescents in a general psychiatric hospital. A.M.A. *Arch. gen. Psychiat.*, 1965, **13**, 240–254.

IONESCO, EUGENE. *Rhinoceros* (D. PRONSE, Trans.). New York: Grove Press, 1960.

MARCUS, DAVID, OFFER, DANIEL, BLATT, SIDNEY, & GRATCH, GERALD. A comparison of communication patterns in the families of disturbed and non-disturbed adolescents. Paper read at Chicago Soc. Adol. Psychiat., April 13, 1965.

OFFER, DANIEL, & BARGLOW, PETER. Adolescent and young adult self-mutilation incidents in a general psychiatric hospital. A.M.A. *Arch. gen. Psychiat.*, 1960, **3**, 194–204.

OFFER, DANIEL, & SABSHIN, MELVIN. The psychiatrist and the normal adolescent. A.M.A. *Arch. gen. Psychiat.*, 1963, 9, 427–432.

OFFER, DANIEL, SABSHIN, MELVIN, & MARCUS, DAVID. Clinical evaluations of "normal" adolescents. *Amer. J. Psychiat.*, 1965, 9, 864–872.

STRAUSS, ANSELM, SCHATZMAN, LEONARD, BUCHER, RUE, EHRLICH, DANUTA, & SABSHIN, MELVIN. *Psychiatric ideologies and institutions.* New York: The Free Press of Glencoe, 1964.

CHAPTER 1

ARIETI, SILVANO (Ed.). *American handbook of psychiatry.* New York: Basic Books, 1959.

BARTON, WALTER E. Viewpoint of a clinician. In MARIE JAHODA (Ed.), *Current concepts of positive mental health.* New York: Basic Books, 1959.

BERNARD, CLAUDE. *An introduction to the study of experimental medicine* [1865]. New York: Macmillan, 1927.

BURROWS, WILLIAM. *Textbook of Microbiology.* Philadelphia: Saunders, 1954.

CANNON, WALTER B. *Bodily changes in pain, hunger, fear and rage.* An account of recent researches into the function of emotional excitement. New York: Appleton, 1929.

CASSEL, J., PATRICK, R., & JENKINS, D. Epidemiological analysis of the health implications of culture change: a conceptual model. *Ann. N.Y. Acad. Sci.*, 1960, **84**, 238.

DUNBAR, FLANDERS. *Psychiatry in Medical Specialties.* New York: The Blakiston Division, 1959.

DUNHAM, H. WARREN. Community psychiatry: the newest therapeutic bandwagon. *A.M.A. Arch. gen. Psychiat.*, 1965, **12**, 303–314.

ENGEL, GEORGE. Homeostasis, behavioral adjustment and the concept of health and disease. In ROY R. GRINKER (Ed.), *Mid-century psychiatry.* Springfield, Ill.: Charles C Thomas, 1953.

ENGEL, GEORGE. A unified concept of health and disease. *Perspect. Biol. & Med.*, 1960, **3**, (4), 459.

ENGEL, GEORGE. Is grief a disease? *Psychosom. Med.*, 1961, **23** (1), 18.

ENGEL, GEORGE. *Psychological development in health and illness.* Philadelphia: Saunders, 1962.

FRANK, JEROME D. *Persuasion and healing.* Baltimore: Johns Hopkins University Press, 1961. P. 35.

GREGORY, IAN. *Psychiatry: biological and social.* Philadelphia: Saunders, 1961.

HENDERSON, SIR DAVID K., & GILLESPIE, R. D. A *textbook of psychiatry.* New York: Oxford University Press, 1950.

JERVIS, GEORGE A. Phenylpyruvic oligophrenia (Phenylketonuria). *Assn. Res. nerv. ment. Dis. Proc.*, 1953, **33**, 259.

KÖLLE, KURT. *Psychiatrie.* Stuttgart: G. Thième, 1961. Pp. 43–45.

LAUGHLIN, HENRY P. *The neuroses in clinical practice.* Philadelphia: W. B. Saunders, 1956. Pp. 1–4.

LEVINE, MAURICE. *Psychotherapy in medical practice.* New York: Macmillan, 1942.

LEWIS, AUBREY. Between guesswork and certainty in psychiatry. *Lancet*, 1958, **1**, 170, 227.

MEYER-GROSS, W., SLATER, E., & ROTH, M. *Clinical psychiatry.* Baltimore: Williams & Wilkins, 1960.

NATHANSON, MORTON. Philosophische grundfragen der psychiatrie: 1. Philosophie and psychiatrie. In *Psychiatrie der gegenwart.* Berlin: Springer Verlag, 1963.

NOYES, ARTHUR P., & KOLB, LAWRENCE C. *Modern clinical psychiatry.* Philadelphia: W. B. Saunders, 1958. P. 662.

REDLICH, FREDRICK C. The concept of health in psychiatry. In ALEXANDER H. LEIGHTON, JOHN A. CLAUSSEN, & ROBERT N. WILSON (Eds.), *Explorations in social psychiatry.* New York: Basic Books, 1957.

RUFF, G. E., & LEVY, E. S. Psychiatric evaluation of candidates for space flights. *Amer. J. Psychiat.*, 1959, **116**, 5.

RUFF, G. E., & KORCHIN, S. J. Psychological response of the Mercury astronauts to stress. Paper presented at a Symposium on "Human Reactions to Threat of Impending Disaster" at the general meeting of American Association for the Advancement of Science, December 28, 1962.

RYLE, J. A. The meaning of normal. *Lancet*, 1947, **1** (1), 4–5.

SABSHIN, MELVIN. Theoretical models in community and social psychiatry. In *Symposium on community psychiatry: what it is and what it is not.* Madison: University of Wisconsin Press, 1966.

STRAUS, ERWIN W. Phenomenology: pure and applied. Lecture given at meeting in Lexington, Ky., May 1963.

STRAUS, ERWIN W. *Phenomenological Psychology.* New York: Basic Books, 1966.

SZASZ, THOMAS S. Some observations on the relationship between psychiatry and the law. *Arch. Neurol. Psychiat.*, 1956, **75**, 297.

Szasz, Thomas S. The myth of mental illness. *Amer. Psychol.*, 1960, **15** (2), 113–118.

Szasz, Thomas S. *The myth of mental illness.* New York: Harper, 1961. (a)

Szasz, Thomas S. The uses of naming and the origin of the myth of mental illness. *Amer. Psychol.*, 1961, **16** (2), 59–65. (b)

Szasz, Thomas S. Some implications for law of the "myth of mental illness." Paper delivered at the Illinois Psychiat. Soc. meeting, March 1963.

Whitehorn, John C. Goals of psychotherapy. In E. A. Rubinstein & Morris B. Parloff (Eds.), *Research in psychotherapy.* Washington: Amer. Psychol. Ass., 1959.

Williams, R. J., & Siegel, F. L. Propetology, a new branch of medical science. *Amer. J. Med.*, 1961, **31**, 3.

CHAPTER 2

Ackerman, Nathan W. Goals in therapy: A symposium. *Amer. J. Psychol.*, 1956, **16**, 9–14.

Ackerman, Nathan W. *The psychodynamics of family life.* New York: Basic Books, 1958.

Adler, Alfred. *Social interest: Challenge to mankind.* New York: G. P. Putnam & Sons, 1939.

Alexander, Franz. *Fundamentals of psychoanalysis.* New York: Norton, 1948. P. 194.

Ansbacher, Hans L., & Ansbacher, Rowena R. (Eds.). *The individual psychology of Alfred Adler.* New York: Basic Books, Inc., 1956. Pp. 102, 446.

Darrah, L. W. The difficulties of being normal. *J. nerv. ment. Dis.*, 1939, **90**, 730–737.

Eissler, Kurt R. The effect of the structure of the ego on psychoanalytic technique. *J. Amer. psychoanal. Ass.*, 1953, **1** (1), 194.

Eissler, Kurt R. The efficient soldier. In Warner Muensterburger & Sidney Axelrod (Eds.), *The psychoanalytic study of society.* New York: International Universities Press, 1960.

Erikson, Erik H. *Childhood and society.* New York: Norton, 1950.

ERICKSON, ERIK H. The problem of ego identity. *J. Amer. Psa. Ass.*, 1956 (4), 56–121.

FORDHAM, MICHAEL. Ego, self and mental health. *Brit. J. Med. Psychiat.*, 1960, **33**, 237.

FREUD, SIGMUND. Analysis terminable and interminable (1937). In Vol. 5 of JAMES STRACHEY (Trans.), *Collected papers of Sigmund Freud.* New York: Basic Books, Inc., 1959.

FREUD, SIGMUND. *Civilization and its discontents* (1930). In Vol. 21 of Standard ed. JAMES STRACHEY (Trans.). London: Hogarth Press, 1961.

FREUD, SIGMUND. *Psychopathology of everyday life* (1901). Vol. 6 of Standard ed., JAMES STRACHEY (Trans.). London: Hogarth Press, 1961.

FREUD, SIGMUND. *Three essays on the theory of sexuality* (1905). New York: Basic Books, 1962.

FREUD, SIGMUND. *The interpretation of dreams* (1900). Standard ed., JAMES STRACHEY (Trans.). London: Hogarth Press, 1961.

FROMM, ERICH. *The sane society.* New York: Rinehart, 1955.

FROMM-REICHMAN, FRIEDA. Remarks on the philosophy of mental disorder. *Psychiatry*, 1946, **19**, 293.

GITELSON, MAXWELL. The analysis of the "normal" candidate. *Int. J. Psychoanal.*, 1954, **35**, 174.

GLOVER, EDWARD. Medico-psychological aspects of normality. In his *On the early development of mind.* New York: International Universities Press, 1956.

GROTJAHN, MARTIN. Trends in contemporary psychotherapy and the future of mental health. *Brit. J. med. Psychol.*, 1960, **33**, 312.

HARMS, ERNEST. Carl Gustav Jung. *Amer. J. Psychiat.*, 1962, **118**, 728–732.

HARTMANN, HEINZ. Psychoanalysis and the concept of health. *Int. J. Psychoanal.*, 1939, **20**, 308.

HARTMANN, HEINZ. Towards a concept of mental health. *Brit. J. Med. Psychol.*, 1960, **33**, 243–248.

JONES, ERNEST. The concept of the normal mind. In S. D. SCHMALHAUSEN, (Ed.), *Our neurotic change.* New York: Farrar & Rinehart, 1931.

JONES, ERNEST. The concept of a normal mind. In ERNEST JONES,

Papers on psychoanalysis. Baltimore, Md.: Williams & Wilkins, 1948.

JONES, ERNEST. Cited in MARTIN BIRNBACH, *Neo-Freudian social philosophy.* Stanford, Calif.: Stanford University Press, 1961. P. 7.

JUNG, CARL G., *Basic writings of Carl G. Jung.* V. STAUB DE LASZIO (Ed.). New York: Modern Library, 1959, pp. 260–261.

KLEIN, MELANIE. On mental health. *Brit. J. Med. Psychol.*, 1960, **33**, 237–241.

KUBIE, LAWRENCE S. The distortion of the symbolic process in neurosis and psychosis. *J. Amer. Psychoanal. Ass.*, 1953, **1** (1).

KUBIE, LAWRENCE S. The fundamental nature of the distinction between normality and neurosis. *Psychoanal. Quart.*, 1954, **23**, 167.

KUBIE, LAWRENCE S. *Neurotic distortions of the creative process.* Lawrence, Kansas: University of Kansas Press, 1958. P. 20.

MENNINGER, KARL. *The human mind.* (3rd ed.) New York: Knopf, 1945.

MICHAELS, JOSEPH J. Character structure and character disorders. In SILVANO ARIETI (Ed.), *American handbook of psychiatry.* New York: Basic Books, 1959.

MONEY-KYRLE, ROGER E. Psychoanalysis and ethics. In MELANIE KLEIN, PAULA HEIMANN, & ROGER E. MONEY-KYRLE (Eds.), *New directions in psychoanalysis.* New York: Basic Books, 1957.

RANK, OTTO. *The artist and other contributions to the psychoanalysis of poetical creation.* (4th enlarged ed.) Leipzig: Internationaler Psychoanalytischer Verlag, 1925.

RANK, OTTO. *Art and artist.* New York: Knopf, 1932. P. 371. Cited in JESSIE TAFT, *Otto Rank.* New York: Julian Press, 1958. P. 283.

RAPAPORT, DAVID. The structure of psychoanalytic theory. *Psychological issues.* Vol. 11, No. 2. New York: International Universities Press, 1960.

REIDER, NORMAN. The concept of normality. *Psychoanal. Quart.*, 1950, **19**, 43.

SAPIRSTEIN, MILTON R. *Emotional security.* New York: Crown Publishers, 1948. P. 86.

SAUL, LEON J. *Emotional maturity*. Philadelphia: J. B. Lippincott Co., 1960. P. 343.

STÄRKE, AUGUST. Psychoanalysis and psychiatry. *Int. J. Psychoanal.*, 1921, **3**, 36.

THOMPSON, CLARA. *Psychoanalysis: evolution and development.* New York: Grove Press, 1957. P. 177.

CHAPTER 3

American Psychological Association. *Directory*. E. S. REED (Ed.). Washington: Author, 1963.

AMES, LOUISE B., LEARNED, J., METRAUX, R. W., & WALKER, R. N. *Child Rorschach responses*. New York: Paul B. Hoeber, 1952.

BECK, SAMUEL J. *Rorschach test*. Vol. 1. *Basic processes*. New York: Grune & Stratton, 1944.

BORING, EDWIN. *A history of experimental psychology*. New York: Appleton-Century-Crofts, 1950. Pp. 476–477.

BUHLER, CHARLOTTE B. Theoretical observations about life's basic tendencies. *Amer. J. Psychother.*, 1959, **13** (3), 561–581.

CATTELL, RAYMOND B. *Descriptions and measurement of personality*. Yonkers, N.Y.: World Books, 1946.

ENGEL, MARY. Some parameters of the psychological evaluation of children. *A.M.A. Arch. gen. Psychiat.* 1960, **2**, 6.

FRIEDES, D. Toward the elimination of the concept of normality. *J. consult. Psychol.*, 1960, **24**, 128–133.

GALTON, FRANCIS. *Hereditary genius* (1869). New York: Horizon Press, 1952.

GOLDSTEIN, KURT. *The organism*. New York: American Book Co., 1939.

HALL, CALVIN S., & LINDZEY, GARDNER. *Theories of personality.* New York: Wiley, 1957.

HATHAWAY, STARKE R., & MONACHESI, ELIO D. *Adolescent personality and behavior: MMPI patterns of normal, delinquent, dropout, and other outcomes.* Minneapolis: University of Minnesota Press, 1963.

HEATH, HELEN A., & OKEN, DONALD. The qualification of "response" to experimental stimuli. *Psychosom. Med.*, 1965, 27 (5), 457–472.

JAHODA, MARIE. *Current concepts of positive mental health.* New York: Basic Books, 1959. P. 99.

JAHODA, MARIE. Towards a social psychology of mental health. In M. J. E. SENN (Ed.), *Symposium on the healthy personality.* New York: Josiah Macy Foundation, 1950.

JAHODA, MARIE. Towards a social psychology of mental health. In ARNOLD M. ROSE (Ed.), *Mental health and mental disorder.* New York: Norton, 1955.

KOCH, H. L. Attitudes of young children towards their peers as related to certain characteristics of their siblings. *Psychol. Monogr.*, 1956, **70**, 19.

KORMAN, M. The concept of normality. *J. consult. Psychol.*, 1961, **25**, 267–269.

LACEY, J. I. The evaluation of autonomic responses: Toward a general solution. *Ann. N.Y. Acad. Sci.*, 1956, **67**, 123.

MASLOW, ABRAHAM H. *Motivation and personality.* New York: Harper & Bros., 1954.

MASLOW, ABRAHAM H., & MITTELMANN, BELA. *Principles of abnormal psychology.* New York: Harper & Bros., 1951.

MEEHL, PAUL E. *Clinical versus statistical prediction.* Minneapolis: University of Minnesota Press, 1954.

MURPHY, LOIS B., & COLLABORATORS. *The widening world of childhood.* New York: Basic Books, 1962.

ROGERS, CARL R. A theory of therapy, personality and interpersonal relationships, as developed in client-centered framework. In Vol. 3 of SIGMUND KOCH (Ed.), *Psychology: a study of a science.* New York: McGraw-Hill, 1959.

SARGENT, HELEN D., & MAYMAN, MARTIN. Clinical psychology. In SILVANO ARIETI (Ed.), *American handbook of psychiatry.* Vol. 2. New York: Basic Books, 1959. P. 1722.

SCHAFER, ROY. *Psychoanalytic interpretation in Rorschach testing.* New York: Grune & Stratton, 1954.

SHOBEN, E. J., Jr. Towards a concept of the normal personality. *Amer. Psychol.*, 1957, **12**, 183–189.

SMITH, M. BREWSTER. Research strategies towards a conception of positive mental health. *Amer. Psychol.*, 1959, **14**, 673–681.

SMITH, M. BREWSTER. Mental health reconsidered: a special case

of the problem of values in psychology. *Amer. Psychol.*, 1961, **16**, 299–306.
SYMONDS, PERCIVAL M. *Adolescent fantasy.* New York: Columbia University Press, 1949.
THURSTONE, L. L. *Multiple-factor analysis: a development and expansion of the vectors of the mind.* Chicago: University of Chicago Press, 1947.
WILDER, JOSEPH. Modern psychophysiology and the law of initial values. *Amer. J. Psychother.*, 1958, **12**, 199.

CHAPTER 4

BECKER, HOWARD S. *Outsiders, studies in the sociology of deviance.* Glencoe, Ill.: Free Press of Glencoe, 1963.
BENEDICT, RUTH. Anthropology and the abnormal. *J. genet. Psychol.*, 1934, **10**, 59. (a)
BENEDICT, RUTH. *Patterns of culture.* Boston: Houghton Mifflin, 1934. (b)
BUCHER, RUE. Personal communication. 1963.
COHEN, ALBERT K. The study of social disorganization and deviant behavior. In ROBERT K. MERTON, LEONARD BLOOM, & LEONARD S. COTTRELL, JR. (Eds.), *Sociology today.* New York: Basic Books, 1959.
COSER, L. A. Some functions of deviant behavior and normative flexibility. *Amer. J. Sociol.*, 1962, **68** (2), 172–181.
DEVEREUX, GEORGE. Normal and abnormal: the key problem of psychiatric anthropology. In J. B. CASAGRANDE & THOMAS GLADWIN (Eds.), *Some uses of anthropology: theoretical and applied.* Anthropological Society of Washington, 1956. P. 23.
DUBOIS, CORA. *The people of Alor.* Minneapolis: University of Minnesota Press, 1944.
ERIKSON, K. T. Social margins: some notes on the sociology of deviants. Paper read at the 55th annual convention of the Amer. Sociological Ass., New York, 1960.
GOFFMAN, ERVING. *Asylums.* New York: Doubleday Anchor Books, 1961.
HERSKOVITS, MELVILLE. In FRANCIS L. K. HSU (Ed.), *Aspects of*

culture and personality. New York: Abelard-Schuman, 1954. P. 279.

Hsu, Francis L. K. (Ed.) *Psychological anthropology: Approaches to culture and personality.* Homewood, Ill.: Dorsey Press, 1961.

Hsu, Francis L. K. Personal communication. 1962.

Kardiner, Abram. *The individual and his society.* With a foreword and two ethnological reports by Ralph Linton. New York: Columbia University Press, 1939.

Kardiner, Abram. With the collaboration of Linton, Ralph, DuBois, Cora, & West, J. *The psychological frontiers of society.* New York: Columbia University Press, 1945.

Linton, Ralph. *Culture and mental disorders.* Springfield, Ill.: Charles C Thomas, 1956. P. 637.

Merton, Robert K. *Social theory and social structure.* Glencoe, Ill.: Free Press of Glencoe, 1949. Pp. 125–149.

Moore, W. E. Predicting discontinuities in social change. *Amer. Soc. Rev.*, 1964, **29**, 3.

Parsons, Talcott. Definitions of health and illness in the light of American values and social structure. In E. Gartley Jaco (Ed.), *Patients, physicians, and illness.* Glencoe, Ill.: Free Press of Glencoe, 1958. P. 176.

Parsons, Talcott. An approach to psychological theory in terms of the theory of action. In Vol. 3 of S. Koch (Ed.), *Psychology: a study of a science.* New York: McGraw-Hill, 1959, p. 643.

Parsons, Talcott. *Social structure and personality.* Glencoe, Ill.: Free Press of Glencoe, 1964.

Singer, M. A survey of culture and personality theory and research. In Bernard Kaplan (Ed.), *Studying personality cross culturally.* Evanston, Ill.: Row, Peterson & Co., 1961.

Srole, Leo, Langer; T. S., Michael, S. T., Opler, Marvin K., & Rennie, Thomas A. C. *Mental health in the metropolis.* New York: McGraw-Hill, 1963.

Stanton, Alfred H., & Schwartz, Morris S. *The mental hospital.* New York: Basic Books, 1954.

Straus, Erwin W. Phenomenology: pure and applied. Lecture given in Lexington, Ky., May 1963.

Strauss, Anselm, Schatzman, Leonard, Bucher, Rue, Ehrlich,

Danuta, & Sabshin, Melvin. *Psychiatric ideologies and institutions.* Glencoe, Ill.: Free Press of Glencoe, 1964.
Wallace, A. F. C. Mental illness, biology, and culture. In Francis L. K. Hsu (Ed.), *Psychological anthropology: approaches to culture and personality.* Homewood, Ill.: Dorsey Press, 1961.
Wegrocki, H. J. A critique of cultural and statistical concepts of abnormality. *J. abnorm. soc. Psychol.,* 1939, **34**, 166.
Zald, M. N. Personal communication. 1964.

CHAPTER 5

Abood, L. G. Some chemical concepts of mental health and disease. In *The effect of pharmacologic agents on the nervous system.* Vol. 37. Proceedings of the Association for Research in Nervous and Mental Disease. Baltimore: Williams & Wilkins, 1959.
Child, C. M. *Physiological foundations of behavior.* New York: Henry Holt & Co., 1924. P. 222.
Coghill, G. E. As described by C. Judson Herrick in his book *George Ellett Coghill, naturalist and philosopher.* Chicago: University of Chicago Press, 1949.
Darwin, Charles. *The origin of species* (1859). London: Everyman's Library, 1947. P. 118.
Dobzhansky, Theodosius. *Mankind evolving.* New Haven: Yale University Press, 1962. P. 126.
Feibleman, J. K. Ecological factors in human maladaption. *Amer. J. Psychiat.,* 1961, **118**, No. 2.
Freedman, L., & Roe, Anne. Evolution and human behavior. In Anne Roe & George Gaylord Simpson (Eds.), *Behavior and evolution.* New Haven: Yale University Press, 1958. P. 461.
Gerard, R. W., & Emerson, A. E. Extrapolations from the biological to the social. *Science,* 1945, **101**, 2632.
Herrick, C. Judson. *The evolution of human nature.* Austin: University of Texas Press, 1956. Pp. 16, 21.
Kallmann, Franz J. The genetics of mental illness. In Silvano

ARIETI (Ed.), *American handbook of psychiatry*. New York: Basic Books, 1959.

LASHLEY, K. S. Structure variation in the nervous system in relation to behavior. *Psychol. Rev.*, 1947, **54**, 333–334.

LENZ, W. *Medizinische genetik*. Stuttgart: G. Thième, 1961.

LOEB, L. *The biological basis of individuality*. Baltimore: Charles C Thomas, 1945. P. 637.

NOVIKOFF, A. B. The concept of integrative levels and biology. *Science*, 1945, **101**, 2618.

ROSENTHAL, DAVID (Ed.), *The Genain quadruplets*. New York: Basic Books, 1963.

VOGEL, F. Personal communication. 1963.

WILLIAMS, ROGER J. *Biochemical individuality*. New York: J. Wiley & Sons, 1956.

WILLIAMS, ROGER J. Normal young men. *Persp. Biol. Med.*, 1957, **1** (1), 97–104.

WILLIAMS, ROGER J. Chemical anthropology—an open door. *Amer. Scientist*, March 1958. Pp. 1–23.

WOLF, STEWART. Disease as a way of life: neural integration in systematic pathology. *Persp. Biol. Med.*, 1961, **4**, 288–305.

CHAPTER 6

BARTON, W. E. Viewpoint of a clinician. In MARIE JAHODA (Ed.), *Current concepts of positive mental health*. New York: Basic Books, 1959.

BENEDICT, RUTH. Anthropology and the abnormal. *J. genet. Psychol.*, 1934, 10, 59.

BUHLER, CHARLOTTE B. Theoretical observations about life's basic tendencies. *Amer. J. Psychother.*, 1959, 13 (3), 561–581.

CHILD, C. M. *Physiological foundations of behavior*. New York: Henry Holt and Co., 1924. P. 222.

COHEN, ALBERT K. The study of social disorganization and deviant behavior. In ROBERT K. MERTON, LEONARD BLOOM, & LEONARD S. COTTRELL, JR. (Eds.), *Sociology today*. New York: Basic Books, 1959.

DUBOIS, CORA. *The people of Alor*. Minneapolis: University of Minnesota Press, 1944.

DUNHAM, H. W. Community psychiatry: the newest therapeutic bandwagon. *A.M.A. Arch. gen. Psychiat.*, 1965, 12, 303–314.

EDWARDS, A. S. A theoretical and clinical study of so-called normality. *J. abnorm. soc. Psychol.*, 1935, 30, 279.

ERIKSON, ERIK H. Identity and the life cycle. *Psychological issues.* New York: International Universities Press, 1959.

FEIBLEMAN, J. K. Ecological factors in human maladaptation. *Amer. J. Psychiat.*, 1961, 118 (2).

FREEDMAN, L., & ROE, ANNE. Evolution and human behavior. In ANNE ROE & GEORGE GAYLORD SIMPSON (Eds.), *Behavior and evolution.* New Haven: Yale University Press, 1958. P. 461.

FREUD, SIGMUND. *Civilization and its discontents* (1930). In Vol. 21 of Standard ed. JAMES STRACHEY (Trans.). London: Hogarth Press, 1961.

GOLDSTEIN, KURT. *The organism.* New York: American Book Co., 1939.

GOLDSTEIN, KURT. Health as value. In ABRAHAM H. MASLOW (Ed.), *New knowledge in human values.* New York: Harper & Bros., 1959.

GRINKER, ROY R., SR. (Ed.). *Toward a unified theory of human behavior.* New York: Basic Books, 1956. P. 370.

GRINKER, ROY R., SR. Normality viewed as a system. *A.M.A. Arch. of gen. Psychiat.*, 1967, 17, 320–324.

GRAY, W., DUHL, F. J., & RIZZO, N. D. *General systems theory and psychiatry.* Boston: Little, Brown & Company, 1969.

HARTMANN, HEINZ. *Ego psychology and the problem of adaptation.* New York: International Universities Press, 1958.

HIRSCH, WALTER. Geistige und seelische stormungen im jugendalter. In *Die jugend von heute.* Berliner Landesausschuss für Gesundheitliche Volksbelehrung, 1962.

KALLMANN, FRANZ J. The genetics of mental illness. In SILVANO ARIETI (Ed.), *American Handbook of Psychiatry.* New York: Basic Books, 1959.

KALLMANN, FRANZ J. Genetic aspects of psychosis. In *The biology of mental health and disease: The Twenty-seventh Annual Conference of the Milbank Memorial Fund.* New York: P. Hoeber, Inc., 1952.

KARDINER, ABRAM. *The individual and his society.* With a foreword and two ethnological reports by RALPH LINTON. New York: Columbia University Press, 1939.

KARDINER, ABRAM. With the collaboration of RALPH LINTON, CORA DUBOIS, & J. WEST. *The psychological frontiers of society*. New York: Columbia University Press, 1945.

LINTON, RALPH. *Culture and mental disorders*. Springfield, Ill.: Charles C Thomas, 1956. P. 637.

LONDON, P. The sources of therapeutic morality. Columbia University *Forum*, 1962, 5 (3).

MASLOW, ABRAHAM M. *Motivation and personality*. New York: Harper & Bros., 1954.

MONEY-KYRLE, ROGER E. Psychoanalysis and ethics. In MELANIE KLEIN, PAULA HEIMANN, & ROGER E. MONEY-KYRLE (Eds.), *New directions in psychoanalysis*. New York: Basic Books, 1955.

PARSONS, TALCOTT. An approach to psychological theory in terms of the theory of action. In Vol. 3 of SIGMUND KOCH (Ed.), *Psychology: a study of a science*. New York: McGraw-Hill, 1959. P. 643.

ROGERS, CARL R. A theory of therapy, personality and interpersonal relationships, as developed in client-centered framework. In Vol. 3 of SIGMUND KOCH (Ed.), *Psychology: a study of a science*. New York: McGraw-Hill, 1959.

ROMANO, JOHN. Basic orientation and education of the medical student. *J. Amer. Med. Assn.*, 1950, *143*, 409.

RUESCH, JURGEN, & BATESON, GREGORY. *Communication: the social matrix of psychiatry*. New York: Norton, 1951. Pp. 69–71.

TROTTER, W. *Instincts of the herd in peace and war*. London: Fisher Unwin, 1916.

VON BERTALANFFY, L. *General system theory*. New York: George Braziller, 1968.

WOLFF, WERNER. *The threshold of the abnormal*. New York: Hermitage House, 1950. Pp. 6–81.

CHAPTER 7

ARISTOTLE. *The student's Oxford Aristotle*. W. D. Ross (Ed.), Vol. 5. *Ethics*. London: 1942.

BECK, A. T. Reliability of psychiatric diagnosis: 1. a critique of systematic studies. *Amer. J. Psychiat.* 1962, **119** (3), 210–216.

BECK, A. T., WARD, C. H., MENDELSON, M., MOCK, J. E., & ERBAUGH, J. K. Reliability of psychiatric diagnosis: 2. A study of consistency of clinical judgements and ratings. *Amer. J. Psychiat.*, 1962, **119** (4), 351–357.

BROMBERG, WALTER. *The mind of man: a history of psychotherapy and psychoanalysis.* New York: Harper Torchbooks, 1959. Pp. 52, 62.

DOSTOYEVSKY, FEODOR. *Notes from the underground.* A new translation with an afterword by A. R. MACANDREW. New York: New American Library of World Literature, 1961.

EISSLER, KURT R. *Leonardo da Vinci: psychoanalytic notes on the enigma.* New York: International Universities Press, 1962.

EISSLER, KURT R. *Goethe: a psychoanalytic study 1775–1776.* Vol. 1. Detroit: Wayne State University Press, 1963.

FREUD, SIGMUND. Dostoevsky and patricide (1928). In Vol. 5 of JAMES STRACHEY (Trans.), *Collected papers of Sigmund Freud.* New York: Basic Books, Inc., 1959.

FREUD, SIGMUND. *Leonardo da Vinci: a psychosexual study of an infantile reminiscence* (1910). A. A. BRILL (Trans.). New York: Dodd & Mead, 1932.

FROMM, ERICH. *The sane society.* New York: Rinehart & Co., 1960. P. 169.

GOETHE, JOHANN WOLFGANG VON. *Faust* (1831). J. F. L. RASCHEN (Trans.). Ithaca, N.Y.: Thrift Press, 1949. P. 27.

GRINKER, ROY R., SR. A dynamic story of the "homoclite." In JULES H. MASSERMAN (Ed.), *Science and Psychoanalysis.* New York: Grune & Stratton, 1963. P. 128.

GUTHRIE, W. K. C. *The Greek philosophers, from Thales to Aristotle.* New York: Harper Torchbooks, 1960.

HIPPOCRATES. On the sacred disease. In J. THATCHER (Ed.), *World great sciences in the original documents.* The Greek world, Vol. 2. Library of Orig. Docts. New York and Chicago: University Research Extension, 1907.

HOFFMAN, M. Psychiatry, nature and science. *Amer. J. Psychiat.*, 1960, **117**, 205.

JOWETT, B. See PLATO.

KRIS, ERNST. *Psychoanalytic exploration in art.* New York: International Universities Press, 1952.

KUBIE, LAWRENCE S. *Neurotic distortions of the creative process.* Lawrence, Kansas: University of Kansas Press, 1958. P. 20.

LONDON, P. The sources of therapeutic morality. *Columbia Univ. Forum,* 1962, **3**, 45–46.

MEERLOO, JOOST A. M. *Suicide and mass suicide.* New York: Grune & Stratton, 1962.

MORA, G. On the 400th anniversary of Johann Weyer's *De praestigiis daemonum*—its significance for today's psychiatry. *Amer. J. Psychiat.*, 1963, **120**, No. 5.

PHILLIPS, WILLIAM. (Ed.) *Art and psychoanalysis.* New York: Criterion Books, 1957.

PLATO. *The dialogues of Plato.* B. JOWETT (Trans.). Vol. 1. New York: Random House, 1937. Pp. 249, 257–258.

RANK, OTTO. *Art and artists.* New York: Knopf, 1932. P. 371. Cited in J. TAFT, *Otto Rank.*

REIK, THEODOR. *The haunting melody.* New York: Grove Press, 1960. P. 262.

ROSS, W. D. See ARISTOTLE.

STERBA, R. F. Therapeutic goal and present-day reality. *J. Hillside Hosp.*, 1960, **9**, 4.

SZASZ, THOMAS S. Some observations on the relationship between psychiatry and the law. *Arch. Neurol. Psychiat.*, 1956, **75**, 297.

SZASZ, THOMAS S. The uses of naming and the origin of the myth of mental illness. *Amer. Psychologist,* 1961, **16** (2), 59–65.

SZASZ, THOMAS S. Some implications for law of the "myth of mental illness." Paper delivered at the Illinois psychiat. soc. meeting, March 1963.

THATCHER, J. See HIPPOCRATES.

VEITH, I. Glimpses into the history of psychotherapy. In JULES H. MASSERMAN & J. C. MORENO (Eds.), *Progress in psychotherapy.* Vol. 3. New York: Grune & Stratton, 1958. P. 9.

WEBSTER'S NEW COLLEGIATE DICTIONARY. Springfield, Mass.: G. & C. Merriam Co., 1951.

WOLFF, R. P. Personal communication. 1963.

ZILBOORG, GREGORY, & HENRY, GEORGE W. A *history of medical psychology.* New York: W. W. Norton, 1941. P. 200.

CHAPTER 8

BAITTLE, B., & OFFER, D. On the nature of adolescent rebellion. In S. C. FEINSTEIN, P. GIOVACCHINI, & A. MILLER (Eds.), *Annals of adolescent psychiatry*. New York: Basic Books, 1971.

BLOCK, JACK. *Lives through time*. Berkeley: Bancroft Books, 1971.

BUTLER, R. N. Privileged communication and confidentiality in research. *A.M.A. Arch. gen. Psychiat.*, 1963, *8* (2).

CHESLER, PHYLLIS. *Women in madness*. New York: Doubleday, 1972.

COX, RACHEL D. *Youth into maturity*. New York: Mental Health Materials Center, 1970.

DASTUR, D. K., MANN, J. D., & POLLIN, W. Hippuric acid excretion, coffee and schizophrenia *A.M.A. Arch. gen. Psychiat.*, 1963, 9 (1).

ESECOVER, H., MALITZ, SIDNEY, & WILKENS, B. Clinical profiles of paid normal subjects volunteering for hallucinogen drug studies. *Amer. J. Psychiat.*, 1961, *117* (10).

FUTTERMAN, E., & HOFFMAN, I. Crisis and adaptation in the families of fatally ill children. In E. J. ANTHONY & C. KOUPERNICK (Eds.), *The child and his family*. New York: John Wiley & Sons, 1973. Vol. 2. Pp. 127–144.

GARBER, B. *A follow-up study of hospitalized adolescents*. New York: Brunner-Mazel, 1972.

GRINKER, ROY R., SR. With the collaboration of ROY R. GRINKER, JR. & J. TIMBERLAKE. A study of "mentally healthy" young males (homoclites). *A.M.A. Arch. gen. Psychiat.*, 1962, *6* (6).

GRINKER, ROY R., & SPIEGEL, J. *Men under stress*. Philadelphia: Blakiston, 1948.

GROUP FOR THE ADVANCEMENT OF PSYCHIATRY. Some observations on controls in psychiatric research. New York: G.A.P., 1959, 3, Report No. 42.

HEATH, D. H. *Explorations of maturity*. New York: Appleton-Century-Crofts, 1967.

HOLMSTROM, R. On the picture of mental health. In *Acta Psychiatrica Scandinavica Supplementum* 231. Munksgaard, Copenhagen, 1972.

KAGEN, J., & MOSS, M. A. *Birth to maturity: a study in psychological development*. New York: John Wiley & Sons, 1962.

KING, S. H. Coping mechanisms in adolescents. *Psychiatric Annals*, 1971, *1* (3), 10–46.

LASAGNA, L., & VON FELSINGER, J. M. The volunteer subject in research. *Science*, 1954, *120*, 359.

LEVITT, E. E., PERSKY, H., & BRADY, J. P. *Hypnotic induction of anxiety: a psychoendocrine investigation*. Springfield, Ill.: Charles C Thomas, 1964.

MASTERSON, J. F. *The psychiatric dilemma of adolescence*. Boston: Little, Brown & Company, 1967.

OFFER, D. *The psychological world of the teen-ager*. New York: Basic Books and Harper Torchbook, 1973.

OFFER, D., FREEDMAN, D. X., & OFFER, J. L. The psychiatrist as researcher. In D. OFFER, & D. X. FREEDMAN (Eds.), *Modern psychiatry and clinical research*. New York: Basic Books, 1972.

OFFER, D., & HOWARD, K. I. An empirical analysis of the Offer self-image questionnaire for adolescents. *A.M.A. Arch. gen. Psychiat.*, 1972, *27*, 529–533.

OFFER, D., & OFFER, J. From teen-age to young manhood: a psychological study. New York: Basic Books, 1975.

OFFER, J. L., OFFER, D., & FREEDMAN, D. X. Summaries of research undertaken by Roy R. Grinker, Sr. In D. OFFER & D. X. FREEDMAN (Eds.), *Modern psychiatry and clinical research*. New York: Basic Books, 1972. P. 275.

OKEN, D. An experimental study of suppressed anger and blood pressure. *A.M.A. Arch. gen. Psychiat.*, 1960, *2*, 441–456.

OSTFELD, A. M., Psychological variables and blood pressure. Unpublished manuscript, University of Illinois College of Medicine, Chicago, 1965.

PERLIN, S., POLIN, W., & BUTLER, R. N. The experimental subject: 1. The psychiatric evaluation and selection of a volunteer population. *A.M.A. gen. Psychiat.*, 1958, *80*, 65.

ROSENTHAL, D., & KETY, S. S. (Eds.). *The transmission of schizophrenia*. New York: Pergamon Press, 1968.

SHEKELLE, R. B., & OSTFELD, A. M. Psychometric evaluations in cardiovascular epidemiology. Unpublished manuscript, University of Illinois College of Medicine, Chicago, 1965.

SILBER, E., COELHO, G. V., MURPHEY, E. B., HAMBURG, D. H., PEARLIN, L. I., & ROSENBERG, M. Competent adolescents coping with college decision. *A.M.A. Arch. gen. Psychiat.*, 1961, *5* (6), 517–528.

SMITH, M. BREWSTER. Normality: for an abnormal age. In D. OFFER & D. X. FREEDMAN (Eds.), *Modern psychiatry and clinical research*. New York: Basic Books, 1972.

SYMONDS, P. M., & JENSEN, A. R. From adolescent to adult. New York: Columbia University Press, 1961.

TAYLOR, I. A., ROSENTHAL, DAVID, & SNYDER, S. Variability in schizophrenia. *A.M.A. Arch. gen. Psychiat.*, 1963, *8*, 2.

VAILLANT, G. E. Theoretical hierarchy of adaptive ego mechanisms. *A.M.A. Arch. gen. Psychiat.*, 1971, *24*, 107–118.

VAILLANT, G. E., & MCARTHUR, C. C. Natural history of male psychological health. *Seminars in psychiatry*, November, 1972, *4* (4), 415–427.

VEECH, R. L., ALTSCHULE, M. D., SULKOWITCH, H., & HOLLIDAY, P. D. The urinary lead-acetate extractable substances in schizophrenia. *A.M.A. Arch. gen. Psychiat.*, 1960, *3*, 6.

WESTLEY, W. A., & EPSTEIN, N. B. *The silent majority*. San Francisco: Jossey-Bass, 1970.

WHITE, R. W. *Lives in progress*. New York: Dryden Press, 1952.

WHITE, W. A. *The meaning of disease*. Baltimore: Williams & Wilkins, 1926.

CHAPTER 9

BART, P. B. (Ed.). *Sexism in family studies*. Special issue, Part 1, *J. of marriage and the family*, 1971, *33* (3). (a)

BART, P. B. (Ed.). *Sexism in family studies*. Special issue, Part 2, *J. of marriage and the family*, 1971, *33* (4). (b)

BECK, A. T. Reliability of psychiatric diagnosis: 1. A critique of systematic studies. *Amer. J. Psychiat.*, 1962, *119* (3), 210–216.

BECKER, HOWARD S. *Outsiders, studies in the sociology of deviance*. Glencoe, Ill.: Free Press of Glencoe, 1963.

BEISER, M. A psychiatric follow-up study of "normal" adults. *Amer. J. Psychiat.*, 1971, *127* (11), 1464–1473.

Chesler, Phyllis. *Women in madness*. Garden City, N.Y.: Doubleday, 1972.

Chu, F., & Trotter, C. *The mental health complex, community mental health centers* (Part I), Center for the Study of Responsive Law. Unpublished manuscript, Washington, D.C., 1972.

Deutsch, H. *The psychology of women*. New York: Grune & Stratton, 1944.

Doi, Takeo. *Reciprocal roles for Asian and North American educators: a view from Japan*. Presented at the 126th annual meeting of the American Psychiatric Association, Honolulu, Hawaii, May 10, 1973.

Eaton, Joseph, & Weil, Robert J. *Cultural and mental disorders*. Glencoe, Ill.: Free Press of Glencoe, 1954.

Ennis, B. J. *Prisoners of psychiatry*. New York: Harcourt and Brace, 1972.

Erikson, Erik H. *Childhood and society*. New York: Norton, 1950.

Erikson, Erik H. Identity and the life cycle. *Psychological issues*. New York: International Universities Press, 1959.

Erikson, Erik H. *Identity: youth and crisis*. New York: W. W. Norton and Company, 1968.

Escalona, Sibylle, & Heider, Grace. *Prediction and outcome*. New York: Basic Books, 1959.

Freud, Anna. The concept of developmental lines. In *The psychoanalytic study of the child*. New York: International Universities Press, 1963.

Freud, Anna. *Normality and pathology in childhood*. New York: International Universities Press, 1965.

Gedo, J., & Goldberg, A. *Models of the mind*. Chicago: The University of Chicago Press, 1973.

Golden, J., Mandel, N., Glueck, B. L., Jr., & Feder, A. A summary description of fifty "normal" white males. *Amer. J. Psychiat*, 1962, *119*, 48.

Golden, J., Silver, R. J., & Mandel, N. The wives of fifty "normal" American men. *A.M.A. Arch. gen. Psychiat.*, 1963, 9 (6).

Grinker, Roy R., Sr. (Ed.). *Toward a unified theory of human behavior*. New York: Basic Books, 1956. P. 370.

Grinker, Roy R., Sr. With the collaboration of Roy R. Grinker,

Jr. & J. Timberlake. A study of "mentally healthy" young males (homoclites). *A.M.A. Arch. gen. Psychiat.*, 1962, *6*, (6).

Grinker, Roy R., Sr. Foreword. In G. V. Coelho, D. A. Hamburg, & J. E. Adams (Eds.), *Coping and adaptation*. New York: Basic Books, 1974.

Grinker, Roy R., & Spiegel, J. *Men under stress*. Philadelphia: Blakiston, 1948.

Hamburg, D. A., & Adams, J. E. A perspective on coping behavior. *Arch. gen. Psychiat.*, 1967, *17*, 277–284.

Hamburg, D. A., Coelho, G. V., & Adams, J. E. Coping and adaptation. In G. V Coelho, D. A. Hamburg, & J. E. Adams (Eds.), *Coping and adaptation*. New York: Basic Books, 1974.

Harris, Irving D. *Normal children and mothers*. Glencoe, Ill.: Free Press of Glencoe, 1959.

Hartmann, H. *Essays on ego psychology*. New York: International Universities Press, 1964.

Heath, D. H. *Exploration of maturity*. New York: Appleton-Century-Crofts, 1965.

Hoffman, M. Psychiatry, nature and science. *Amer. J. Psychiat.*, 1960, *117*, 205.

Hsu, Francis L. K. (Ed.). *Psychological anthropology: approaches to culture and personality*. Homewood, Ill.: Dorsey Press, 1961.

Jahoda, Marie. *Current concepts of positive mental health*. New York: Basic Books, 1959. P. 23.

Janis, I. L. Vigilance and decision making in personal crises. In G. V. Coelho, D. A. Hamburg, & J. E. Adams (Eds.), *Coping and adaptation*. New York: Basic Books, 1974.

Jones, E. Cited in M. Birnbach, *Neo-Freudian social philosophy*. Stanford, Calif.: Stanford University Press, 1961. P. 7.

Kaplan, A. *The conduct of inquiry*. San Francisco: Chandler Publishing Co., 1964.

Kaplan, A. A philosophical discussion of normality. *A.M.A. Arch. gen. Psychiat.*, September, 1967, *17*, 325–330.

Kardiner, Abram. *The individual and his society*. With a foreword and two ethnological reports by R. Linton. New York: Columbia University Press, 1939.

Kardiner, Abram. With the collaboration of R. Linton, Cora

DuBois, & J. West. *The psychological frontiers of society.* New York: Columbia University Press, 1945.

Knapp, Peter H. (Ed.). *Expressions of the emotions in man.* New York: International Universities Press, 1963.

Kohut, H. *The analysis of the self.* New York: International Universities Press, 1971.

Lazarus, R. S., Averill, J. R., & Opton, E. M., Jr. The psychology of coping: issues of research and assessment. In G. V. Coelho, D. A. Hamburg, & J. E. Adams (Eds.), *Coping and adaptation.* New York: Basic Books, 1974.

Leiderman, P. Herbert, & Shapiro, D. (Eds.). *Psychosocial approaches to social behavior.* Stanford, Calif: Stanford University Press, 1964.

Leighton, Alexander H. *My name is legion.* New York: Basic Books, 1959. P. 250.

LeVine, R. A. *Culture, behavior and personality.* Chicago: Aldine, 1973.

London, P. The sources of therapeutic morality. Columbia University *Forum,* 1962, 5 (3).

Masterson, J. F., Jr. *The psychiatric dilemma of adolescence.* Boston: Little, Brown & Company, 1967.

Murphy, Lois B., & collaborators. *The widening world of childhood.* New York: Basic Books, 1962.

Offer, D. *The psychological world of the teen-ager.* New York: Basic Books and Harper Torchbook, 1973.

Offer, D., & Freedman, D. X. (Eds.). *Modern psychiatry and clinical research.* New York: Basic Books, 1972.

Parsons, Talcott. Definitions of health and illness in the light of American values and social structure. In E. Gartley Jaco (Ed.), *Patients, physicians, and illness.* Glencoe, Ill.: Free Press of Glencoe, 1958. P. 176.

Parsons, Talcott. An approach to psychological theory in terms of the theory of action. In Vol. 3 of Sigmund Koch (Ed.), *Psychology: a study of a science.* New York: McGraw-Hill, 1959. P. 643.

Parsons, Talcott. Field theory and system theory: with special reference to the relations between psychological and social systems. In D. Offer & D. X. Freedman (Eds.), *Modern psychiatry and clinical research.* New York: Basic Books, 1972.

Robinson, Robert L. Criticisms of psychiatry. Unpublished paper presented at the American College of Psychiatry, New Orleans, January, 1973.

Sabshin, M., Diesenhaus, H., & Wilkerson, R. Dimensions of institutional racism in psychiatry. *Amer. J. Psychiat.*, 1970, *127* (6), 787–793.

Saul, L. J., & Pulver, S. E. The concept of emotional maturity. *Comprehensive Psychiat.*, 1965, *6* (1), 6–21.

Scott, W. A. Research definitions of mental health and mental illness. *Psychol. Bull.*, 1958, *55* (1).

Sells, S. B. (Ed.). *The definition and measurement of mental health.* U.S.P.H.S., National Center for Health Statistics, September, 1967.

Smith, M. B. Mental health reconsidered: a special case of the problem of values in psychology. *Amer. Psychol.*, 1961, *16*, 299–306.

Smith, M. B. Normality: for an abnormal age. In D. Offer & D. X. Freedman (Eds.), *Modern psychiatry and clinical research.* New York: Basic Books, 1972.

Spitz, René A. *No and yes: on the genesis of human communication.* New York: International Universities Press, 1957.

Srole, Leo, Langer, T. S., Michael, S. T., Opler, Marvin K., & Rennie, Thomas A. C. *Mental health in the metropolis.* Manhattan studies. New York: McGraw-Hill, 1963.

Vaillant, G. E. Theoretical hierarchy of adaptive ego mechanisms. *A.M.A. Arch. gen. Psychiat.*, February, 1971, *24*, 107–118.

Ward, C. H., Beck, A. T., Mendelson, M., Mock, J. E., & Erbauch, J. K. The psychiatric nomenclature: reasons for diagnostic disagreement. *A.M.A. Arch. gen. Psychiat.*, 1962, *7*, 3.

Weinshel, E. M. The ego in health and normality. *J. Am. Psa. Assn.*, 1970, *18* (3), 682–735.

White, R. W. *Competence and the psycho-sexual stages of development.* Nebraska symposium on motivation. Lincoln: University of Nebraska Press, 1960. Pp. 97–138.

White, R. W. The concept of healthy personality: what do we really mean? *The counselling psychologist*, 1973, *4* (2), 3–13.

Index